ELEVEN YEARS
IN
CEYLON

ELEVEN YEARS

IN

CEYLON

COMPRISING

SKETCHES OF THE FIELD SPORTS

AND

NATURAL HISTORY OF THAT COLONY

AND AN ACCOUNT OF ITS

HISTORY AND ANTIQUITIES

MAJOR FORBES

IN TWO VOLUMES
VOL. I

ISBN : 978-93-5324-359-3 (Set)

ISBN : 978-93-5324-360-9 Vol. 1 (HB)

First Published, London, 1840

Published, 2020

Published by

Facsimile Publisher
12 Pragati Market
Ashok Vihar, Ph-2
Delhi-110052
E-mail: books@facsimilepublisher.com

Printed at: G. Print Process, Delhi.

Eleven Years in Ceylon

Major Forbes

ELEVEN YEARS IN CEYLON.

COMPRISING

SKETCHES OF THE FIELD SPORTS

AND

NATURAL HISTORY OF THAT COLONY,

AND AN ACCOUNT OF ITS

HISTORY AND ANTIQUITIES.

BY MAJOR FORBES, 78TH HIGHLANDERS.

A land of wonders! which the sun still eyes
With ray direct, as of the lovely realm
Enamour'd, and delighting there to dwell.
THOMSON.

IN TWO VOLUMES.

VOL. I.

LONDON:
RICHARD BENTLEY, NEW BURLINGTON STREET,
Publisher in Ordinary to Her Majesty.
1840.

CONTENTS

OF THE FIRST VOLUME.

INTRODUCTION.

CHAPTER I.

CHAPTER II.

CHAPTER III.

HISTORY OF THE BRITISH IN CEYLON CONTINUED.

CHAPTER VI.

ELEPHANT SHOOTING NEAR HANGWELLÉ.

CHAPTER VII.

JOURNEY TO ADAM'S PEAK.

CHAPTER VIII.

ASCENT OF THE PEAK.

CHAPTER XI.

FROM ANURÁDHAPOORA TO MANÁR PEARL FISHERY.

CHAPTER XII.

SHOOTING EXCURSION ALONG THE WEST COAST OF CEYLON.

CHAPTER XIII.

VISIT TO KANDY. — MORAL LAWS OF GAUTAMA BUDDHA.

CHAPTER XIV.

KANDIAN FESTIVALS.

CHAPTER XV.

THROUGH MÁTALÉ TO DAMBOOL.

ILLUSTRATIONS.

VOL. I.

VOL. II.

RESIDENCE IN CEYLON.

INTRODUCTION.

Patience! and ye shall hear what he beheld
In other lands, where he was doom'd to go:
Lands that contain the monuments of Eld.—BYRON.

Great Importance of the Island — Its Population numerous and comparatively civilized at an early period.—Possesses a continued History for Twenty-three Centuries. — Liberal Policy of Great Britain to the Cingalese; consequent Prosperity of the Island.—Compared with the Continent of India.—Prospects of Christianity. — My first Acquaintance with Cingalese History, and Determination to examine the Antiquities of the Island.

THE beautiful scenery of Ceylon, its mild climate, rich vegetation, and some of its valuable natural productions, have already been made known to the British public. The immense consequence of this island, from its position, and the harbour of Trinkomalee, could never have been overlooked; so long as the British crown holds sway in India, or British merchants shall trade to the East, its importance can hardly be overrated: now, however, not only are the resources of this country, its most remote valleys and elevated plains, better known to Europeans; but the history of its inhabitants and of the island, its former state and late improvement, equally excite curiosity and demand attention. From the native chronicles we find, that the ancestors of a people whom Britons long regarded as savages, and for some time treated as slaves, existed as a numerous* and comparatively civilized nation at a period antecedent to the discovery of Great Britain and its semi-barbarous inhabitants.

The ancient and continued annals of the Cingalese race have been preserved for upwards of twenty-three centuries, and describe the erection or formation of all those extensive works,—cities, tanks, temples,—whose ruins and numerous inscriptions remain to verify the historical records. For a great proportion of that long period the natives of Ceylon will be found to have remained stationary, or to have retrograded in arts, perhaps in intelligence; whilst Britons, advancing in civilization with extraordinary rapidity, benefiting by experience, and improving in policy, have voluntarily

* I think no one who examines the great and general remains that evince the extent of population once scattered over Ceylon, will be inclined to reckon the number that must have been at one time in the island at less than five millions of people.

abandoned their arbitrary rule in the island, for a mild, free, but still efficient Government. From this circumstance Ceylon is already advancing beyond that barrier of mediocrity, which in Asia seems to have arrested mind and manners at a particular point of civilization.

Institutions suddenly, yet not rashly reformed; direct taxes on cultivated land first moderated, then carefully arranged, fairly levied, and finally redeemed; a whole people passing in an instant * from a state worse than slavery to all the blessings of freedom, with perfect safety to the Government, and incalculable benefit to the subject; a rapid improvement in the face of the country; a most beneficial change in the native character; generally diminished taxation; rapidly increasing revenue; a prosperous and happy people; and, it is not too much to say, an improved climate, — are the effects of the later years of British authority in Ceylon.

Additional interest is given to the changes so happily introduced into this island, by its contiguity to the vast possessions of Great Britain in

* The order of the King in council, abolishing compulsory labour in Ceylon, was, according to instructions, immediately promulgated. Thus the people were at once freed from oppression, or dependence on any individual, and, owing no obedience except to the laws and Government, could no longer be compelled; — of course, they would not from choice rise up in behalf of their former oppressors, whose dignity at first suffered by this act of sound policy and active benevolence.

India; for although the same legislation that has proved so successful in Ceylon, might be inapplicable to the neighbouring continent, yet the relative prosperity of their inhabitants cannot fail to provoke comparison, as it certainly invites inquiry.

Another subject of very great interest is, the general introduction and rapid diffusion of the English language: this paves the way for Christianity, which, it requires but little foresight to predict, must gradually, perhaps rapidly, extend itself over the great majority * of the natives of Ceylon.

Immediately after my arrival in Ceylon, attracted to the jungle by the novelty of elephant shooting, I enjoyed the excitement of that noble sport, the display of luxuriant forest landscapes and distant views of the Kandian mountains, from which rose the famed and mysterious Peak of Samanala.† Admiration of mountain scenery, and a partiality for antiquities, next induced me to visit the Peak; and on my way I had the good fortune to meet Mr. Turnour (then agent of Government in Saffragam),‡ and by him was informed that, notwithstanding the disparaging assertions of English writers on Ceylon, there were still extant con-

* I see little prospect of converts from among those professing the religion of Mohammed.

† Called Adam's Peak by Europeans.

‡ The district in which Adam's Peak is situated.

tinued native records of great antiquity. I found that he had already arranged an Epitome of the History of Ceylon from B. C. 543, and that he had visited the gigantic monuments and far-spread ruins of its most ancient capital. I also heard with satisfaction that the sites of several of the ancient cities mentioned in Cingalese history were still unknown, or at least had remained unnoticed by Europeans. This information determined me to acquire some knowledge of the Cingalese language, and to search for those vestiges of antiquity which could farther verify the native chronicles.

On ascertaining the nature of my pursuits on this subject, Mr. Turnour afterwards allowed me to transcribe his epitome of native history, which has since been published.* By his permission, that epitome is contained in this work. In return for his kindness and liberality, I am pleased to think that, in visiting all the ancient cities of note mentioned in their records, I have been the means of furnishing many new proofs of the authenticity of the native annals, and that I have this opportunity of stating my admiration of the judgment and accuracy with which Mr. Turnour has arranged and abridged the Cingalese history.

I now submit to the public an account of journeys undertaken in prosecution of the design which

* In the Ceylon Almanac for 1833.

I had adopted; with remarks, which are the result of my observations during eleven years' residence in Ceylon. For the greater part of that time, along with a military command, I held civil employment as assistant-agent and district judge of Mátelé in the Kandian provinces. In the course of my wanderings I omitted no opportunity of sketching the scenery, antiquities, or subjects of sporting interest that passed before me; at the same time, I was enabled to procure drawings of the varied costumes of its inhabitants, and of the brilliant flowers and magnificent forest-trees that blossom in the "Eden of the Eastern wave."

For some time I directed much of my attention to the discovery of inscriptions, which I found in great numbers sculptured on rocks in every part of the country. Many of these (not copied with sufficient accuracy, or in the Nagara character) remain undeciphered; but from what has already been translated, and the ruins which have been examined, I am satisfied that farther proof of the general accuracy of the native chronicles is not required. "Cingalese history is authenticated by the concurrence of every evidence that can contribute to verify the annals of any country." *

* Turnour's Introduction to Mahawanso.—That most important historical work of Ceylon (the Mahawanso) has been translated from the Pali, and the first volume is already published. It is found to contain fragments of Indian (continental)

I have indulged a hope that these illustrations may excite an interest in the British public, and enable it to form some idea of the features of a country surpassingly rich and beautiful, and of the history of an ancient people (lately freed from tyranny and despotism) now increasing in prosperity, and rapidly raising themselves in the scale of civilization.

The authentic history of the country having been scrutinised and abridged by Mr. Turnour, I afterwards turned my attention to a period of time and a people generally supposed to be for ever "flooded in the night of Eld," and commenced an inquiry into the traditions and legends of Lanka, and its aboriginal inhabitants, previous to the invasion of the Singha race, B. C. 543. In this department my success has not been great; but my endeavours may excite attention, even if my views fail to produce conviction, or should eventually prove erroneous. At all events, I indulge a hope that individuals possessing greater advantages, and with more leisure, may hereafter profit by the facts

history, particularly of that last period of the ascendancy of Buddhism and its general prevalence in Hindostan; also of that period where the writers of the East and of the West meet in the only point which has, as yet, been found common to the records of the Greeks and the history of any Indian nation, viz. the reign of the Buddhist sovereign of India contemporary with Alexander the Great and Seleucus, called Sandracottus in the Greek, Chandragupta in the Sanscrit, and Chandagutto in the Pali annals.

I have collected, the localities I have ascertained, and the traditions I have recorded, during my search for history amidst those dim receding ages into which the ever-rolling wave of time has cast back the earliest records of our race.

CHAPTER I.

NAMES OF THE ISLAND OF CEYLON.

Embassies from regions far remote,
*   *   *   *   *
From India and the Golden Chersonese,
And utmost Indian isle Taprobane.—MILTON.

Names of the Island of Ceylon in Ancient and Modern Times — Their Derivation. — Geographical Description of the Island — Its Temperature. — Geological Character. — Population.— Mountains.

LAKA, Lanká, Lankáwa, Laka-diwa, Lanka-dwipia, or some variety derived from these words by different terminations, or epithets prefixed, are the most ancient appellations of Ceylon to be found in Sanscrit or Cingalese writings † Laka is the Elu (ancient Cingalese), Lanka the Sanscrit name

† The names given to Ceylon in the times of Gautama's three predecessors as Buddhas, were:

In the time of Kakusanda Buddha, it was called Oja-dwipia.
In the time of Konagamma, it was called Waradwipia.
In the time of Kásyapa, it was called Madadwipia.

These names are only mentioned in the account of the Buddhas.

of the island. I think it probable this name was derived from Laka, or Laksha (one hundred thousand, or multitude), and diva, or dwipia (islands); for Cingalese traditions mention that thousands of isles attached to the kingdom of Lanka were overwhelmed by the sea B.C. 2387, along with the splendid capital of Sri-Lanka-poora, which stood to the westward of any part of the present island. I am aware that other derivations have always been given, but I see no reason to approve of them, when the same name, Lakadive, which is that of the cluster of islands at no great distance from Ceylon, has always borne the same simple derivation that I now suggest. If there is any truth in the Ramayan, or the Rawena Katawa of Ceylon, the Maldives and Lakadives were then part of the kingdom of Rawena; and along with the great extent of Lanka, which was submerged, and the southern peninsula of India, formed the kingdom over which he ruled.

Naga Dwipia,—island of Nagas,—if not used for the whole island, is a name employed by Buddhist writers for that part of its western coast which lies around Kellania; but does not appear to have been in use after the invasion of Vijeya, B.C. 543.

I am inclined to suggest that the name of Tambapani, Tambapanni, Tambrapanni, of the Pali historians, which has been corrupted into Taprobane by those of the western world, may have nad its origin when Vijeya and his followers made knowr their first conquests in Lanka to the race from which he was descended, and from whom he had been expelled. It was in the district of Tamena, or Tambana, or Tambapanni, that Vijeya landed, and for a considerable time his force seems to have been confined to that portion of the country; in fact, until after his surprise and massacre of the inhabitants at Sri Wasta Poora, not less than three years after his landing.* After this, he founded the city of Tamena.†

* It appears that Kuwani, the daughter of one of the aboriginal chiefs, bore three children to Vijeya, and he discarded her after he had made himself master of the country by this massacre.

† Various reasons induce me to conjecture that the district of Tamana was the present district of Tamankada ("Kada" is limit or frontier). There are many villages called Tamana, from a tree of that name, common in the flat and northern parts of the island; and there is a commonly received opinion amongst Cingalese, that one of them, on the western side of the country, near Putlam, occupies the site of Vijeya's capital, although there are no remains of it. But the antiquarian accuracy of natives can no more be trusted than their etymological deductions: as a specimen of the latter, I shall quote, from Turnour's translation of the Mahawanso, the derivation of the name of Tambrapanni.

"At the spot where the seven hundred men, with the king (Vijeya) at their head, exhausted by (sea) sickness, and faint from weakness, had landed out of the vessel, supporting themselves on the palms of their hands pressed on the ground, they sat themselves down. Hence to them the name of 'Tambapannis' (copper-palmed, from the colour of the soil): from this circumstance, that wilderness obtained the name of Tambapanni; from the same cause, also, this renowned land became celebrated (under that name)." This derivation is manifestly

The most common name of the island is Singhala, —variously written Sihala, Sihalen, Singhalen, Ceylon, — derived from Singha, or Siha,* the race to which Vijeya and his followers belonged. They were exiled by his father, who ruled over a country, Lála, whose capital, Singhapura, is probably the same as Singhea on the banks of the Gunduck, where the site of an ancient city is discernible, encumbered with numerous ruins and Buddhist monuments.

GENERAL DESCRIPTION OF THE ISLAND.

The island of Ceylon is in length, from Point Pedro to Dondera Head, two hundred and seventy-five miles, with an average breadth of one hundred miles, and a superficial area of twenty-five thousand square miles. The northern and eastern provinces are flat, and subject to long-continued droughts. The central, the western, and

absurd; for, besides the numerous villages, and a district in Ceylon called Tamana, there is the district and river of Tambraparni in the southern peninsula of India; and the writer of the Mahawanso, in a previous chapter, had already stated that Vijeya "landed in the division, Tambapanni, of this land, Lanka."

* From Singha (the Cingalese word), Siha (the Pali), with the addition of dwipa, diva, dua, div, dib, all signifying island, we have numerous corruptions of Seren, Zeilan, Ceylon, — Seren dib, Seilan div, &c.

southern provinces are moist, comparatively cool, and favourable to the cultivation of cocoa-nut, coffee, and cinnamon.* Although the island is situated between 6° and 10° of north altitude, and between 80° and 82° of east longitude, it enjoys a much more temperate climate than countries whose geographical position would be considered more favourable. From its size, the sea-breezes range across it; and the great elevation of the mountains not only insures a certain degree of cold, but attracts so many clouds and so much moisture as to insure the evergreen of its forests, and unceasing cultivation of the fields, over one half of the country. The side of the great Kandian range of hills nearest to the eastern coast partakes in part of the deficiency of moisture which distinguishes the maritime provinces nearest the range; and it is remarkable that on one side of these hills the climate is moist and cool, its vegetation rich and continually refreshed by showers, while on the other side, except during the rainy season, there prevail oppressive heats and parching winds.

"At Colombo, the mean daily variation of the temperature does not exceed 3°, while the annual range of the thermometer is from 76° to 86½° of Fahrenheit. At Trinkomalee, the greatest daily variation is 17°, and the annual range from 74½°

* I believe sugar-cane has also been successfully cultivated within the last two years.

to 91½°. At Kandy, the mean daily variation is 6°, and the annual range from 66° to 86°. Higher up the hills, at Nuwara Ellia, a military convalescent station, the mean daily variation is as high as 11°, while the annual range of the thermometer is from 35½° to 80½°. In Colombo, the quantity of rain that fell during the year 1830 was one hundred and two inches; of which eighty-one inches fell in the months of April, May, October, and November."*

There is no appearance whatever of volcanoes in Ceylon, or that such ever existed; and, with regard to its rocks, I shall quote Dr. Davy, the best authority on the subject, who says, "Uniformity of formation is the most remarkable feature in the geological character of the island. As far as my information extends, the whole of Ceylon, with very few exceptions, consists of primitive rock." The gems found in Ceylon are not in general of much value; and the ruby, the most valuable, is rarely met with.

The rise of the tides in Ceylon does not exceed three feet; and the harbours are inlets of the sea, in nowise depending upon the tides, and altogether unconnected with the rivers.

Although there are no natural lakes in the island, probably no country is better watered by rivers, and innumerable streams and rills, than the

* Colonel Colebrooke's Report; Commission of Inquiry, 1831.

hilly country of the interior, and the adjacent territory; whilst the ingenuity and labour of the earlier inhabitants, by the construction of immense reservoirs,—artificial lakes,—had almost rendered them independent of such droughts as usually occur in the revolution of seasons.

With regard to the population of the island, as might naturally be expected, the returns, until the abolition of compulsory service, were so much under the real numbers, that from them no guess can be formed of the general increase; but it is probable that, in as short a time as can be calculated on from data in other most favoured portions of the globe, Ceylon will again contain the same numerous population it must once have possessed, and which it is still capable of supporting. By the last census, in 1835, the returns gave the amount of population about 1,250,000, and showed that the number of males exceeded that of the females by one-tenth part. The return of 1824 only gave a total of 852,000.*

Adam's Peak was, for many years after the British possessed the country, considered the

* The returns of the maritime provinces prior to the taking of the Kandian country showed an increase of population so rapid, that I should be inclined to attribute it to the inaccuracy of the lists from the cause above mentioned:

Population	of maritime	provinces	in 1814,	475,883
„	of ditto	ditto	in 1824,	595,105
			Increase	119,222

highest mountain in the island, although its height is only seven thousand four hundred and twenty feet: while the Wilmantalawe (part of the Horton plains) is now found to be seven thousand feet; and three mountains, Suduhugalla, Totapella, and Lunugalla, rise from that elevated region, and reach from seven to eight hundred feet above its level. Although to European constitutions the cool temperature of the elevated plains is peculiarly agreeable, they were entirely uninhabited by Kandians; the limit of rice cultivation and native population being the same, as the one is partly dependent on the other, and both are checked by the cold at an elevation not exceeding four thousand feet. The convalescent station of Nuwara Ellia is six thousand two hundred and ten feet; and the mountain Pedro-tallagalla, which bounds it on one side, rises to a height of eight thousand two hundred and eighty feet above the level of the sea.*

* These heights were furnished to the Ceylon Almanac by Lieutenant-colonel Fraser, Deputy Quartermaster-general.

CHAPTER II.

HISTORY OF THE BRITISH IN CEYLON.

——The nightly ambuscade,
The daily harass, and the fight delay'd,
The long privation of the hoped supply,
The tentless rest beneath the humid sky.—BYRON.

Succession of British Governors.—British Embassy to Kandy, 1763.—*Fort Ostenburgh taken, and another Embassy sent to Kandy,* 1782.—*Maritime Provinces of Ceylon taken,* 1796.—*Placed under the Madras Government.—Made a King's Colony, and Hon. F. North appointed Governor.—Pilámé Taláwe.—His Character.—Makes proposals to the British Governor,* 1799.—*Repeats them in* 1800.—*General Macdowal sent Ambassador to Kandy.—Extraordinary proposals to the King.—Failure of the Mission.—War with the King of Kandy.—His Capital taken.—Mootoo Sámy proclaimed King.—Treaty concluded with Him—Another Treaty concluded with Pilámé Taláwe.—His Conference with the British Governor.—British Treatment of Mootoo Sámy.—British Garrison in Kandy attacked.—They abandon the Town.—Surrender.—Are massacred by the Kandians.—Fate of Mootoo Sámy.—Escape of Corporal Barnsley.—Major Davie.—Ensign Grant.—Defence of Dambadennia.—Noble Conduct of the Malay Officers.—Captain Nouradeen.—Kandians attack the Maritime Provinces—Are Repulsed.—The Kandian Army Routed.*—1804, *Captain Johnson enters the Kandian Country.—Takes Kandy.—Passes on to Trinkomalee.*

Succession of British Governors in Ceylon, *from the taking of the Island in* 1796 *to* 1837.

The Honourable the Governor of Madras in Council. Administration commenced 26th February, 1796, terminated 12th October, 1798.

Honourable Frederick North, (afterwards Earl of Guildford,) 12th October, 1798, to 19th July, 1805.

Lieutenant-general the Right Honourable Sir Thomas Maitland, G.C.B., 19th July, 1805, to 19th March, 1811.

Major-general John Wilson, Lieutenant-governor, 19th March, 1811, to 11th March, 1812.

General Sir Robert Brownrigg, Bart., G.C.B., 11th March, 1812, to 1st February, 1820.

Major-general Sir Edward Barnes, K.C.B., Lieutenant-governor, 1st February, 1820, to 2nd February, 1822.

Lieutenant-general the Honourable Sir Edward Paget, K.C.B., 2nd February, 1822, to 6th November, 1822.

Major-general Sir James Campbell, K.C.B., Lieutenant-governor, 6th November, 1822, to 18th January, 1824.

Lieutenant-general Sir Edward Barnes, G.C.B., 18th January, 1824, to 13th October, 1831.

Major-general Sir John Wilson, K.C.B., 13th October, 1831, to 23rd October, 1831.

The Right Honourable Sir R. Wilmot Horton, G.C.H., 23rd October 1831, to 1837.

Summary of the history of British affairs in Ceylon, from A.D. 1763 to 1837.

In 1763, the Madras Government despatched an embassy to the Kandian King, Kirti Sri Raja Singha, which not only failed to produce any satisfactory result, but is known to have left no favourable impression of British power or policy on the minds of the Kandians. In 1782, Fort Ostenburgh, at Trinkomalee, was taken possession of by the British fleet, under Sir Edward Hughes, and a body of troops commanded by Sir Hector Munro. Soon after this event, and during the short period which the British force retained possession of this harbour, the Government of Madras sent another embassy, under the charge of Mr. Boyd, who landed at Trinkomalee, and in travelling from that place to the residence appointed for him in the vicinity of Kandy, appears to have occupied a whole month, although the distance is only a hundred and thirty miles. The natives along this route had been directed to furnish provisions for the persons composing the embassy, but were forbidden to receive payment, and in returning, Mr. Boyd was informed, that two natives of Wehigalla, whom he had remunerated for supplies which they had furnished, had been executed for disobeying the King's commands. From the mild and humane character of the King who then reigned, Rájadhi Raja Singha, I disbelieved the story, and, on inquiring at the village, ascertained that no such execution had taken place;

for, although it was forty-eight years since the embassy had passed, I found several persons who recollected the most minute circumstances which occurred on that occasion. The falsehood told to the ambassador was no doubt intended to convince him of the energetic despotism of the King, as well as to exalt the royal hospitality.

In 1796, a British armament from the south of India, under the command of Colonel Stewart, took possession of all the towns and territory held by the Dutch in Ceylon, comprising the whole sea-coast, and a belt of unequal breadth all round the island; it is this territory which is usually denominated the Maritime Provinces. However able the arrangements, or efficient the force, the warlike operations were not of a nature to excite interest, or require detail,—even Colombo, strongly fortified, and fairly garrisoned, made no resistance.

Ceylon remained for two years under the government of Madras, and during that short period, some disturbances occurred, and considerable dissatisfaction was created by the employment of natives from the continent of India, in collecting the revenue, and other duties, which, under the Portuguese and Dutch, had always been efficiently performed by the Cingalese headmen.

In 1798, Ceylon was taken from under the authority of the East India Company, and the Honourable Frederick North arrived as Governor. In the same year, the Kandian King, Rájadhi Raja

Singha* died without issue, and the interest and intrigues of Pilame Tálawe, (the first Adikar,) enabled him to raise to the throne Kannasamy, a nephew of one of the Queens, by the title of Sri Wikrema Raja Singha. The King was then only eighteen years of age, and Pilámé Taláwe, under sanction of the royal authority, commenced a system of falsehood, cruelty, and bloodshed. His deceptions, and he appears to have been most unaccountably successful in them, were principally practised on the British Governor, and those employed by him in diplomatic and military affairs; as for the Kandians, they knew the first Adikar too well to be deceived by his cunning, although they succumbed to his power, and suffered by his cruelty. His objects were to get rid of his enemies, amongst whom he reckoned all who could resist, or might interfere with his schemes of ambition, and to allow the odium of murders committed by his direction, to fall on the handsome puppet on whom he had placed a crown, which he intended to transfer to his own brows; this result he expected to accomplish, either by the open assistance of the British Government, or by secret treason, and the assassination of the King.

In 1799, Pilámé Taláwe sounded the British Governor, as to the degree of assistance he might

* The King who had co-operated with the British when they took possession of the maritime provinces from the Dutch.

hope for in carrying into effect the schemes of ambition he had for some time meditated, and was now impatient to execute. He proposed that the British should aid him to ascend, and then support him in possession of the Kandian throne, which was to become vacant for the minister by the assassination of his master. In return for their co-operation, this King in prospect, regicide in intention, and traitor in fact, proffered his friendship; and promised political advantages to the British Government.

Again in 1800, Pilámé Taláwe persevered in bringing forward the same insulting proposals, and urged the British Governor to connive at, or assist in his schemes of villainy.

Soon after these overtures, General Macdowal was sent as ambassador to Kandy to propose to the King that, for his own protection, he should retire into the British territory; and from there should exercise supreme authority, whilst Pilámé Taláwe was to possess a delegated power in the Kandian provinces, protected by a British subsidiary force. One can hardly believe that these proposals were intended to insure the personal safety of the King, although this is implied by the historian of that period, Cordiner, who was himself on the spot; they appear much more fitted to accomplish all the views of the first Adikar; and as the quarter from which danger to the King might be expected was not to be communicated to him, the interference of the British Governor was sure to be deemed impertinent, and must have been regarded with suspicion. From these arrangements, it might at first appear that the Adikar was to acquire substantial power, while the British Governor was to play protector to a royal semblance; but the real scope of these proposals can scarcely be regarded as so short-sighted in point of policy, although it may be difficult to defend them on the ground of morality. British troops were to be insinuated into the Kandian country; and considering the character of the intended native viceroy, Pilámé Taláwe, they must either have fallen victims to his crooked policy, or have secured the country to the British Crown.

It is difficult to imagine what delusion could have led any one to expect that a suspicious, jealous, and haughty despot, who styled himself, in his counter-proposals, "King of Lanka, as great amongst men as Iswara amongst the gods!" would delegate all power to his minister, and transfer his own person from possible danger to certain restraint. As might have been predicted, the mission was a total failure; and the same consequences resulted from this, as from former embassies, viz: that they ministered to the vanity of the Kandian monarch, and exalted him in the eyes of his ignorant subjects, who contrasted the studied splendour of the royal pageantry, with the degrading ceremonies enforced upon the British representative.

Our embassies and negotiations were numerous from 1798 to 1803; and, certainly, they neither raised us in the estimation of the Kandians, nor procured from them protection for our native subjects.

Pacific measures, on the part of the British Governor, having been invariably followed by increasing insults from the Kandian court, active operations and open warfare were at length commenced. On the 31st January 1803, a division of the army under General Macdowal, marched from Colombo to attack Kandy, at the same time that Colonel Barbut was advancing with a large force from Trinkomalee. The two divisions, amounting to about three thousand regular troops, united on the banks of the Mahawelliganga, three miles from Kandy, and next day, 21st February, having crossed that river, the British forces entered the Cingalese capital, which had been abandoned by the enemy, and was on fire in several places.

Colonel Barbut, with a strong party, then returned to Trinkomalee, and escorted from there Mootoo Sámy, a brother of one of the Queens of Rajadhi Raja Singha. This prince asserted that he had a better right to the Kandian throne than its possessor; but this may be doubted, as, in addition to the right of possession, the King, de facto, had been duly inaugurated, after being formally approved by the Kandian people; however, the British Government, deeming it advisable to support the pretensions of Mootoo Sámy, proclaimed him King of Kandy, and then entered into a treaty with him as an independent sovereign.

The stipulations were impolitic and ungenerous, for the articles to which this titular King assented, would have transferred from the Kandian monarchy the only valuable possessions of which he had not already been despoiled; and, although the chiefs of the districts to be ceded* might be insensible to the calls of patriotism, self-interest formed a surer bond to unite them against a nominal king, who had made such ruinous concessions.

The articles of convention between Mootoo Sámy and the British, were arranged about the 8th of March, and one of the clauses provided that he was to receive an auxiliary force from the British settlements, if it should be found necessary for the maintaining of his authority. Yet, on the 29th of the same month, we find that at a conference held between General Macdowal and Pilámé Taláwe, it was agreed that the de facto King should be delivered over to the care of the British Government, that Pilámé Taláwe should be invested with supreme authority in Kandy; that he should pay about three thousand pounds annually for Mootoo Sámy,

* The seven Korles, Matalai, and Tamankada.

and, besides other advantages, cede to the British the same valuable provinces that Mootoo Sámy had agreed to sacrifice.

Previous to this conference, on the 12th of March, the British commander, still duped by the Adikar, and at his instigation, had despatched two strong parties under Colonel Bailie and Colonel Logan on a meteor chase to seize the King; these detachments were of course unsuccessful, and returned after suffering considerable loss.

After this, at the request of Pilámé Taláwe, the British Governor agreed to meet him personally, and for that purpose proceeded to Dambadennia in the Kandian provinces, and there the Adikar arrived on the 3rd of May. At this conference, the treaty previously arranged between the traitor minister of the Kandian King, and the British Commander of the Forces, was formally ratified by the representative of his Britannic Majesty "who now thought that the Adikar was sincere, and that he had at length determined to act with good faith."* It was afterwards ascertained that the Adikar had intended to seize the person of the Governor, and was only prevented from carrying his plan into execution, by the accidental and opportune arrival of Colonel Barbut with a strong party of Malays. The treatment of Mootoo Sámy by the British authorities at this time is indefensible on the plea of necessity, and nothing less

* Cordiner.

could afford any justification. Mootoo Sámy is described as being mild and amiable; his right to the Kandian throne was proclaimed by the British; they brought him to the capital; they saluted him as King; they offered to support him with a military force; yet, but a very few days after this, without any fault on his, or misfortune on their part, they deliberately conclude, and afterwards ratify a treaty, by which he was to become a pensioner on one they knew to be a villain, ready to commit the very worst of crimes, yet whom they were about to raise to supreme authority over the Kandians.

The garrison in Kandy becoming sickly, a great part of the troops were withdrawn from there to the maritime provinces; and on the 1st of April the garrison was reduced to three hundred Europeans, and seven hundred Malays, and Indian artillery, besides a considerable number left sick in hospital. Colonel Barbut, who held the command, after attending the Governor at Dambadennia, was seized with fever, and being conveyed to Colombo, died there on the 21st of April. On the 23rd of May, General Macdowal returned to Kandy, but was attacked with fever, and left it for Colombo on the 11th of June; after which, Major Davie of the Ceylon regiment, succeeded to the command in Kandy.

After seizing the Kandian capital, no measures of sufficient energy secured the advantages acquired by the British troops; the surrounding country was left unsubdued, and the King, at a short distance off, was permitted to assemble the people, who began to recover from their panic. The season proved unhealthy; the natives gradually approached, and closing around the town, cut off the communications and supplies of this fated garrison, until on the night of the 23rd of June (emboldened by their knowledge of the general sickness from which the British force was suffering), the Kandians took possession of lines, which, within musket-shot reach, commanded and looked down upon the frail buildings in which the British forces were assembled.

Next day, they were attacked by large bodies of Kandians, goaded on by their chiefs, who were aware that on an eminence, secure from danger, a merciless monarch was watching their conduct, and would assuredly take a cruel revenge on whoever should prove timid or unsuccessful. After seven hours' fighting, and suffering considerable loss, Major Davie, who commanded the British troops, displayed a flag of truce, commenced negotiations, and accepted terms, which appear to have been dictated by Pilámé Taláwe, although the slightest reflection ought to have convinced the British commander that treachery and cunning formed the only stable principles of the first Adikar's policy. Major Davie abandoned his sick, trusting to the faith of a barbarian, who promised that they would be sent after he had departed, and then proceeded with all the troops that were able to march, to the Wattepolowa ferry on the Mahawelliganga. He found the river swollen from the heavy rains which had fallen in the mountains, and of course the canoes, which were to be furnished by the Kandian minister, were not only withheld, but everything which could facilitate the passage of the river had been removed.

Major Davie made no attempt to recede from the position which he first occupied,—a green hillock, crowned by a shady bo-tree, close to the bank of the river;—yet, by a vigorous attack, he might have dispersed the rabble of half-armed, unenergetic, and timid natives by whom he was surrounded, and might then have ensured his passage of the river, or by some other route have regained the British territory. Two circumstances which happened in the following year, I consider fully justify these remarks; the first was the total defeat of the Kandian military array (united under the eye of the King), by only a hundred men, mostly convalescents, under Captain Pollock; the second event was, the triumphant march of Captain Johnson's party, from one extremity to the other of the Kandian country, in the course of which he took its capital. The circumstances connected with these affairs will be detailed in their proper order of time; but it must be remembered that on these occasions the success of the Kandians (over Major Davie's troops), had given them a confidence in their own courage, which they had never before felt, and soon discovered to be fallacious.

Major Davie must have been devoid of energy, and destitute of mental resources, when he proceeded to violate the British faith, and the first duty of a soldier, by surrendering to certain death the unfortunate prince whom we had tempted to assume a nominal sovereignty. Mootoo Sámy, his five relations, and a deserter, were given up at the demand of the Kandian chiefs, who, in return, promised to fulfil their former engagement, of furnishing canoes for the troops to cross the river. "Is it possible, that the triumphant arms of England can be so humbled as to fear the menaces of such cowards as the Kandians?" was the just and natural exclamation of the unfortunate prince, on hearing that he was to be delivered into the hands of his furious rival. Mootoo Sámy and his friends being taken before the King, he ordered their instant execution, which took place on their removal from the royal presence, by the krises of the Kandian Malay guard: at the same time, the deserter was impaled; and, six weeks after, eight of the prince's attendants, deprived of their noses and ears, made their appearance at the fort of Trinkomalee.

Major Davie had no right to expect, and did not deserve that such conduct should free him from the difficulties of his situation; on the contrary, it elevated the spirits of the King, and stimulated him to attempt that act of atrocious cruelty, which suited so well with his cowardly character. He desired the Adikar and the chiefs to put the English to death. Some of his favourites were afterwards employed to request that he would mitigate the order, saying, "It is just that your enemies should be deprived of their property, and be detained as prisoners, but not that those who submit should suffer death." The King was furious at this opposition to his wishes, and hinted at the former treasons of his minister, whose overtures to the British Governor were known, although their extent was not then suspected by the King; for Pilámé Taláwe had sufficient art to deceive the tyrant, by deluding and betraying the British, when he found them unwilling to forward his nefarious schemes to their fullest extent. He was now, however, disinclined to commit an act which he was aware would for ever prevent his renewal of the secret negotiations with the British, through whose assistance he still hoped to reach the summit of his ambition. The danger of retaliation, and just revenge, was also put in his view by more than one of the chiefs; but the indirect threats of the King having dissipated the selfish scruples of the minister, he immediately proceeded to gratify his royal master, by carrying into effect the order he had received, with that mixture of cunning and cruelty which were the prominent features of his character. He first persuaded the wretched commander of the British troops to leave his men, and to bring some of his officers to the place, a little nearer Kandy, where the chiefs had established themselves, and which was removed from the view of the British position. The remainder of the party were then informed that these officers had crossed the river a mile higher up, and that all, leaving their arms behind, were to be removed in small parties to join the officers on the opposite bank. In this manner, unarmed, and only two or three at a time, the soldiers were conducted by Caffres, renegade Malays, and the lowest Kandians,* until each party arrived at the edge of a bank, where they could no longer be seen by their remaining comrades; they were then suddenly stabbed, or butchered in various ways, and their dead bodies were rolled down into the ravine beneath.

At the same time that the European troops were massacred near the river, the whole of the sick, in number a hundred and fifty,† one hundred and twenty of whom were soldiers of the 19th British regiment, who had been left behind in hospital,

* The Gahalas, who were compelled by custom, and inured by practice, to perform cruel executions, which were certainly repugnant to the Cingalese character and Buddhist religion, although apathy and terror prevented successful resistance to the crimes of tyrannical rulers.

† "The massacre of one hundred and fifty sick soldiers, lying helpless in the hospital of Kandy, left under the pledge of public faith, and the no less treacherous murder of the whole British garrison, commanded by Major Davie, which had surrendered on a promise of safety, impress upon the Governor's

were slaughtered in the town of Kandy; the dead, dying, and sick, having been thrown promiscuously into a pit prepared on purpose.*

As nearly as can be ascertained, the troops, under the command of Major Davie, on the banks of the river, consisted of seventeen officers, twenty European soldiers, two hundred and fifty Malays, and one hundred and forty gun Lascars. How many of the Malays and Lascars were sacrificed on the 26th of June, I could not ascertain; but from the information of survivors, I believe but few suffered, as the King vainly expected them to enter his army and serve him faithfully. Major Davie and Captain Rumley were intentionally preserved from the slaughter of Europeans; Captain Humphreys, and a sub-assistant surgeon, during the confusion, rolled themselves down the side of the ravine into which the bodies of their comrades were tumbled. After concealing themselves for some days, they were discovered, taken before the King, and ordered to be confined. The sub-assistant, in September, escaped to Colombo; Captains Rumley and Humphreys were soon cut off by sickness; Major Davie survived several years, and died about 1810: he ex-

mind an act of perfidy unparalleled in civilized warfare, and an awful lesson recorded in characters of blood, against the momentary admission of future confidence."

Extract from Sir Robert Brownrigg's official declaration on taking possession of the Kandian country.

* Davy's Ceylon.

isted unmolested, latterly almost unnoticed, in Kandy, and, I am informed, was not easily to be distinguished from a native. This unfortunate man therefore expiated his errors of judgment by lingering out his existence in a miserable captivity; and we may mitigate our severe opinion of the indefensible acts of this unfortunate commander, by imagining how much the scenes of sickness and suffering which he constantly witnessed may have affected his mind. We also see that his superiors, with better opportunities of information, were equally the dupes, and only by good fortune escaped becoming the victims of Kandian treachery.

Amidst the mass of dead in the ravine near Wattepolowa, grievously wounded, and tormented by thirst, lay Corporal Barnsley, of the 19th regiment, having a deep cut of a sword on his neck, and a contusion from the blow of a club on his head. Towards night, having felt returning strength, he determined to exert his remaining energies in attempting to escape. When it became dark, he contrived to disengage himself from the festering heap of his slaughtered fellow-soldiers, and, although suffering excruciating pain. swam across the river. In his feeble state the kindness of various natives relieved him from hunger and thirst, at great peril to themselves, and this is one of many proofs that the cruelties of which Kandians have been guilty were to be attributed to the vices of their rulers, and is no inherent part of the native character. Corporal Barnsley reached the post of Fort Macdowal, in Mátalé, eighteen miles from Kandy, and, along with its garrison, escaped to Trinkomalee, and recovered from his wounds. On hearing from this man the fate of the troops under Major Davie, the officer who commanded at Fort Macdowal abandoned nineteen sick Europeans,* and that same night commenced his retreat to Trinkomalee. At this period the conduct of Ensign John Grant, of the Malay corps, deserves to be particularly remembered, as exhibiting a proof of what the firmness and courage of a few men well commanded could effect against a multitude of undisciplined natives, even in the intoxication of their undeserved success over larger parties. Ensign Grant had only fourteen European convalescents and twenty-two invalid Malays to defend the unhealthy post of Dambadennia † against thousands of Kandians; but having strengthened the place by a breastwork of rice bags and other stores which had been under his charge, he bade defiance to the open attacks of the natives, and treated with contempt their treacherous offers of protection and promised safe conduct in case of his surrender. After maintaining his post for ten days, a reinforcement arrived, and the gallant party retired to Colombo.

After the surrender of the force under Major Davie, the native officers of the Malay corps in the British service behaved with that stern fidelity and

* Cordiner.

† In the Seven Korles.

gallant spirit that shows how well they might have been depended on had not the wavering timidity of their superior in rank wrought out so miserable a catastrophe. When brought before the King, they indignantly refused the tempting offers which were made to induce them to enter into his service; the threats, even the certainty of death, had no influence on their decision; they died refusing to violate their oath of allegiance, or compromise their strict feelings of honour. The principal officer of the Malays, Captain Nouradeen, and his brother, following his example, when brought before the tyrant, saluted him respectfully; but neither promises nor threats would induce them to prostrate themselves as they were required to do. They were then imprisoned for two months, and again sent for, and offered the alternative of a command in the Kandian troops, or instant death; they did not hesitate, but firmly refused to violate their engagements to the King of England. They were ordered to immediate execution, and their unburied bodies were left a prey to dogs and jackals. If any circumstance could add to the admiration with which such noble feelings of honour in these native officers should be regarded, it is, that their brother was at the same time in the service of the Kandian King.

Many of the Malay private oldiers entered the Kandian King's service, but took the first favourable opportunity of escaping to their old masters; and at

Hangwelle they had formed a plot for capturing the King and carrying him into the British lines, but his cautious timidity and sudden flight prevented the attempt from being made.

After the destruction of the garrison of Kandy, the Kandians began to press upon the maritime provinces, and in August, not without support from many of its inhabitants, overran the rich district of Matura, and occupied the small fort of Tangalle, which had been abandoned. Captain Beaver, of the 19th regiment, being sent against them, soon expelled the invaders, with little loss to his own party; and a few examples having been made of those British subjects who had assisted the Kandians, these valuable provinces of the south were reduced to their former peaceable state. Ensign Pendergast had already repulsed the mountaineers from Hambantotte, which was garrisoned with invalid Malays, and with them he made a sortie, which effectually dislodged the Kandians from the neighbourhood of the salt Leways. On the 24th of August, Mohammed Ally Ibrahim, a native officer, sallied out from the fort of Chilaw, and drove off a large body of Kandians with considerable loss. About the same time Major Evans surprised and defeated a body who had assembled for the purpose of attacking Putlam, and the King, on hearing the result, ordered the chief of the Kandian party to be executed. In short, in every direction inroads were made, and all of them were repelled with loss;

amongst others, Chilaw was again attacked, and successfully defended by Messrs. Campbell and Deane of the Ceylon civil service, and twenty-five Sepoys; when their shot was expended they fired copper coins upon the Kandians, and maintained the post until relieved from Colombo.

The Kandian tyrant, insensible to advice, and inflated by the praises of those who attributed to his power the effects of his falsehood and cruelty, summoned the whole force of his country, and advanced in the direction of Colombo, in hopes of expelling the British from the Maritime provinces. Having reached Hangwelle, eighteen miles from Colombo, on the 6th of September, 1803, he proceeded to attack the fieldwork there, which was garrisoned by one hundred men, mostly convalescents, under Captain Pollock, 51st regiment. Thirty of these he had despatched under Lieutenant Mercer, 51st regiment; and when the Kandians attacked the post in front, and were suffering severely from its fire, this party, coming on their flank by a circuitous path, through a thick jungle, caused the whole Kandian army to give way, and following the example of their King, they fled in the utmost confusion. The British had only two men wounded; but the slaughter of Kandians was great, as the Coolies employed for the purpose buried two hundred and seventy bodies next day. Many of the Malays and gun Lascars made their escape during this rout, and returned to their regiments: the

Lascars (in this affair) had been compelled to serve the Kandian guns, but pointed them so that no injury was done by their fire. In the fatiguing marches and desultory warfare of this year, the names of Captain John Buchan, Captain Frederick Hankey, Captain F. Von Driberg, Lieutenants Jewel and Johnson, are particularly mentioned for their energetic exertions in clearing the maritime provinces of the intruders, and securing those traitors who abetted the Kandians.

In 1804, Captain Johnson, in command of a small body of troops, had been ordered to proceed from Batticaloe to form a junction with another party on the verge of the British possessions; after which the united force was to push forward into the Kandian country. It appears that if this arrangement was ever really intended, the plan was subsequently abandoned for a desultory warfare of petty inroads, by separate parties advancing from various points, but with orders not to remain in permanent possession of the country they might overrun. As the original orders given to Captain Johnson were not cancelled by subsequent instructions, as was the case with other officers who were to command detached parties, he entered the Kandian country, traversed its most difficult defiles, crossed its largest river, took its capital, and only then discovered that he was unsupported, and that on his own resources must depend the safety of a detachment, which at starting only mustered three hundred and five men, and these were now isolated in the very centre of an enemy's country.

It was under these discouraging circumstances that Captain Johnson departed from Kandy to fight his way through forests for one hundred and thirty miles to Trinkomalee; and before crossing the Mahawelliganga, the feelings of his gallant band had to be farther depressed by passing through the field of slaughter, and the scattered bones of their comrades who had composed the force under Major Davie: neither could they fail to call to mind that it was a party superior in numbers to their own, which had left so sad a memorial. However, the same prudence, decision, and spirit in their commander, who had conducted them so far, sufficed to lead them through a host of enemies cowering in the long continuance of the Mátalé forests: finally, with a loss of two officers and forty-eight men, the party reached Trinkomalee, well nigh worn out with continual fatigue, anxiety and suffering. Although unsuccessful for any immediate military advantage, and discreditable to those who had exposed a portion of the army to unnecessary hardships, and probable destruction, yet the gallantry of Captain Johnson and his party taught the Kandians a respect for British troops which they had not before felt, and afterwards reluctantly admitted. One of the chiefs who harassed Captain Johnson in his retreat, assured me that the commander of the party must have been in alliance with supernatural powers, as his personal escape whilst passing through a continued ambush, and his superior judgment and energy were unaccountable, unless this explanation was admitted.

In the period from which I have sketched these details, our troops were grievously harassed and uselessly sacrificed; we neither conciliated our own subjects, nor gained respect from our enemies; our negotiations were despicable, our policy unsuccessful.

After these exertions, the British sank into a feverish repose in a defensive attitude; an undignified and impolitic position to assume before a cruel and treacherous enemy, to whom we might have dictated terms, instead of appearing to forget injuries. I have no means of ascertaining whether our pacific or passive policy after this time, was influenced by the common and most erroneous belief entertained of the general unhealthiness of the Kandian country; but that impression did exist, and certainly continued long after experience had proved that, if not altogether unfounded, the insalubrity, even of the worst portions of the Kandian provinces, had been greatly exaggerated. The principal causes of the general sickness and grievous mortality amongst the British troops that had been marched into the interior, arose from the injudicious choice of wrong seasons and unhealthy routes, in which our troops were moved; whilst the permanent posts were too often established in the most pestilential places.

It was during this long season of distrust and inactivity, as regarded the British and Kandians, that their King was progressing in a career of guilt, which finally led to his own overthrow, and fixed the "emerald gem of the eastern world" in the crown of the British monarch.

CHAPTER III.

HISTORY OF THE BRITISH IN CEYLON CONTINUED.

Ruin seize thec, rtuhless King,
Confusion on thy banners wait.—GRAY.

Proceedings at the Kandian Court. — Attempt to Assassinate the King. — Execution of Pilámé Taláwe, 1812. — *Eheylapola.— Unparalleled Cruelty of the King to the Family of Eheylapola,* 1814. — *Other Acts of his Cruelty. — Sir Robert Brownrigg Governor. — The British Army enters the Kandian Country— Is joined by the Natives. — The King taken and Dethroned.— The whole Island united under the British Authority. — The last Kandian King. — His Death. — Character. — Kandian Rebellion of* 1817.—*Rebellion suppressed,* 1818. —*Fate of the Rebel Leaders. — Wilbawe, the pretended King. — Authority of the Native Chiefs abridged. — Moormen. — Sir Edward Barnes's Government. — Public Roads. — Sir Robert Wilmot Horton, Governor. — Abolition of all compulsory Services,* 1832. — *The Charter,* 1833. — *Natives declared eligible to fill every Office. — Admitted into the Legislative Council. — New Judicial System. — Abortive Conspiracy of Native Chiefs and Priests,* 1834. — *Rapid Improvement of the Country. — Christianity. — Education.*

TRAINED to bloody deeds and treacherous conduct, the Kandian King at last became jealous of the chief who had raised him to the throne, and instructed him in cruelty; the intrigues of Pilámé Taláwe were certainly sufficient to excite alarm, and if their scope had been known, to excuse any severity which the King might have adopted. Various acts of caprice and indecision on the part of the monarch with regard to his minister, terminated in 1812, by the dismissal of the first Adikar from all his offices. The degraded chief immediately commenced planning his revenge, and soon contrived to bribe a considerable body of Malays in the Kandian service to assist his schemes, which were to be commenced with the assassination of the monarch. Two districts near Kandy,* in which Pilámé Taláwe had much family influence, were gained over to assist the traitor, whose plans ultimately failed from the premature insurrection of these districts, before the murder of the King had been perpetrated. This deed had been delayed in consequence of their spy, one of the King's household, making it known to the assassins, that the King was awake at the hour when they expected to find him asleep, and seal his fate. The Malay conspirators escaped to Colombo; six inferior chiefs suffered death by torture; Pilámé Taláwe and his nephews were beheaded, and their extensive estates were added to the royal domains.

Pilámé Taláwe was succeeded in his office of first Adikar by Eheylapola, who two years afterwards, without having committed any crimes deserving

* Oodenuwara and Yattenuwara, near Kandy.

punishment like his predecessor, nevertheless saw unequivocal symptoms of being destined to a similar fate, and escaped from the country of the jealous tyrant, to place himself under the protection of the British Government. For this step, his wife, children, relations, and former adherents were put to death in various ways, with unparalleled cruelty,* and at this time the appetite of the royal monster for blood appears to have so increased with the number of victims, that in 1814 it had swallowed up every dread of consequences, while it rejected every circumstance of precaution. He had disgusted his subjects and alienated their affections by a severe exaction of compulsory labour, in forming the lake of Kandy; he had terrified the chiefs by confiscations and numerous executions from their number, and the class to which they belonged; he had combined the priesthood in hostility to his government by putting to death the second High-priest Paranataley, and finally reached the climax of reckless cruelty, when he ordered the mutilation of ten native traders, British subjects, whom he tortured, so that only three survived to reach the maritime provinces.†

* The particulars of this will be found in the account of Eheylapola.

† "Of this animosity" (on the part of the Kandian King), "a daring instance was exhibited in the unprovoked and barbarous mutilation of ten innocent subjects of the British Go-

At this time, the Governor and commander-in-chief was Sir Robert Brownrigg, who had determined (in opposition, it is said, to the advice of the Council), to revenge the intolerable insults and wanton aggressions which a powerless and merciless despot had offered to the British power, by dethroning the tyrant, and uniting the island under the authority of the British crown. For this determination there are abundant excuses on the plea of justice, protecting our own subjects from aggression, and relieving the Kandian people from a monstrous tyranny. On the score of policy, it is now admitted to be unobjectionable; our position, as masters of the maritime provinces, being one of extreme weakness, extending for eight hundred miles in a narrow belt all round the circumference of the island, whilst an enemy in possession of the interior could always assemble a force, and direct it against the most vulnerable post before the British authorities might ascertain the point to be attacked, or could send the necessary assistance to the place.

Having completed his hostile preparations, and immediately after the outrage (on the ten native traders) already mentioned,* the Governor declared

vernment, by which seven of the number lost their lives; a measure calculated, and apparently intended to put a final negative to every probability of friendly intercourse."—*Sir R. Brownrigg's official declaration.*

* A party of Kandians at the same time had advanced into the British territory and set fire to a village.—*Davy's Ceylon.*

war on the 10th of January, 1815, and the next day the British troops entered the Kandian territory. The arrangements for this invasion were complete and able, so that if the different divisions of the army had encountered opposition, the result would not have been doubtful; but the principal chiefs joined the British forces, and every one fled from the falling despot. On the 14th of February, our troops entered Kandy, and on the 18th the King was brought in prisoner, having been captured in the mountains of Dombara. On the 2nd of March, the British Governor and the native chiefs on the part of the Kandian people dethroned the tyrant, and the Kandians transferred their allegiance to the British Monarch.

Sri Wikrema Raja Singha was removed to Colombo, from thence to Madras, and finally to the Fort of Vellore, in which place he died of dropsy, 30th of January, 1832, aged fifty-two years;* the last seventeen of these he passed in confinement. His features were handsome, his figure manly, and his general appearance dignified; but the qualities of his mind appear to have been a compound of the meanest with the most violent passions, without one redeeming virtue to weigh against selfishness, cruelty, and cowardice: he was equally destitute of any amiable quality which could excite compas-

* The King left an only son, an infant; who, along with some other of his relations, receive trifling pensions from the Cingalese Government.

sion for his fate, even amongst those who served about his person, or had been advanced by his power.

The Kandian leaders were left in possession of their former offices, and the people were governed according to their ancient laws; but the chiefs soon felt that their influence had suffered by submitting to a regular and efficient Government, and that too a foreign one, which as yet they had not learned to respect, and from former examples hoped to overthrow. These were the first stimulants to a desire for change, and the over-conciliatory manner in which their headmen were treated by the highest British authorities, not only inspired them with a vain confidence in their own importance, but comparing this treatment with that of their late ruler, they came to the conclusion that so glaring a want of dignity could only proceed from conscious deficiency of power.

A rebellion was the consequence; it suddenly broke out in October, 1817, and soon after its commencement, the influential chiefs, with very few exceptions, were either in open rebellion, in confinement for favouring the rebels, or were only deterred by fear or policy from immediately joining a cause, to which they meant to adhere so soon as anticipated success should enable them to show their zeal, without incurring personal danger, or possible confiscation of property. Even Eheylapola, whose wife and family had been destroyed by the dethroned despot, and who had himself declined office, and only requested that he might be styled "The friend of the British Government," was arrested on well-grounded suspicion of his fidelity, and his brother-in-law, Kaepitapola, was the acknowledged leader of the rebels, and the undoubted instigator of their treason. He it was who had employed the pretender, who appeared as King, and was announced as Durra Sawmy, a member of the deposed royal family. The first open act of rebellion was the murder of a Moorman in the forest of Welasse, by order of this puppet of a King, the tool of those chiefs who were admitted into the secret. This act was soon followed by the death of Mr. Wilson, of the Ceylon civil service, who had proceeded to the spot with a small party of military, on receiving information of the murder, and some mysterious whisperings of intended treason; he fell by the arrows of the Veddahs, who had been summoned by the chiefs, and were assembled in considerable numbers, and on his death the party retired to Badulla.

The rebellion now spread rapidly; and in less than six months, most of those districts which had not already appeared in open insurrection, were secretly organised for revolt, and only awaited the fitting opportunity of joining the rebels. Luckily, the private animosity subsisting between Eheylapola and the first Adikar, Mollegodda, induced the latter to exert his influence in support of the

British supremacy, which he had good reason to identify with his own safety. By his influence in the district of the Four Corles, the people there were generally restrained from insurrection; a service of great importance at this period to the British interest, as through that province lay the principal defiles and mountain passes of the road, which led from Colombo to the Kandian capital.

A protracted warfare of small military posts established throughout the country, and detached parties in continual motion, pursuing an armed population in a mountainous and wooded country, was naturally productive of considerable loss to the British force; for, although few fell by the weapons of the Kandians, exposure and privations proved fatal to many. Driven from their villages, their cocoa-nut trees cut down, their property and crops destroyed, and, unable to till their land, the natives suffered severely from sickness and famine, besides those who fell by the fire of the British troops, or suffered execution for their treasonable actions. Dr. Davy, who had the best opportunities of ascertaining the loss of life occasioned by this rebellion, estimates that of the British at one thousand; and I believe he certainly is not over the amount, when he says, that ten thousand natives were cut off by war or its consequences at this period.

After the rebellion had continued for nine months, no favourable impression had been made by the great exertions of our troops, who were nearly exhausted by incessant fatigue, and extreme privations in a tropical climate; it is even understood that arrangements were in contemplation for withdrawing the British force from the interior, when a sudden change occurred. This was principally caused by disunion amongst the leaders of the rebels, who were incapable of continued perseverance in any one object, or of sacrificing their petty jealousies and personal disputes, even to forward a cause in which they had perilled their lives and hereditary properties, — things almost equally dear to a Kandian chief.

Madugalla, an influential headman of Dombara, coming to an open rupture with Kaepitapola, detected, and openly exposed the impostor King, whom he placed in the stocks, and it was then ascertained beyond a doubt, that the pretender was a native of the village from which he took the name of Wilbawe, and that he had formerly been a Buddhist priest.

Wilbawe contrived to extricate himself from durance, and escaped to the remote province of Nuwara Kalawia; there he had the good fortune to remain unnoticed for fourteen years, although at one time he was compelled to assist a party who were searching for him near the deserted city of Annurâdhapoora. The large reward that still remained offered for his apprehension, having stimulated the perseverance of a Buddhist priest (who was familiar with his features), he at last in his wanderings recognised the object of his search, and, having given information, Wilbawe was secured in 1829. When arrested, it was found that he had received a severe injury in the shoulder from a wild elephant, and that hard labour and anxiety had greatly changed his appearance, and given him a peculiarly melancholy cast of countenance; he had been a handsome man, and with features strongly resembling the Kandian royal family, of which native scandal said he was an illegitimate member. He was tried and convicted, but afterwards received a pardon by orders from Britain. After the detection of Wilbawe, our parties were uniformly successful, the insurgents gradually dispersed, their leaders fled, and the three of most influence, viz. Kaepitapola, Madugalla, and Pilámé Taláwe, were apprehended and brought to trial. Pilámé Taláwe, a weak and indolent man, was a son of the late first Adikar of the same name, but as free from the cruel propensities of his father as from his abilities and energy; — he was transported to the Mauritius. Madugalla * and Kaepitapola were beheaded; the latter, a man of ability, activity,

* The eldest son of Madugalla, a boy about six years old at the time of his father's death, having been educated at one of the missionary's establishments, was afterwards admitted into the office of Government at Matali, as a volunteer, where he proved himself useful and intelligent. He was then removed, and received a good appointment in the revenue department. Soon after this promotion, having proceeded to his native village to take possession of some of his father's lands, which had been restored to the family, in an unlucky dispute with his aunt,

and influence, but of great duplicity of character, when he found that cunning and subtlety were ineffectual to save him from punishment, met death without apathy, yet with a firmness and courage worthy of a different fate, and better cause. Eheylapola was not tried, nor were his lands confiscated; but he was banished to the Isle of France, along with several chiefs of inferior note. On the termination of hostilities and return to order, an entire change in the management of the Kandian provinces was accomplished. The paramount influence of the chiefs in the different districts was destroyed, by placing civilians, or British officers, in authority over them, to collect the revenue, and administer justice; while all the inferior headmen, instead of being appointed annually by the chief, received their situations direct from Government. This arrangement, not only gave increased security to the Government, but enabled the poor native suitor to obtain that justice which he had little chance of receiving under the former system, where money or influence might alike bias the judge, or direct the evidence.

We could not blame the chiefs if they had at-

having used some disrespectful expressions, her husband cleft the young man's head with an axe which lay near. This uncle, also called Madugalla, was the first native of rank tried before the supreme court, when it was introduced into the Kandian provinces in 1834. His jury of Kandian chiefs found him guilty of manslaughter, and he received sentence of seven years' transportation.

tempted to re-establish a native dynasty, which was hallowed in their eyes by its antiquity, and by conformity to the established religion; but, to call their exertions in this rebellion patriotism, would be to dignify it with a name of which their motives were unworthy. Self-interest, and to restore their own power over the mass of the people, whom they had so long oppressed, was their principal aim and final object: the restoration of a native monarchy was a secondary consideration, but a necessary step; the means by which they endeavoured to accomplish their purpose were often cruel, and generally treacherous. It is true, the British had acquired the quiet possession of the Kandian country by a convention with the people, represented by their chiefs, and not by direct conquests; but this circumstance was more a point of honour, than a substantial difference to the people. Their history contained the records of many attempts to expel foreign invaders from the land, and hitherto, whether against Europeans or Asiatics, success had always sanctified these endeavours. This was a powerful incentive to the headmen, and must be considered as a proportionably strong excuse for their rebellion, by which they hoped to regain that position and precedence so much valued by Kandians, and which they perceived had passed from them to rest with Europeans. Many of them must also have felt that their indolent and intriguing dispositions were more suited to a despot's court, than to acquiring the habits of activity, and the information expected from chiefs employed under British authorities. Others judged rightly, in thinking it would be better to trust to the caprice of a tyrant, than to have their merits for office too closely scanned, or their administration of justice too minutely examined.

After the rebellion was suppressed, no unnecessary punishments were inflicted; even to the rebel leaders, or their descendants, great consideration was shown, as soon as it could be done, without exciting the idea that our clemency was the offspring of timidity. Indeed, I cannot help thinking, that hundreds of British, and thousands of native lives might have been saved, if, at the commencement of the rebellion, a stern and severe example had been made of the persons and property of those who first committed acts of treason and murder, and had taken the field in arms against the British Government. It would have struck terror into all classes, and have been a sufficient excuse to the lower ranks for withdrawing to those homes which, in the event of their remaining absent, would be rendered desolate; for it was no affection for their leaders, or pretence at principle, that induced the multitude to rise in insurrection: they had no interest in the cause, and ventured their lives on no stronger temptation than ancient habits of blind obedience to the chiefs, or for fear of revenge in the event of their success.

The Moormen (as the Mohammedan inhabitants are called), who are numerous in several districts, attached themselves on every occasion, and zealously, to the British interest; and at the commencement of the rebellion, promises were made to them, by proclamation, with regard to their not again being put under Kandian (Cingalese) headmen, which I do not think were afterwards fairly and fully performed; for while compulsory labour existed, they were called out by, and performed duties under, Cingalese headmen: this never appeared to me either politic or just.

After the departure of Sir Robert Brownrigg, Sir Edward Barnes, who succeeded to the government, planned and superintended with unceasing vigilance the opening up of the Kandian provinces, by the formation of extensive carriage roads, and building substantial bridges. Under him, the country derived all the benefit that could be produced by unrecompensed compulsory labour, which was exacted according to the customs of that despotism, to the powers of which the British Government had succeeded. The untiring vigilance and personal activity which Sir Edward Barnes exerted in superintending public works, alone caused so vicious a system to be of public benefit; under any man of less energy, unrecompensed compulsory labour would have been an unmitigated curse, enforcing caste, depopulating the country, and producing no adequate results. Each subdivision of class or caste, was called out for service by its own headman, who, as he received no pay, depended for the amount of his perquisites and peculations on the number under him; it was, therefore, a motive paramount to all others in natives, self-interest, which insured the headman retaining all the members of his department in their original vocation and due subjection. Not only did this system maintain caste with the utmost strictness, but it retained and supported in full power over the people, those headmen whose interests could never be otherwise than opposed to a regular Government.

It must also be considered, that without injustice to individuals, regularity of system, backed by power to enforce all legal rights, enabled the British Government to exact much more, both of labour and revenue, than any native despot would have ventured to demand.

In 1831, Sir Robert Wilmot Horton arrived as Governor; and next year, in consequence of the report of His Majesty's Commissioners of inquiry, the Magna Charta of Ceylon, the order of the King in council * abolishing all compulsory service, reached the island, and the native inhabitants passed in a day from a state more bitter than slavery to the most perfect freedom. In their former oppressed state, it is true, that justice was impartially

* Dated the 12th April 1832, it reached Ceylon, and was immediately proclaimed on the 28th September 1832.

administered to the rich and to the poor, in so far as the facts of the case could be ascertained; yet the rich man was disgusted by impartial conduct in the judges, while the poor suitors did not benefit by it; for the rich litigant could bribe the influential native in office, and he could command the oaths of those who, placed and secured under his control, were not only liable to be overworked by his orders, but were even subject to punishment at his caprice.*

A charter soon followed the abolition of forced labour, and the people, having already obtained freedom, now found easy access to substantial and speedy justice, whilst every situation was thrown open to their competition, and the acquirements and character of the individual, not the colour of his skin, became the only tests of fitness for every office. Three gentlemen, natives of Ceylon, were introduced into the legislative council on terms of perfect equality with the other unofficial members, although it required some firmness on the part of Government to carry into effect this liberal provision of the supreme Government.

Of the new system for administering justice in Ceylon I shall attempt an outline, as it appears to me extremely simple, at the same time that it has

* These remarks are made from my own observations in the Kandian country, in which I held office four years before, and for a still longer period after the abolition of compulsory labour.

proved most efficient.* In the first place, a district judge, with three assessors, selected daily by lot, form the District Court, which exercises exclusive original jurisdiction within certain geographical limits. All civil cases whatever, arising within its bounds, must first be decided in that court; but every decision there pronounced may be appealed from, and revised before a judge of the Supreme Court, with three assessors, on half yearly circuit; or might be appealed to the three judges of the Supreme Court at Colombo. In criminal cases the power of district courts was restricted, and persons accused of great crimes were committed for trial before the Supreme Court on circuits, where they were prosecuted by the King's advocate, and tried by a jury of thirteen intelligent persons of any class or colour. In civil cases, where judgments were appealed against from a District Court, the appellant was prevented from benefitting by delay; and in criminal cases the judge, notwithstanding the appeal, might carry the sentence into effect on his own responsibility. Soon after the beneficial and important changes consequent upon the abolition of compulsory labour, and the introduction of the improved system of administering justice began to be felt, the chiefs, seeing that their tyrannical power and undue influence were thereby abolished, con-

* This plan was the proposal of C. H. Cameron, Esq. one of his Majesty's Commissioners of Inquiry for Ceylon. The arrangements for carrying it into practice were most ably perfected by the Chief Justice, Sir C. Marshall.

spired together, and contemplated, along with some intriguing priests, to overthrow the British power. The highest class did not perceive any immediate benefit to themselves from the new system of liberal policy, and of course were jealous of the advantages conferred on the great body of the people, whom they had hitherto held in subjection; but this conspiracy showed how wise, as well as humane, the policy was that broke at once the rod of the oppressor, for it was by it that the chiefs were enabled to goad the people into open rebellion against the British Government in 1817 — now in 1834, as not one of their former followers, or present dependents, would assist in again putting the yoke on their own necks, it was proposed to have recourse to deception, and rouse them, during a religious festival, by a false announcement, that the British Government had restored forced labour, and abolished the Buddhist religion. Poison and massacre were spoken of as means to be used against the Europeans in the Kandian country, but no plan had been fixed; and the utter absurdity of their views and hopelessness of such an attempt would possibly have led to its abandonment, but it was found necessary to check their wild designs, and several of the principal chiefs and a few priests were arrested. One of the circumstances which seemed to have been a bond of union amongst those who at least contemplated treason, was, that the charter of justice, by putting all power of punishment in the hands of the District Courts, and introducing the English criminal law, effectually prevented the ill-treatment of slaves, and rendered their services of much less value. The open, even violent, manner in which several Europeans declaimed against the abolition of compulsory labour, and the other benefits conferred upon the mass of the people in Ceylon, no doubt had its effect on the chiefs, and in some degree palliates their offence, which was little more than arranging to destroy improvements which some of their superiors too openly condemned.

In January, 1835, several chiefs and priests were tried for treason before a judge of the Supreme Court, and a jury composed of six Europeans and seven natives of high rank from the maritime provinces. The prisoners had objected to being tried by Kandians (even chiefs), and the event justified their foresight; the evidence against them was strong, but the prisoners were acquitted. It is understood that the six Europeans were unanimous for conviction, but that the seven natives (being the majority) were of a contrary opinion, and the verdict accordingly was, not guilty. No evil consequences ensued from this verdict, and the people learned from the trial what would have been attempted against their new liberties. Government removed from office those chiefs whom the evidence had proved to be unworthy of confidence, and rewarded those who had been instrumental in developing the plans of the conspirators.

The great changes recommended by the commissioners of inquiry had been only a short time introduced, when an immense improvement in the condition of the people, as well as in the face of the country, became apparent, for increased cultivation of grain by the natives, and the formation of coffee and other plantations by them and Europeans was the natural consequence of destroying the monopoly of a nation's labour. From the genial climate little clothing is requisite in Ceylon, and abundance of food (at the worst, fruit and yams) with fuel at command, probably places the peasant of Ceylon in a more enviable position than the inhabitant of any other country. As to the higher classes (except the old chiefs) they have lost the recollection of barbarous power, and, whilst giving their children an English education, are teaching them to aspire to those offices which confer real importance and just influence on the possessors. The highest rank of natives in general have mild manners and quick abilities; and from the laudable ambition with which they are inspired, we may expect, ere long, that many of them will be found filling with respectability the high official situations which so justly and so liberally have been opened to their competition.

Before closing this account of British rule, I shall give my opinion of the state and prospects of Christianity in Ceylon. This religion was introduced into the northern provinces at a very early period by Nestorian missionaries from Persia, and was adopted by many of the inhabitants on the north-west coast nearest to Malabar. The Portuguese in the beginning of the sixteenth century, by persuasion or compulsion, made many converts, and the principal Portuguese officers became sponsors to the Cingalese chiefs who embraced Christianity; they at the same time adopted the surname of their godfather, in addition to their native family name, and thus we find amongst the Cingalese the names of Perera, De Silva, Liveyra, and most others which appear in the list of those Portuguese who held the highest offices in the island, from 1518 to 1658. After that period, the Dutch having dispossessed the Portuguese of all the territory they held in Ceylon, attempted to supersede the Roman Catholic religion by the Protestant, and took an effectual way of making hypocrites under the pretence of improving that system of Christianity which had been already introduced. The Dutch declared that, to enable a native to hold office, it was necessary he should profess the reformed faith. In consequence of this rule, those who aspired to office apostatised, while those who had nothing to gain by a change, remained steadfast in their religion.

However objectionable their mode of conversion may have been, the Dutch deserve credit for their perseverance in educating the natives in Christianity, and in establishing a general system of schools for their instruction. In 1796, the British superseded the Dutch in their power over the maritime provinces of the island, but under the Government of Madras which continued for two years, "the catechists and schoolmasters no longer received their salaries;" and "the duties of public worship, and the education of the youth began to be feebly discharged or entirely neglected."* When the island ceased to be under the Honourable East India Company, and Governor North arrived in 1798, he re-established and remodelled the places of education, and in 1801, there were one hundred and seventy schools, and "the number of native Protestant Christians exceeded three hundred and forty-two thousand. The Christians professing the religion of the church of Rome, are supposed to be still more numerous."

"Early in the year 1803, instructions in His Majesty's name were received at Colombo, directing that the expense of all the schools in the island should be limited to the amount of fifteen hundred pounds per annum."† In the report of the commissioners of inquiry, December, 1831, I find that "the Government schools have continued to be maintained by the British Government, but they are extremely defective and inefficient;" and again, "as the control exercised is insufficient to secure

* Cordiner's Ceylon. † Ibid.

the attendance either of the masters or of the scholars, many abuses prevail, and the Government schools, in several instances, exist only in name." The wretched parsimony of the British home Government, in reducing the funds necessary and previously given for education, at the same time that so many situations for Europeans were invented, and such lavish expenditure in salaries was sanctioned, apparently admits of no justification. Much, however, has been done by the exertions of missionaries in propagating true Christianity, and in educating the natives.

After the report of the commission of inquiry, and the arrival of Sir R. W. Horton, as Governor, the subject of education attracted more attention, and arrangements were made for having the English language generally taught. If this is zealously persevered in, I should be inclined to adopt the language of Cordiner, who, writing in 1807, regarding the introduction of Christianity, says, "There is no doubt that if ever the Government of England pay attention to this subject, the religion of Christ will become as clearly understood, and as well practised, in Ceylon, as in any part of the King's dominions."

In Ceylon, the face of the country rapidly improving, trade increasing, diminished taxation, an increasing revenue, with a happy and contented people, are undeniable evidences to prove that the radical changes made in this colony are correct in theory, and have been carried into effect honestly and ably, by the executive of Ceylon, under the Government of Sir Robert Wilmot Horton.

CHAPTER IV.

ANCIENT INSTITUTIONS AND SUCCESSION OF NATIVE KINGS OF CEYLON.

They were of most ancient time:
Of primeval age and clime.—READE.

Preservation of the Native Annals from B.C. 543, *to* A.D. 1815.— *Ancient Cingalese Courts.* — *Plurality of Husbands.* — *Trial by Ordeal.* — *Caste.*—*Extraordinary Murder.*—*The Rhodias.* — *Complaint against a Rhodia.* — *Kandian Form of Government.* — *Number of Cingalese Kings.* — *Comparative length of their Reigns at different periods.*—*Proportion of violent Deaths.* —*Female Sovereigns : Anoola*—*Singhawallee*—*Leelawatee*— *Kalyanawattee* — *Donna Catherina.* — *Duties of a Cingalese Monarch.* — *List of the Kings of Ceylon, from* 543 B.C. *to* A.D. 1815.

As this narrative of travels is intended to illustrate the history and antiquities, as well as the scenery and field sports of Ceylon, it would be imperfectly understood without some knowledge of the native history, as well as of British dominion in the Island; I have, therefore, prefixed this sketch of the ancient institutions of the country, and the succession of its Kings.

The possession of the Kandian country has enabled us to prove the truth of Cingalese history, so long despised by Europeans, by examining remains of antiquity, and inscriptions which, situated in forests, covered with vegetation, and sunk in obscurity, have been lately recalled from oblivion to bear witness to the authenticity of the native records, and to the minute accuracy with which Cingalese historians detailed the particulars of the building of religious edifices, and the embellishment of their ancient capitals. To the historical being blended with the religious in the native annals, in so far as relates to the erection and endowment of religious edifices, and the gifts bestowed to the Buddhist priesthood, we probably owe the complete preservation of the Cingalese chronicles through so many ages, and in despite of repeated attempts at their destruction.*

At whatever time we find that the religion of the island was prosperous, then the history is distinct; and when Buddhism wanes, we have to grope our way through doubtful and meagre details of historical events. Miracles and prophecies are to be found in every ancient history; — in that of Ceylon they are not more numerous than in the early chronicles of other countries, and fewer

* Mágha, a foreign invader, who ruled from A.D. 1214 to 1235, and Raja Singha, the apostate, who reigned from A.D. 1581 to 1592, are particularly mentioned as attempting to destroy the ancient records.

than might have been expected, if we consider the allegorical style of Eastern writing, and how generally inventions have been set up to cast a shade which might prevent any other than the privileged eyes of priesthood from seeing too minutely into history and religion. Cingalese historians seem in some degree to have associated the ideas of corporeal size with mental superiority, and political power with numbers; yet they may only mean multitudes, when they express *laksha* (a hundred thousand), as *yodhya*, usually translated giant, is a word applicable to great power of mind, as well as to uncommon stature, and, consequently, is used for an eminent man, whether sage or warrior.* If the events be compared, and Buddhist miracles are excluded from Cingalese history, we shall find records of accurate detail and great antiquity commencing with Vijeya and the invasion of the Singha race, B.C. 543, and terminating in A.D. 1815, with Wikremo Singha, the last and worst of a faded dynasty and fallen nation.

When we compare the remains of the many extensive and permanent works of the earlier inhabitants, with those, few in number and frail in construction, which later generations in Ceylon have reared, I am tempted to suggest, as one

* I have examined a royal grant, not a hundred years old, in which the grantee is termed *yodhya*, and his services are stated to have been forming a tank, and checking smallpox by the power of charms.

cause of their inferiority, that from the time when Buddhism declined in India, and its most valued relic, the Dalada, found refuge in Ceylon, A.D. 309, there appears to have been a decay of all friendly communication and general intercourse between the island and the continent. From that time, the Cingalese, having nothing to excite them to emulation, no foreign example to stimulate their energies, and prevented by caste from improvement,* slowly and gradually declined in the arts; yet, carefully preserving hereditary prejudices, and inheriting the pride, without the power, of their ancestors, they became distinguished by presumptuous vanity and contented ignorance of everything beyond the limits of their country.

Ceylon, previous to the invasion of the Singha race, appears to have been divided into separate principalities; but the nature of its institutions in that early period cannot now be traced. If the inhabitants then, like the Veddahs now, were exempt from caste, it was imposed upon them by their conqueror Vijeya, and was subsequently confirmed by the policy of succeeding Kings, and the prejudices of those classes who accompanied Mehindoo to Ceylon, B.C. 307. In a Cingalese work, there is a fanciful account of the descent of Vijeya from Sammata Raja, King of India, a person of the

* Caste, although contrary to the tenets of Gautama Buddha, was always maintained by the policy of Cingalese Kings and the pride of the higher classes.

solar race, described as being the first mortal who was elected and acknowledged as a chief by those who peopled the earth immediately after the fall. The powers voluntarily conferred upon Sammata Raja, are declared to have been unlimited; and from the wealth of his subjects, his necessities were to be supplied. The Kings of Ceylon, according to the example of their supposed ancestor, claimed the same prerogative, and appear to have admitted the necessity of election, previous to their inauguration; even the last King of Kandy went through the farce of receiving a confirmation of his right to the throne from the voices of the people.

In the constitution of Kandian society, the Gam-sabae and Ratta-sabae (the village and district councils) afford specimens of free institutions, which one could not expect to find surviving through so long a period of arbitrary rule. The village council was composed of the head of every family residing within its limits, however low his rank, or small his property: from this tribunal, there was an appeal to the district council, which consisted of intelligent delegates from each village in the Pattoo or subdivision of a district. Village councils were indispensable, in a country where landed property is so minutely divided, and consanguinity so entangled as in Ceylon; but in 1828, district councils only lingered in the remote province of Nuwara-kalawia, and even there, were seldom used. Equal division of property amongst the children, and plurality of husbands amongst the women, besides other causes, offer sufficient reasons for intricacy in the settlement of inheritance. Trial by ordeal, dipping the hands in boiling oil, or heated cow-dung; also, oaths in a temple, or under a bo-tree, were in use for deciding cases prior to 1815; but when the British agents were appointed to administer justice, these forms of chance judgment were no longer permitted.

The Cingalese consider their ancient royal race, called Sákya, Ikshwaku, Okàka, and Suraya-wanzae,* to be of the highest caste; but as none, even of the chiefs, are of the Brahman caste, they are at no trouble to decide on the relative precedence of the royal "race of the sun," with the sacerdotal race of Brahmans, but acknowledge both to be superior to any of the families now existing in Ceylon. In the Kandian country, there were none of the Cingalese inhabitants who lived exclusively by mercantile pursuits; and the highest caste is that of the cultivators, called Goya-wanzae, the same as is known in the maritime provinces by the appellation of Wellale; to this belong the chiefs and principal families, and with these were ranked the Christians. The labourers and tradesmen, alotted to particular services and trades, formed the other caste, called Kshudra-wanzae; and in it, not only each service or trade was separated from another,

* *Suraya*, sun; *Wanzae*, race, or lineage.

but was also subdivided into branches, the families of which did not intermarry. A Kandian of the Seven Korles having discovered that an intimacy subsisted between his daughter and a person of somewhat inferior rank, put her to death, and placed her body on a sort of temporary stage, such as is used for making offerings to the devils. According to an ancient superstition, he believed this horrid act rendered pure and unimpeachable the honour of his family, which had been sullied by the misconduct of one of its members. When apprehended by order of the British authorities, the infatuated father avowed the deed, and suffered as a murderer. A very few such cases have caused an erroneous impression on many persons, not intimately acquainted with the Cingalese character, that they are naturally a cruel people. Although the death of the man was perhaps a necessary example for murder committed under the influence of a mistaken zeal for family honour, yet it cannot fail to strike one as in strange contrast to the practice with regard to Britons in their own affairs (as they are called) of honour, when, if not enforced in spite of the law, certain classes are at least encouraged to stake their own or take another's life, and that on points certainly of less consequence to them, than the degradation of a whole family and their posterity.

The particulars regarding the castes, and their classification, however much condensed, would be tiresome to a general reader, and to those who take an interest in the subject, an abridgment would be of little value;* I shall, therefore, pass to the outcast Rhodias who have inherited the dreadful punishment to which their remote ancestors, either for sins or misfortunes, had been condemned. These punishments, after enduring for upwards of two thousand years, and intended to be perpetual in the posterity of the original victims, are now at an end, as well as the dynasty which established and continued these atrocious cruelties. There are several fabulous accounts of the institution of these outcasts: one generally believed by natives, is, that this race were originally the hunters and purveyors of game for the royal table, and that on a certain occasion, having failed to procure game, they substituted the flesh of a child. Another account is, that continuing to eat beef after it was prohibited, was the cause of the disgrace and sufferings of the Rhodias; but treason and sacrilege, if not the original crimes for which they were condemned, are certainly those which in later times have continued or increased the numbers of the outcasts. About the middle of the eighteenth century, the sacrilegious act of one was made the excuse for degrading a whole family of rank to the situation and community of Rhodias. This punishment, considered worse than

* A correct account of them has already been given in Dr. Davy's Travels in Ceylon.

death, was only adjudged to those of the highest rank, who it might be supposed would feel the full extent of a punishment intended to be interminable to the race of those condemned. Rhodias were not allowed to build a house, but were forced to live in sheds without any wall, and open at one side,—they could not possess or cultivate lands,—they were prohibited from approaching a temple,—their touch was contamination, and they might be killed with impunity. Two Rhodias, who were hanged for murder at Kandy, in 1834, repeated some Pali hymns immediately before their execution, which shows that this unfortunate race had cherished the Buddhist religion, although abandoned by its teachers, and excluded from its temples.*

When the crops of a village had been reaped, and cleaned in the threshing-floors of the field, the Rhodias generally received a small portion of paddy as a gift from each of the cultivators; the alms thus given with the semblance of charity, was intended by the donor as an insurance against aggression on his property, or injury to his family from the practice of *hunaim* (witchcraft) by the outcasts; and the most liberal of the villagers was likely to have fewest sudden deaths amongst his

* Dr. Davy mentions a solitary instance of which he had heard, of a Buddhist priest preaching to the Rhodias, for which, having incurred the royal displeasure, and on being rebuked by the King, the teacher replied, "Religion should be common to all."

cattle, which fed in the forests where the Rhodia *cupaya* (hamlet) was established. On one occasion, a Rhodia, irritated at the small quantity of paddy bestowed on him by a proprietor, took up the stinted allowance, and, advancing to the threshing-floor, deliberately sprinkled the handful over the large grain-heap of the churl, whose property was thus rendered useless. A complaint having been made to a British authority, the cultivator was told in what manner he might obtain redress, but any form of legal proceeding seemed to him derogatory to his dignity when a Rhodia was his adversary. Finding that his offer "to shoot the outcast" was rejected, and being moreover informed that such an act would certainly bring him to the gallows, the cultivator walked off, apparently resigned to the loss of his rice, and no doubt wondering at the value which a foreign nation ignorantly placed on the life of a Rhodia.

Under the native dynasty the Kandian gaoler appointed some low-caste person, generally a charcoal-burner, to communicate orders to the Rhodias, —for the Government which sanctioned their persecution was mean enough to profit by the labour of people whom it would not protect, and compelled them to furnish ropes of hides for the purpose of catching elephants. They were fortune-tellers; and this circumstance, conjoined with the good looks of their women and the activity of the men, who made ropes, whips, and other useful articles, was the cause of Rhodias being less oppressed than was intended by the cruel lawgiver who established their position beyond the pale of society.

The authorities under the Kandian dynasty were thus arranged:—

First.—The King,—then the Adikars or ministers of state, having general authority and superintendance over the chiefs and people. Some Kings had only one Adikar, the usual number was two, and the last King of Kandy,—not that he followed their advice, but from jealousy of their power, and doubt of their fidelity,—increased the number, and had three Adikars; after these ministers came—

The Dessauves, chiefs of large districts; the Rate Mahatmeás, chiefs of inferior districts; Basnaike Nilamés, chiefs of Temples; officers of the palace.

Under all these were innumerable subordinates, whose powers were again subdivided, so that every separate class in each village had several persons exercising authority, and greedy for plunder. The King alone could order a capital punishment, and all cases might, if the appellant had sufficient influence, be reheard at the Maha Wasala, ("the great gate,") before the King in person. Latterly, the Kandian Government was a despotism, delegated and exercised through a multitude of tyrants from the King to the charcoal-burner, who communicated across a stream with the Gasmadoo, as the influential man in a Rhodia hamlet was usually termed. The people, particularly those in remote districts, suffered severely from the rapacious exactions of those in office, and appeals against injustice, had to toil up these numerous steps of office, down which the penal powers of the executive descended with accumulating severity. Yet a short road to justice was frequently found by clamorous and persevering appeals to the King in person, particularly if they were directed against rich subjects, or influential chiefs, who were always objects of jealousy and pillage.

A Kandian Monarch preserved before strangers a semblance of authority and wealth, far greater than what he really possessed, by general seclusion and occasional pompous display, while his own subjects were imposed upon by the high-sounding titles which he assumed, and by a respect shown to him as if he were a god. To the principal chiefs he delivered his orders in a style calculated to show their immeasurable inferiority, and while receiving his commands they remained in the most humiliating positions. The King did not permit any person to have a house two stories high, nor to build one with windows, nor even to roof with tiles, nor whitewash mud walls, without obtaining the royal sanction; by such arts the mean buildings of the royal residence at Kandy remained in the eyes of natives the most splendid palace in the world; their King was considered as the greatest monarch, and, mistake greater than any, they fancied themselves the bravest and most powerful of nations. Ambassadors to the Kandian court were lodged at some distance from the town, and the receptions were publicly held at night, when the mean appearance of the Kandian houses was less visible, and whatever of wealth or power the King could command was displayed to advantage by torch-light. The part of the audience-hall where the ambassadors were placed was secretly heated, previous to their reception, by means of glowing charcoal placed in cocoa-nut shells, that the natives might see how poor foreigners were influenced and overcome by the awful presence of Kandian Majesty.

In the Cingalese chronicles, the notice of many of the sovereigns is brief, merely stating the duration of their reign, and whether their deaths were caused by violence; of some pious King you may find it recorded that he departed to the region of the gods, *i. e.* died;—while an impious or unjust sovereign on departing this life is declared to have gone to the lowest hell. With the rulers of Ceylon, as with the Kings of most other eastern nations, despotism was the form of government, and passion the guide of conduct; those amongst them who have performed their duties with diligence, distinguished themselves by courage, increased the prosperity of the country by useful works, or its fame and sanctity by religious monuments, have been lauded by devout historians, and are placed on an equality with a few royal fanatics, who, reversing the customs of their race and country, have obtained distinction by public penance and apparent humility. Of the remainder, there was probably nothing that deserved to be recorded; they "had a more splendid trough and wider sty" than their subjects, and from this circumstance their names are saved from oblivion in the chronicles of Cingalese Kings.

I have already mentioned that the throne of Ceylon was not hereditary, and this will be sufficiently apparent on reviewing the succession of one hundred and fifty-nine Cingalese Kings from 307 B.C. until A.D. 1815.* In that period thirty-nine eldest sons, or nearly one-fourth, succeeded to their fathers: but twenty-nine, or more than one-fifth, were succeeded by brothers. Also, several Kings are mentioned as having appointed their successors, and two childless widows are found amongst the list of Sovereigns. In theory the Cingalese monarchy was elective in the descendants of the solar race; in practice it was either hereditary, or became the prize of the strongest of those who claimed to be of royal lineage.

* I have not in this summary of facts extracted from Cingalese history, taken into consideration the reign of six kings with whom the epitome commences, because in the native records previous to B.C. 307, there are discrepancies, both as regards the number of sovereigns and the length of their reigns.

In the same number of Kings, viz. 159, we find,—

15 reigned for a period less than			.	1 year.
30 for a period more than 1 and less than				5 years.
31 more than 5, less than			. .	10
30	„	10	„ . .	15
15	„	15	„ . .	20
16	„	20	„ . .	25
4	„	25	„ . .	30
6	„	30	„ . .	35
4	„	35	„ . .	40
5	„	40	„ . .	45
2	„	50	„ . .	55
1 reigned	.	.	. . .	55

A REVISED CHRONOLOGICAL LIST OF THE SOVEREIGNS OF CEYLON.

"In the chronological portion of the Epitome of the History of Ceylon some trifling errors were committed, occasioned partly by the haste in which that contribution for the Almanac of 1833 was compiled, and in part by inaccuracies of the press. As none of these errata can now be rectified without deranging, to the extent of each error, all the subsequent dates, this Revised list has been prepared.

The following are the dates at which the anachronisms, unavoidably created from the form in which the native histories have been compiled, admit of correction.—

B.C. 543. The landing of Wejaya, in the year of Budha's death.

B.C. 307. Bud. 236. The arrival of the mission sent by Dharmaasooka, Emperor of Dambadiva, to establish Budhism in Ceylon, in the first year of Dewenipeatissa's reign.

B.C. 104. Bud. 439th year, 9th month, 10th day. The deposition of Walagambahoo in the fifth month of his reign, and the conquest of Ceylon by the Malabars.

B.C. 90. Bud. 453. 10. 10. This is the date at which, according to the Mahawanse, Walagambahoo, on his restoration, founded Abbayaagiri, being in the 217th year, 10th month, and 10th day after Budhism was orally promulgated by the mission sent by Dharmaasooka. But, according to Singhalese authority, it is the date at which the doctrines of Budhism were first reduced to writing in Ceylon, while Walagambahoo was still a disguised fugitive. In the former case, there would be an anachronism of at least two years at the restoration of this sovereign,—which, however, in this uncertainty as to the event to which the date is applicable, I have not attempted to rectify.

A.D. 209. Bud. 752. 4. 10. The date of the origin of the Wytooliya heresy, which occurred in the first year of the reign of Waiwahara Tissa. The anachronism up to this period is consequently six years, and the error is adjusted accordingly.

A.D. 252. Bud. 795. The date of a revival of the Wytooliya heresy, in the fourth year of the reign of Goloo Abhaa. At the accession of this sovereign, so recently after the foregoing adjustment, there is no anachronism.

A.D. 275. Bud. 818. Accession of Mahasen — anachronism four years — adjusted.

A.D. 301. Bud. 844. 9. 20. Death of Mahasen — anachronism four years — adjusted.

A.D. 545. Bud 1088. The date of another revival of the Wytooliya heresy, in the twelfth year of the reign of Ambahaira Sala Maiwan — anachronism one year, six months — adjusted.

A.D. 838. Bud. 1381. The date of the origin of the Wijrawaadiya heresy, in the reign of Mitwella Sen, but the year of the reign is not given. Supposing it to have originated even in the year of his accession, the anachronism would amount to four years — adjusted to that extent.

A.D. 1153. Bud. 1696. The accession of Praakramabahoo 1st. error six years — adjusted.

A.D. 1200. Bud. 1743. The accession of Sahasa Mallawa, which is corroborated by the inscription on the Dambulla rock.

A.D. 1266. Bud. 1809. The accession of Panditta Praakrama Bahoo 3rd. — error seven years — adjusted.

A.D. 1347. Bud. 1890. The accession of Bhuwaneka Bahoo 4th. — As the term of the reign of the three immediately preceding sovereigns is not given, the extent of the anachronism at this date cannot be ascertained.

In the remaining portion of the History of Ceylon, there is no want of dates for the adjustment of its chronology, which, however, it would be superfluous to notice here." GEORGE TURNOUR.

KANDY, 11th DECEMBER 1833.

*** The names of places printed within brackets signify the seat of Government. The names printed in italics are those of subordinate or contemporary Princes. The dates denote the period of accession of the Kings.

1. Wejaya. [Tamananowera.] B.C. 543. Bud. 1. Reigned 38 years. The founder of the Wejayan dynasty.
2. Oopatissa 1st. [Oopatissanowera.] B.C. 505. Bud. 38. Reigned 1 year. Minister — regent.
3. Panduwaasa. [Oopatissanowera.] B.C. 504. Bud. 39. Reigned 30 years. Paternal nephew of Wejaya.

3. *Raama.* [*Raamagoona.*]
Roohoona. [*Roohoona.*]
Diggaina. [*Diggaamadulla.*]
Oorawelli. [*Mahawelligama.*]
Anooraadha. [*Anooraadhapoora.*]
Wejitta. [*Wejittapoora.*]
} *Brothers-in-law of Panduwaasa.*

4. Abhaya. [Oopatissanowera.] B.C. 474. Bud. 69. Reigned 20 years. Son of Panduwaasa, dethroned.
Interregnum. B.C. 454. Bud. 89. Seventeen years.

5. Pandukaabhaya. [Anooraadhapoora.] B.C. 437. Bud. 106. Reigned 70 years. Maternal grandson of Panduwaasa.

6. Mootaseewa. [Anooraadhapoora.] B.C. 367. Bud. 176. Reigned 60 years. Paternal grandson of Panduwaasa.

7. Devenipeatissa. [Anooradhaapoora.] B.C. 307. Bud. 236. Reigned 40 years. Second son.
Mahanaaga. [*Maagama.*] *Brother.*
Yataalatissa. [*Kellania.*] *Son.*
Gotaahbhaya. [*Maagama.*] *Son.*
Kellani-tissa, [*Kellania.*] *Relationship not specified.*
Kaawan-tissa. [*Maagama.*] *Son of Gotaabhaya.*

8. Oottiya. [Anooraadhapoora.] B.C. 267. Bud. 276. Reigned 10 years. Fourth son of Mootaseewa.

9. Maha-seewa. [Anooraadhapoora.] B.C. 257. Bud. 286. Reigned 10 years. Fifth son of Mootaseewa.

10. Suratissa. [Anooraadhapoora.] B.C. 247. Bud. 296. Reigned 10 years. Sixth son of Mootaseewa — put to death.

11. Sena and Goottika. [Anooraadhapoora.] B.C. 237. Bud. 306. Reigned 22 years. Foreign usurpers—put to death.

12. Asela. [Anooraadhapoora.] B.C. 215. Bud. 328. Reigned 10 years. Ninth son of Mootaseewa—deposed.

13. Elaala. [Anooraadhapoora.] B.C. 205. Bud. 338. Reigned 44 years. Foreign usurper—killed in battle.

14. Dootoogaimoonoo. [Anooraadhapoora.] B.C. 161. Bud. 382. Reigned 24 years. Son of *Kaawantissa.*

15. Saidaitissa. [Anooraadhapoora.] B.C. 137. Bud. 406. Reigned 18 years. Brother.

16. Toohl, or Thullathanaka. [Anooraadhapoora.] B.C. 119. Bud. 424. Reigned 1 month and 10 days. Younger son—deposed.
17. Laiminitissa 1st, or Lajjetissa. [Anooraadhapoora.] B.C. 119. Bud. 424. Reigned 9 years and 8 months. Elder brother.
18. Kaloonna, or Khallaata-naaga. [Anooraadhapoora.] B.C. 109. Bud. 434. Reigned 6 years. Brother—put to death.
19. Walagambahoo 1st, or Wattagaamini. [Anooraadhapoora.] B.C. 104. Bud. 439. Reigned 5 months. Brother—deposed.
20. Paluhatta. [Anooraadhapoora.] B.C. 103. Bud. 440. Reigned 3 years.
    Baayiha. [Anooraadhapoora.] B.C. 100. Bud. 443. Reigned 2 years.
    Panaymaaraa. [Anooraadhapoora.] B.C. 98. Bud. 445. Reigned 7 years.
    Peliyamaaraa. [Anooraadhapoora.] B.C. 91. Bud. 452. Reigned 7 months.
    Daathiya. [Anooraadhapoora.] B.C. 90. Bud. 453. Reigned 2 years.
    Total 14 years and 7 months—Foreign usurpers—successively deposed and put to death.
21. Walagambahoo 1st. [Anooraadhapoora.] B.C. 88. Bud. 455. Reigned 12 years and 5 months. Reconquered the kingdom.
22. Mahadailitissa, or Mahachoola. [Anooraadhapoora.] B.C. 76. Bud. 467. Reigned 14 years. Son.
23. Choora Naaga. [Anooraadhapoora.] B.C. 62. Bud. 481. Reigned 12 years. Son—put to death.
24. Kooda Tissa. [Anooraadhapoora.] B.C. 50. Bud. 493. Reigned 3 years. Son—poisoned by his wife.
25. Anoola. [Anooraadhapoora.] B.C. 47. Bud. 496. Reigned 5 years and 4 months. Widow.
26. Makalantissa, or Kallakanni Tessa. [Anooraadhapoora.] B.C. 41. Bud. 502. Reigned 22 years. Second son of Koodatissa.
27. Baatiyatissa 1st, or Baatikaabhaya. [Anooraadhapoora.] B.C. 19. Bud. 524. Reigned 28 years. Son.
28. Maha Dailiya Maana or Daathika. [Anooraadhapoora.] A.D. 9. Bud. 552. Reigned 12 years. Brother.

29. Addagaimoono, or Aamanda Gaamini. [Anooraadhapoora.] A.D. 21. Bud. 564. Reigned 9 years and 8 months. Son—put to death.

30. Kinihirridaila or Kanijaani Tissa. [Anooraadhapoora.] A.D. 30. Bud. 573. Reigned 3 years. Brother.

31. Kooda Abhaa or Choolaabhaya. [Anooraadhapoora.] A.D. 33. Bud. 576. Reigned 1 year. Son.

32. Singhawallee or Seewalli. [Anooraadhapoora.] A.D. 34. Bud. 577. Reigned 4 months. Sister—put to death.

Interregnum. A.D. 35. Bud. 578. 3 years.

33. Elloona or Ila Naaga. [Anooraadhapoora.] A.D. 38. Bud. 581. Reigned 6 years. Maternal nephew of Addagaimoonoo.

34. Sanda Moohoona, or Chanda Mukha Seewa. [Anooraadhapoora. A.D. 44. Bud. 587. Reigned 8 years and 7 months. Son.

35. Yasa Siloo, or Yataalakatissa. [Anooraadhapoora.] A.D. 52. Bud. 595. Reigned 7 years and 8 months. Brother—put to death.

36. Subha. [Anooraadhapoora.] A.D. 60. Bud. 603. Reigned 6 years. Usurper—put to death.

37. Wahapp, or Wasahba. [Anooraadhapoora.] A.D. 66. Bud. 609. Reigned 44 years. Descendant of Laiminitissa.

38. Waknais, or Wanka Naasika. [Anooraadhapoora.] A.D. 110. Bud. 653. Reigned 3 years. Son.

39. Gajaabahoo 1st, or Gaaminee. [Anooraadhapoora.] A.D. 113. Bud. 656. Reigned 12 years. Son.

40. Mahaloomaana, or Mallaka Naaga. [Anooraadhapoora.] A.D. 125. Bud. 668. Reigned 6 years. Maternal cousin.

41. Baatiya Tissa 2d, or Bhaatika Tissa. [Anooraadhapoora.] A.D. 131. Bud. 674. Reigned 24 years. Son.

42. Choola Tissa, or Kanitthatissa. [Anooraadhapoora.] A.D. 155. Bud. 698. Reigned 18 years. Brother.

43. Koohoona, or Choodda Naaga. [Anooraadhapoora.] A.D. 173. Bud. 716. Reigned 10 years. Son—murdered.

44. Koodanaama, or Kooda Naaga. [Anooraadhapoora.] A.D. 183. Bud. 726. Reigned 1 year. Nephew—deposed.

45. Kooda Sirinaa or Siri Naaga 1st. [Anooraadhapoora.] A.D. 184. Bud. 727. Reigned 19 years. Brother-in-law.

46. Waiwahairatissa, or Wairatissa. [Anooraadhapoora.] A.D. 209. Bud. 752. Reigned 22 years. Son—murdered.

47. Abha Sen, or Abha Tissa. [Anooraadhapoora.] A.D. 231. Bud. 774. Reigned 8 years. Brother.

48. Siri Naaga 2d. [Anooraadhapoora.] A.D. 239. Bud. 782. Reigned 2 years. Son.

49. Weja Indoo, or Wejaya 2d. [Anooraadhapoora.] A.D. 241. Bud. 784. Reigned 1 year. Son—put to death.

50. Sangatissa 1st. [Anooraadhapoora.] A.D. 242. Bud. 785. Reigned 4 years. Descendant of Laiminitissa—poisoned.

51. Dahama Sirisanga Bo, or Sirisanga Bodhi 1st. [Anooraadhapoora.] A.D. 246. Bud. 789. Reigned 2 years. Descendant of Laiminitissa—deposed.

52. Goloo Abhaa, Gothaabhaya, or Meghawarna Abhaya. [Anooraadhapoora.] A.D. 248. Bud. 791. Reigned 13 years. Descendant of Laiminitissa.

53. Makalan Detoo Tissa 1st. [Anooraadhapoora.] A.D. 261. Bud. 804. Reigned 10 years. Son.

54. Maha Sen. [Anooraadhapoora.] A.D. 275. Bud. 818. Reigned 27 years. Brother.

55. Kitsiri Maiwan 1st, or Keertissree Megha-warna. A.D. 302. Bud. 845. Reigned 28 years. Son.

56. Detoo Tissa 2d. [Anooraadhapoora.] A.D. 330. Bud. 873. Reigned 9 years. Brother.

57. Bujas or Budha Daasa. [Anooraadhapoora.] A.D. 339. Bud. 882. Reigned 29 years. Son.

58. Oopotissa 2d. [Anooraadhapoora.] A.D. 368. Bud. 911. Reigned 42 years. Son.

59. Maha Naama. [Anooraadhapoora.] A.D. 410. Bud. 953. Reigned 22 years. Brother.

60. Senghot, or Sotthi Sena. [Anooraadhapoora.] A.D. 432. Bud. 975. Reigned 1 day. Son—poisoned.

61. Laimini Tisso 2d, or Chatagaahaka. [Anooraadhapoora.] A.D. 432. Bud. 975. Reigned 1 year. Descendant of Laiminitissa.

62. Mitta Sena, or Karalsora. [Anooraadhapoora.] A.D. 433. Bud. 976. Reigned 1 year. Relationship not specified—put to death.

63. Paandu. [Anooraadhapoora.] A.D. 434. Bud. 977. Reigned 5 years.
Paarinda Kooda. [Anooraadhapoora.] A.D. 439. Bud. 982. Reigned 16 years.
Khudda Paarinda. [Anooraadhapoora.] A.D. 455. Bud. 998. Reigned 2 months.
Daatthiya. [Anooraadhapoora.] A.D. 455. Bud. 998. Reigned 3 years.
Pitthiya. [Anooraadhapoora.] A.D. 458. Bud. 1001. Reigned 7 months.
Total 24 years and 9 months—Foreign usurpers.

64. Daasenkelleya, or Dhaatu Sena. [Anooraadhapoora.] A.D. 459. Bud. 1002. Reigned 18 years. Descendant of the original royal family—put to death.

65. Seegiri Kasoomboo, or Kaasyapa 1st. [Seegiri Galla Nowera.] A.D. 477. Bud. 1020. Reigned 18 years. Son—committed suicide.

66. Moogallaana 1st. [Anooraadhapoora.] A.D. 495. Bud. 1038. Reigned 18 years. Brother.

67. Koomaara Daas, or Koomaara Dhaatu Sena. [Anooraadhapoora.] A.D. 513. Bud. 1056. Reigned 9 years. Son—immolated himself.

68. Kirti Sena. [Anooraadhapoora.] A.D. 522. Bud. 1065. Reigned 9 years. Son—murdered.

69. Maidee Seewoo, or Seewaka. [Anooraadhapoora.] A.D. 531. Bud. 1074. Reigned 25 days. Maternal uncle—murdered.

70. Laimini Oopatissa 3d. [Anooraadhapoora.] A.D. 531. Bud. 1074. Reigned 1 year and 6 months. Brother-in-law

71. Ambaherra Salamaiwan, or Silaakaala. [Anooraadhapoora.] A.D. 534. Bud. 1077. Reigned 13 years. Son-in-law.

72. Daapuloo 1st, or Daatthaapa Bhodhi. [Anooraadhapoora.] A.D. 547. Bud. 1090. Reigned 6 months and 6 days. Second Son—committed suicide.

73. Dalamagalan, or Moogallaana 2d. [Anooraadhapoora.] A.D. 547. Bud. 1090. Reigned 20 years. Elder Brother.

74. Kuda Kitsiri Maiwan 1st, or Keertisree Megha-warna. [Anooraadhapoora.] A.D. 567. Bud. 1110. Reigned 19 years. Son—put to death.

75. Senewee or Maha Naaga. [Anooraadhapoora.] A.D. 586. Bud. 1129. Reigned 3 years. Descendant of the Okaaka branch.

76. Aggrabodhi 1st, or Akbo. [Anooraadhapoora.] A.D. 589. Bud. 1132. Reigned 34 years and 2 months. Maternal nephew.

77. Aggrabodhi 2d, or Soola Akbo. [Anooraadhapoora.] A.D. 623. Bud. 1166. Reigned 10 years. Son-in-law.

78. Sanghatissa. [Anooraadhapoora.] A.D. 633. Bud. 1176. Reigned 2 months. Brother—decapitated.

79. Boona Moogalan, or Laimini Bonaaya. [Anooraadhapoora.] A.D. 633. Bud. 1176. Reigned 6 years. Usurper—put to death.

80. Abhaseggaaheka, or Asiggaaheka. [Anooraadhapoora.] A.D. 639. Bud. 1182. Reigned 9 years. Maternal grandson.

81. Siri Sangabo 2d. [Anooraadhapoora.] A.D. 648. Bud. 1191. Reigned 6 months. Son—deposed.

82. Kaloona Detootissa, or Laimina Katooreya. [Dewoonooweara, or Dondera.] A.D. 648. Bud. 1191. Reigned 5 months. Descendant of Laiminitissa—committed suicide.

— Siri Sangabo 2d. [Anooraadhapoora.] A.D. 649. Bud. 1192. Reigned 16 years. Restored, and again deposed.

83. Daloopeatissa 1st, or Dhatthopatissa. [Anooraadhapoora.] A.D. 665. Bud. 1208. Reigned 12 years. Laimini branch—killed in battle.

84. Paisooloo Kasoombo, or Kaasaypa 2d. [Anooraadhapoora.] A.D. 677. Bud. 1220. Reigned 9 years. Brother of Sirisangabo.

85. Dapuloo 2d. [Anooraadhapoora.] A.D. 686. Bud. 1229. Reigned 7 years. Okaaka branch—deposed.

86. Daloopeatissa 2d, or Hattha-Datthopatissa. [Anooraadhapoora.] A.D. 693. Bud. 1236. Reigned 9 years. Son of Daloopeatissa 1st.
87. Paisooloo Siri Sanga Bo 3d, or Aggrabodhi. [Anooraadhapoora.] A.D. 702. Bud. 1245. Reigned 16 years. Brother.
88. Walpitti Wasidata or Dantanaama. [Anooraadhapoora.] A.D. 718. Bud. 1261. Reigned 2 years. Okaaka branch.
89. Hooneonaru Riandalaor Hatthadatha. [Anooraadhapoora.] A.D. 720. Bud. 1263. Reigned 6 months. Original royal family—decapitated.
90. Mahalaipaanoo, or Maanawamma. [Anooraadhapoora.] A.D. 720. Bud. 1263. Reigned 6 years. Original royal family.
91. Kaasiyappa 3d, or Kasoombo. [Anooraadhapoora.] A.D. 726. Bud. 1269. Reigned 3 years. Son.
92. Aggrabodhi 3d, or Akbo. [Anooraadhapoora.] A.D. 729. Bud. 1272. Reigned 40 years. Nephew.
93. Aggrabodhi 4th, or Kuda Akbo. [Pollonnaroowa.] A.D. 769. Bud. 1312. Reigned 6 years. Son.
94. Mihindoo 1st, or Salamaiwan. [Pollonnaroowa.] A.D. 775. Bud. 1318. Reigned 20 years. Original royal family.
95. Dapoola 2d. [Pollonnaroowa.] A.D. 795. Bud. 1338. Reigned 5 years. Son.
96. Mihindo 2d, or Dharmika-Seelaamaiga. [Pollonnaroowa.] A.D. 800. Bud 1343. Reigned 4 years. Son.
97. Aggrabodhi 5th, or Akbo. [Pollonnaroowa.] A.D. 804. Bud. 1347. Reigned 11 years. Brother.
98. Dappoola 3d, or Kuda Dappoola. [Pollonnaroowa.] A.D. 815. Bud. 1358. Reigned 16 years. Son.
99. Aggrabodhi 6th. [Pollonnaroowa.] A.D. 831. Bud. 1374. Reigned 3 years. Cousin.
100. Mitwella Sen, or Selaamaiga. [Pollonnaroowa.] A.D. 838. Bud. 1381. Reigned 20 years. Son.
101. Kaasiyappa 4th, or Maaganyin Sena, or Mihindoo. [Pollonnaroowa.] A.D. 858. Bud. 1401. Reigned 33 years. Grandson.

102. Udaya 1st. [Pollonnaroowa.] A.D. 891. Bud. 1434. Reigned 35 years. Brother.

103. Udaya 2d. [Pollonnaroowa.] A.D. 926. Bud. 4469. Reigned 11 years. Son.

104. Kaasiyappa 5th. [Pollonnaroowa.] A.D. 937. Bud. 1480. Reigned 17 years. Nephew and Son-in-law.

105. Kaasiyappa 6th. [Pollonnaroowa.] A.D. 954. Bud. 1497. Reigned 10 years. Son-in-law.

106. Dappoola 4th. [Pollonnaroowa.] A.D. 964. Bud. 1507. Reigned 7 months. Son.

107. Dappoola 5th. [Pollonnaroowa.] A.D. 964. Bud. 1507. Reigned 10 years. Relationship not specified.

108. Udaya 3d. [Pollonnaroowa.] A.D. 974. Bud. 1517. Reigned 3 years. Brother.

109. Sena 2d. [Pollonnaroowa.] A.D. 977. Bud. 1520. Reigned 9 years. Relationship not specified.

110. Udaya 4th. [Pollonnaroowa.] A.D. 986. Bud. 1529. Reigned 8 years. Relationship not specified.

111. Sena 3d. [Pollonnaroowa.] A.D. 994. Bud. 1537. Reigned 3 years. Relationship not specified.

112. Mihindoo 3d. [Pollonnaroowa.] A.D. 997. Bud. 1540. Reigned 16 years. Relationship not specified.

113. Sena 4th. [Pollonnaroowa.] A.D. 1013. Bud. 1556. Reigned 10 years. Son—minor.

114. Mihindoo 4th. [Anooraadhapoora.] A.D. 1023. Bud. 1566. Reigned 36 years. Brother—carried captive to India—during the Soleean conquest.

Interregnum [Pollonnaroowa.] A.D. 1059. Bud. 1602. 12 years. Soleean vice-royalty.

Maha Lai, or Maha Laala Keerti. [*Roohoona*].
Wikrema Paandi. [*Kalutotta.*]
Jagat Paandi, or Jagati Paalie. [*Roohoona.*]
Prakrama Paandi, or Prakrama Bahoo. [*Roohoona.*]
Lokaiswera. [*Kaacharagama.*]

} *Subordinate native Kings during the Soleean Vice-royalty.*

115. Wejayabahoo 1st, or Sirisangabo 4th. [Pollonnaroowa.] A.D. 1071. Bud. 1614. Reigned 55 years. Grandson of Mihindoo 4th.

116. Jayabahoo 1st. [Pollonnaroowa.] A.D. 1126. Bud. 1669. Reigned 1 year. Brother.

117. Wikramabahoo 1st. [Pollonnaroowa.] *Maanaabarana.* [*Roohoona.*] 118. Gajaabahoo 2d. [Pollonnaroowa.] *Siriwallaba, or Kitsiri Maiwan.* [*Roohoona.*]	A.D. 1127. Bud. 1670. Reigned 20 years.	A disputed succession.

119. Prakramma Bahoo 1st. [Pollonnaroowa.] A.D. 1153. Bud. 1696. Reigned 33 years. Son of Maanaabarana.

120. Wijayabahoo 2d. [Pollonnaroowa.] A.D. 1186. Bud. 1729. Reigned 1 year. Nephew—murdered.

121. Mihindo 5th, or Kitsen Kisdaas. [Pollonnaroowa.] A.D. 1187. Bud. 1730. Reigned 5 days. Usurper—put to death.

122. Kirti Nissanga. [Pollonnaroowa.] A.D. 1187. Bud. 1730. Reigned 9 years. A prince of Kaalinga.

— Weerabahoo. [Pollonnaroowa.] A.D. 1196. Bud. 1739. Reigned 1 day. Son—put to death.

123. Wikramabahoo 2d. [Pollonnaroowa.] A.D. 1196. Bud. 1739. Reigned 3 months. Brother of Kirti Nissanga—put to death.

124. Chondakanga. [Pollonnaroowa.] A.D. 1196. Bud. 1739. Reigned 9 months. Nephew—deposed.

125. Leelawatee. [Pollonnaroowa.] A.D. 1197. Bud. 1740. Reigned 3 years. Widow of Prakramabahoo—deposed.

126. Saahasamallawa. [Pollonnaroowa.] A.D. 1200. Bud. 1743. Reigned 2 years. Okaaka branch—deposed.

127. Kalyaanawati. [Pollonnaroowa.] A.D. 1202. Bud. 1745. Reigned 6 years. Sister of Kirti Nissanga.

128. Dharmaasooka. [Pollonnaroowa.] A.D. 1208. Bud. 1751. Reigned 1 year. Relationship not specified — a minor.

129. Nayaanga or Neekanga [Pollonnaroowa.] A.D. 1209. Bud. 1752. Reigned 17 days. Minister—put to death.

— Leelawatee. [Pollonnaroowa.] A.D. 1209. Bud. 1752. Reigned 1 year. Restored, and again deposed.

130. Lokaiswera 1st. [Pollonnaroowa.] A.D. 1210. Bud. 1753. Reigned 9 months. Usurper—deposed.

— Leelawatee. [Pollonnaroowa.] A.D. 1211. Bud. 1754. Reigned 7 months. Again restored and deposed a third time.

131. Pandi Prakrama Bahoo 2d. [Pollonnaroowa.] A.D. 1211. Bud. 1754. Reigned 3 years. Usurper—deposed.

132. Maagha. [Pollonnaroowa.] A.D. 1214. Bud. 1757. Reigned 21 years. Foreign usurper.

133. Wejayabahoo 3d. [Dambadeniya.] A.D. 1235. Bud. 1778. Reigned 24 years. Descendant of Sirisangabo 1st.

134. Kalikaala Sahitya Sargwajnya, or Paandita Prakrama Bahoo 3d. [Dambadeniya.] A.D. 1266. Bud. 1809. Reigned 35 years. Son.

135. Bosat Wejaya Bahoo 4th. [Pollonnaroowa.] A.D. 1301. Bud. 1844. Reigned 2 years. Son.

— *Bhuwaneka Bahoo.* [*Yapahoo, or Subhapabattoo.*]

136. Bhuwaneka Bahoo 1st. [*Yapahoo, or Subhapabattoo.*] A.D. 1303. Bud. 1846. Reigned 11 years. Brother.

137. Prakrama Bahoo 3d. [Pollonnaroowa.] A.D. 1314. Bud. 1857. Reigned 5 years. Son of Bosat Wejayabahoo.

138. Bhuwaneka Bahoo 2d. [Kurunaigalla, or Hastisailapoora.] A.D. 1319. Bud. 1862. Duration of reign not stated. Son of Bhuwenekabahoo.

139. Pandita Prakrama Bahoo 4th. [Kurunaigalla, or Hastisailapoora. Duration of reign not stated. Relationship not specified.

140. Wanny Bhuwaneka Bahoo 3d. [Kurunaigalla, or Hastisailapoora. Duration of reign not stated. Relationship not specified.

141. Wejaya Bahoo 5th. [Kurunaigalla, or Hastisailapoora.] Duration of reign not stated.

142. Bhuwaneka Bahoo 4th. [Gampola, or Gangaasiripoora.] A.D. 1347. Bud. 1890. Reigned 14 years.

143. Prakrama Bahoo 5th. [Gampola, or Gangaasiripoora.] A.D. 1361. Bud. 1904. Reigned 10 years.

(141–143: Relationship not specified.)

144. Wikrambahoo 3d. [Partly at Kandy or Sengadagalla Nowera.] A.D. 1371. Bud. 1914. Reigned 7 years. Cousin.

145. Bhuwaneka Bahoo 5th. [Gampola, or Gangaasiripoora.] A.D. 1378. Bud. 1921. Reigned 20 years.

146. Wejaya Bahoo 5th, or Weera Bahoo. [Gampola, or Gangaasiripoora.] A.D. 1398. Bud. 1941. Reigned 12 years.

147. Sree Praakrama Bahoo 6th. [Kotta, or Jayawardanapoora.] A.D. 1410. Bud. 1953. Reigned 52 years.

(145–147: Relationship not specified.)

148. Jayaabahoo 2d. [Kotta or Jayawardanapoora.] A.D. 1462. Bud. 2005. Reigned 2 years. Maternal grandson—put to death.

149. Bhuwaneka Bahoo 6th. [Kotta, or Jayawardanapoora.] A.D. 1464. Bud. 2007. Reigned 7 years. Relationship not specified.

150. Pandita Praakrama Bahoo 7th. [Kotta, or Jayawardanapoora.] A.D. 1471. Bud. 2114. Reigned 14 years. Adopted son.

151. Weera Praakrama Bahoo 8th. [Kotta, or Jayawardanapoora.] A.D. 1485. Bud. 2028. Reigned 20 years. Brother of Bhuwanekabahoo 6th.

152. Dharma Praakrama Bahoo 9th. [Kotta, or Jayawardanapoora.] A.D. 1505. Bud. 2048. Reigned 22 years. Son.

153. Wejaya Bahoo 7th. [Kotta, or Jayawardanapoora.] A.D. 1527. Bud. 2070. Reigned 7 years. Brother—murdered.

— *Jayaweera Bandara.* [*Gampola.*]

154. Bhuwaneka Bahoo 7th. [Kotta.] A.D. 1534. Bud. 2077. Reigned 8 years. Son.

Maayaadunnai. [*Seetaawaka.*]

Raygam Bandara. [*Raygam.*]

Jayaweera Bandara. [*Kandy.*]

155. Don Juan Dharmapaala. [Kotta.] A.D. 1542 Bud. 2085. Reigned 39 years. Grandson.

A Malabar. [*Yapahoo.*]

Portuguese. [*Colombo.*]

Weediye Raja. [*Pailainda Nowera.*]

Raajasingha. [*Aiwissawelle.*]

155. *Idirimaaney Suriya.* [*Seven Korles.*]
Wikrama Bahoo. [*Kandy.*] *Descendant of* Sirisangabo 1st.

156. Raajasingha 1st. [Seetaawaka.] A.D. 1581. Bud. 2124. Reigned 11 years. Son of *Maayaadunnai.*
Jaya Suriya. [*Seetaawaka.*]
Weediye Raja's Queen. [*Seetaawaka.*]

157. Wimala Dharma. [Kandy.] A.D. 1592. Bud. 2135. Reigned 12 years. Original royal family.

158. Senaaratena, or Senerat. [Kandy.] A.D. 1604. Bud. 2147. Reigned 31 years. Brother.

159. Raaja-singha 2nd. [Kandy.] A.D. 1635. Bud. 2178. Reigned 50 years. Son.
Koomaara-singa. [*Ouvah.*] *Brother.*
Wijaya Paala. [*Matelle.*] *Brother.*

160. Wimala Dharma Suriya 2nd. [Kandy.] A.D. 1685. Bud. 2228. Reigned 22 years. Son of Raaja-singha.

161. Sreeweera Prakrama Narendra-singha, or Koondasaala. [Kandy.] A.D. 1707. Bud. 2250. Reigned 32 years. Son.

162. Sreewejaya Raaja-singha, or Hanguranketta. [Kandy.] A.D. 1739. Bud. 2282. Reigned 8 years. Brother-in-law.

163. Kirtisree Raaja-singha. [Kandy.] A.D. 1747. Bud. 2290. Reigned 34 years. Brother-in-law.

164. Raajaadhi Raaja-singha. [Kandy.] A.D. 1781. Bud. 2324. Reigned 17 years. Brother.

165. Sree Wickrema Raaja-singha. [Kandy.] A.D. 1798. Bud. 2341. Reigned 16 years. Son of the late King's wife's sister, deposed by the English, and died in captivity.

Dividing these one hundred and fifty-nine Sovereigns, and the period of two thousand one hundred and twenty-two years over which their reigns extended, into four nearly equal parts, and taking the proportional length of a reign in each period, we find there was a much greater security for its longer duration in the last five centuries than in either of the three preceding periods of the same length of time; yet it was in the earlier and more precarious times that every work of magnitude or durability which now exists was executed; and this is one of many convincing proofs, that it was by means of a much more numerous population; and neither from the internal prosperity of the kingdom, nor the power of knowledge, that the earliest Kings were enabled to execute undertakings so much beyond the capacity of the nation for the last five hundred years.

In a period of five hundred and thirty-eight years, viz. from B.C. 307 until A.D. 231, there were forty-one Kings, which gives an average to each reign of rather more than thirteen years.

From A. D. 232 until A. D. 769, a period of five hundred and thirty-eight years, there were forty-six Kings, which gives an average to each reign of less than twelve years.

From A.D. 770, until A.D. 1301, a period of five hundred and thirty-two years, there were forty-two Kings, the average duration of their reigns falling short of thirteen years.

From A.D. 1302, until A.D. 1815, a period of five hundred and fourteen years, there were only thirty Kings, whose reigns average upwards of seventeen years.

In the first period, nearly two out of every five

Kings met violent deaths; in the second period, about one in three; in the third period, only one in seven; and in the fourth period, one in six, came to death by violent means.

The violent deaths of Cingalese Kings may be classed thus.—

Twenty-two murdered by their successors.

Six murdered by individuals.

Thirteen killed in feuds and war.

Four committed suicide.

If we add to these, eleven Kings who were dethroned, and whose after-fate is unknown, it will appear that not more than two-thirds of those Princes who ascended the Cingalese throne, reached the funeral-pile without violence, and retained sovereign authority at the time of their death.

An account of the lives of the female Sovereigns, who have ruled Ceylon, may, perhaps, give the most correct, though not a favourable, picture of the state of society at the times in which they lived.

The first Queen, in order of time, was Anoola, who ascended the throne after having poisoned the King, her husband, Kuda Tissa, B.C. 48. She then married, and raised to the throne in succession, five ministers, all of whom she despatched by poison, viz. Balat-Swama, after sharing her throne for fourteen months; Wattooka, after thirteen months; the Brahman minister and household priest, Nilia, who succeeded, was only permitted to retain the precarious rank to which he was elevated, for six months: Sakkoo, was his successor in the dangerous dignity, and existed for eleven months, then fell, and was followed by Ballatissa, whose life and authority was terminated in fifteen months. Four months longer this female fiend, setting decency at defiance, ruled over the island, and was then put to death by her step-son and successor, Makalantissa, who had escaped from her violence, and remained concealed in the garb of a priest.

The next Queen, who ruled over Ceylon, was Singhawallee, who succeeded to the throne on the death of her brother, A.D. 34; and after a reign of four months, fell a victim to the ambition of her cousin Elloona, who put this Queen to death, and reigned in her stead.

From this time, until A.D. 1197, when Leelawatee usurped the throne, by the assistance of her husband, no female sovereign intervenes. She was the widow of Prákrama Bahoo 1st, the most active and renowned sovereign of the Sooloowanzae, or succession of Kings, posterior to A.D. 301. For some time after his death, Cingalese history contains little, except a record of royal murders, for which ambition furnished victims, blood-stained Princes, who snatched a sceptre, that in their gory hands and feeble grasp, still pointed onwards to a bloody tomb. Of the six Kings who followed Prákrama Bahoo, four were murdered, one died a natural death, and the sixth, Chondakanga, was deposed and had his eyes put out, by order of the minister Kirti, who had married Leelawatee, and now raised her to the throne, while he exercised the supreme authority under sanction of her name. These six reigns only occupied ten years; and three years after her accession, Leelawatee was deposed by the King Sáhasamallawa, who only enjoyed his dignity for two years, and was then deposed by the influence of the minister Neeckanga, who placed on the throne the Queen Kalyánawati.

Kalyánawati, the sister of a former King, commenced her reign A.D. 1202, and appears, notwithstanding the turbulence of those times, to have died in possession of the throne which she had occupied for six years, and left to an infant, her successor Dharmasoka, from whom it was usurped by the same Neeckanga who had been instrumental in raising Kalyanawati to sovereign power. Seventeen days numbered Neeckanga's short-lived dignity, and then the usurper fell by the hand of his minister Manoda, who restored the deposed Queen Leelawatee. Again, for one year she enjoyed power, and was then deposed by an usurper, Lokaiswara, who, in his turn, was expelled by the Queen, after a reign of nine months. Leelawatee again reigned for seven months, and was deposed for the third and last time by the usurper Pándi Prákrama Bahoo 2nd, A.D. 1211.

A short account of Donna Catherina, who was proclaimed by the Portuguese as Queen of Kandy, in the latter part of the sixteenth century, but who is not acknowledged as a sovereign by Cingalese historians, will be found in the account of Nuwara Ellia. Donna Catherina, the daughter of a deposed King, was educated as a Catholic by the Portuguese, who afterwards proclaimed her as Queen, and supported her cause. Her allies being defeated, and herself left a prisoner, Donna Catherina married her victorious rival, and, after his death, espoused his brother and successor: finally, she died lamented by her subjects, to whose worship and customs she seems to have conformed, if indeed she did not entirely abandon the religion in which she had been educated.

I shall conclude this sketch of the native dynasty, with the acknowledged duties of a Cingalese monarch, which will show that it was in defiance of unexceptionable rules for their guidance, that Buddhist Kings proved cruel rulers, as I shall afterwards have occasion to remark how slightly a Buddhist people are restrained by their excellent moral laws.

Be willingly charitable to the deserving.

Be mild of speech.

Let your conduct and actions be such as to conduce to the good of your people.

Let the love of your people equal the love of yourself.

Favour no one to the injury of another.

Injure no one to benefit another.

Let no fear prevent your doing justice.

Avoid doing evil through ignorance, or the want of correct information.

Be munificent.

Strictly follow the rules of your religion.

Remunerate the deserving.

Let your conduct be upright.

Let your conduct be mild.

Be patient.

Be without malice.

Inflict not torture.

Be merciful.

Attend to good council.

These are the principal rules * by which a Buddhist monarch should regulate his conduct.

* These rules, as above translated, are from Dr Davy's Ceylon.

CHAPTER V.

ELEPHANT SHOOTING AT AVISAVELLE.

'Tis sweet to contemplate the fleeting shades
That o'er thy towering forests lightly creep,
When cloth'd in clouds the sun's effulgence fades;
Or when his beams athwart their verdure sweep,
To view thy starry leaves, a vast expanse,
Wave in the sportive breeze their trembling hues;
And as they catch each transient light, they glance
Unnumber'd colours bathed in ever-vernal dews.

Lines to Adam's Peak,
By the Honourable Wm. Granville.

Start from Colombo for the purpose of Elephant Shooting.—Kellania Ganga. — Canoe. — Death of King Bhuwaneka Bahoo Seventh. — Banks of the River. — Native Breakfast.— Jungle Crow. — Pariah Dogs. — Lebuna. — Hangwelle. — Rev. Mr. Chayter. — Missionaries. — Evening in the Interior of Ceylon.—Anecdote.—Road to Avisavelle.—Jungle-fowl.—Bamboo.—Monkeys.—Curlew.—Kaendatta.—Rogue Elephants — Wild Elephant. — Snakes. — Pigeon Shooting. — Land Leeches. — Chatty Bath. — Rest-house Dinner. — Tobacco Smoking.—Moschetto Curtains.—Breakfast.—Driving large Herd of Elephants.—Elephant Shooting.—Lieutenant H—— seized by an Elephant. — Rapid return to Colombo. — A Cordial: — Elephant's Head.

My first two excursions into the interior of Ceylon were undertaken for the purpose of elephant shooting soon after my arrival in the country, and while still in ignorance of the proper manner of pursuing elephants, or the exact place to fire at when I should encounter them. Yet I record my earliest essays, (unlucky and unsuccessful though they were), because then my impressions were more vivid, both of that most magnificent of all field sports, and also of the unequalled richness of Ceylon landscape. Both expeditions were made ere experience had inured me to the presence and habits of these huge animals, and before my eye had become accustomed to, or sated with, the eternal luxuriance of the evergreen forests which clothe alike the most level districts and the steepest pinnacle of Kandian mountains.

In November, 1826, on receiving information that a number of elephants had made their appearance near the banks of the Kellania Ganga, twenty-five miles from Colombo,* a party, of which I was a member, immediately agreed to go in search of them, and to commence our career as elephant shots. After perfecting our arrangements, I had not even started, when I discovered how incorrect were the ideas I had formed of the manner of travelling in Ceylon, and how much the instructions and advice with which I had been liberally supplied, required to be modified before I could proceed. We had been informed, that to reach Hangwellé (our place of rendezvous), with comfort, convenience, and speed, it was only necessary to engage a boat, and by embarking in the evening we might enjoy a good night's rest, and reach our destination before morning, without losing sight of our servants and supplies. Colonel L—— and myself having determined on choosing this luxurious mode of conveyance, were a little disappointed at finding, that as there were obstructions in the canal, we had to walk, and our baggage to be carried, four miles to the boat, which was waiting on the Kellania Ganga.* After a delay of several hours we fairly embarked, people, furniture, provisions, wines, guns, ammunition, in short, all the necessaries of a determined sporting party, on a sort of platform fixed on two canoes, and over which a cocoa-nut-leaf room was erected. The native boatmen encouraged us by saying that, as heavy rain had fallen in the mountains, the water in the river was so deep that we could not find any impediment or delay in crossing sand-banks or shallows.

The Kellania Ganga is formed by the union of several torrents, which have their source in the western division of the mountainous range connected with Adam's Peak. The length of its course is seventy miles; for the first half of this distance it flows through a thinly inhabited forest-covered country, and here its waters are clear, its bed rocky, and its current precipitous; for the

* Ganga River.

last thirty-five miles this river is navigable for boats, and well adapted for the purpose of inland communication. It runs into the sea four miles from Colombo, and is connected with that fort by a canal, which was completed before the British took possession of the country, for they have done but little, either to improve the navigation of the river, or to connect it by roads with a promising and healthy country lying between Colombo and the mountains.*

I remained for some time admiring the luxuriant vegetation and lofty trees on the river banks, and their deep shadows over which we floated. It was here on this river, nearly three hundred years ago, that Bhuwaneka Bahoo the Seventh, the hundred and fifty-fourth King of the Singha race was shot through the heart by a Portuguese gentleman who accompanied him on a party of pleasure. It is distinctly mentioned that the act was unintentional, and as it was for the Portuguese interest that this King should have lived, we may readily admit that his death was by accident. This monarch would have been unable to support himself on the throne without the assistance of his European allies, in return for which he placed himself and his country entirely at their disposal, and sent

* I have heard that since this was written, and about the time I left the country, several lines of road were projected, traced, and about to be commenced, leading to this river from various points of the interior of the country.

to Portugal a native ambassador* with the golden image of a Prince whom he had adopted and intended as his successor. This Prince was christened in effigy in the royal palace of Lisbon, A.D. 1540, and received the name of Don Juan, being called after Don Juan of Austria. He succeeded to the throne on the death of Bhuwaneka Bahoo, and adopted the Christian faith, but his power never extended beyond those parts in which he was protected by the forces of his Portuguese allies.

When I retired to sleep and to prepare for the adventures of the next day, I soon found that this combination of house and vessel possessed in perfection the bad qualities of both; it had the scanty accommodation which is the characteristic of every floating conveyance, and carried such an abundance of bugs as is rarely to be met with in the dirtiest hovel. Driven again to the open air, I found the lines of cocoa-nut trees apparently as interminable as ever, while their white stems and tufted tops reflected on the river above, below, and all around, seemed more stubbornly monotonous than they were previous to my retreating under cover. Morning at length dawned, and the perfume exhaled from the shadock, orange, lime, and areka-nut-tree flowers, which grew everywhere along the bank,

* Salappoo Arachy. The inferior rank of Arachy which this ambassador held, shows that either no native of rank acknowledged the King supported by the Portuguese, or that none of them could be persuaded to trust themselves into the hands of his faithful Majesty.

became more powerful, but was still delicious. We could now distinguish objects at a distance, and to our severe disappointment recognised buildings by which we knew that in the ten hours' rowing we had only advanced three miles, and had therefore the alternative of walking twelve miles, or running the risk of being too late for the sport.

We disembarked at the first native cottage, and while the servants were preparing coffee, the woman of the house was employed in making cakes from a liquid composition of rice-flower and cocoanut milk, which, being passed through small holes in the bottom of a dish, assumed the appearance of vermicelli; it was then received on a wicker tray placed over boiling water, and there being cooked by steam, became a very palatable cake. She also prepared from the meal of a small grain another kind of cake, of a dark colour, which, in shape and taste, bore a considerable resemblance to an oatmeal bannock. Having made a hearty breakfast on these delicacies, we commenced our walk, and were repeatedly serenaded by the loud hoarse call of "Ouk! ouk! ouk!" which we found to proceed from a bird commonly called the Jungle Crow, which, in habits and shape, nearly resembles the magpie: its body, head, and tail are black, but its wings are of a light-brown colour, and its eyes bright red.

Having reached the rest-house of Hangwellé, I may as well describe what a rest-house in some places now is, and this one was in 1828. The house consisted of a large roof, covered with thatch, which reached within seven feet of the ground, and projected so far beyond the four mud walls that supported it, as to allow a considerable space under the eaves, which was dignified with the name of verandah; two empty rooms, of moderate size, were contained within the walls, and the floors of these, as well as of the verandah, were plastered with cow-dung. This coating of the floors is a common native custom, and is practised because fleas, and some other kind of vermin, have sufficient taste to abstain from trespassing on this vile composition, until it has lost that evil savour in which lies its virtue. From this description it may be inferred, that these establishments afford shelter from rain, when the roofs are in good repair, and from wind and fogs, when the doors will shut; if to these combined advantages are superadded an absence of vermin, and the possession of a travelling bed, then, with some confidence, the sojourner may reckon on enjoying repose in a rest-house. On arriving at one of them, you are immediately attended by several carrion crows, and, as soon as you are seated, and have composed yourself in a comfortable attitude, one or more of these harpies, having settled beyond your reach, and, in defiance of all threatening gestures, commences forthwith to screech at you, with expanded beak and drooping wings, until to your vexed ear each succeeding sound of their eternal *khaa! khaa! khaa!* appears louder and hoarser than the preceding guttural. Besides being a severe trial to one's patience, they are much in the habit of levying a tax on the supplies; and perhaps at the very momont that you are meditating revenge against the noisy performer in front, another of the gang is quietly winging his way out at some side window with your breakfast loaf. Their scent, or their sagacity, is unrivalled amongst birds of their own size; for, halt where you will, unpack when you may, only look up into the tree above, and you will find one crow at least with his head on one side peering into your provision-baskets, as if he were sent to take an inventory. On the stranger's arrival at a rest-house, not less certain than the clamour of the crows is the worrying of Pariah dogs, which assemble in numbers, and with every variety of lank sides, lame legs, blind eyes, and blotched bodies; these wretched animals having ascertained the position of those packages which they covet, next proceed to examine the physiognomy of the traveller, and may be seen cautiously approaching and staring in his face, apparently for the purpose of discovering whether they may hope to be allowed to pick up the crumbs and fragments of his feast. A kind look is sufficient to attach one of these dogs; and, as they hold that position in the canine, that vagrants and vagabonds do amongst the human castes, they have also been gifted with that sharpness of wits, and facility of digestion, that enables them to exist where the hound of higher descent might starve. When more than usually pressed by hunger, they feed on fallen jack-fruit; and a juvenile Pariah dog is as precocious and unscrupulous in providing his own supplies, as the most thorough-bred brat of a travelling tinker. At a later period of my residence in the island, an accident having deprived me of a watch-dog, I accosted civilly a large Pariah that passed me as I was riding; the animal showed his acknowledgment by wagging his tail and following me home; and from that time he commenced attending regularly at dinner: he also took upon himself the task of barking at all strange people, and biting all strange dogs that approached my house; and, in short, from the first day, Lebuna diligently performed the duties of an accomplished watch-dog. This animal became very fat; yet, although overfed, he could not forbear stealing from habit, as he had formerly done from necessity, and was at last cut down by the cleaver of a Malay butcher, while feloniously waddling off with a quarter of mutton.*

* I had honoured this outcast with a European name, but was unable to enforce my nomenclature; the native servants called him *lebuna* (the tolerated); and under that appellation he lived and died.

My European servants were Scotch (Aberdeenshire), and from them the natives picked up the language and accent with wonderful facility and accuracy, so that strangers have some-

The rest-house is situated within the small redoubt of Hangwellé; and the only defence to a post of so much consequence, during the Kandian war, appears to have been a dry ditch, which is now choked up with vegetation. This trifling field-work commanded the navigation of the Kellania Ganga, as well as the direct road from Kandy to Colombo;. and while waiting for my servants and baggage, I strolled out to examine the ground where the last of Kandian Kings, with the whole force of his country, was routed with disgrace by a handful of invalid Europeans. On returning from my walk, I was surprised to find a stranger, a comfortable-looking European gentleman, seated in the verandah, enjoying the quiet scene and cool air of the river bank: as we approached, his dress announced him to be of the missionary profession, and his frank manner did not leave us long in suspense as to his name and situation. The Rev. Mr. Chayter had been for some time in Ava, and after suffering many hardships there, had removed in 1812 to Colombo, and then commenced the Baptist missionary establishment in Ceylon. This gentleman, soon after his arrival in the island, devoted himself to the study of the native lan-

times been astonished at hearing Kandians calling "Hisky, hisky,"—"hae Dougy, Dougy." So also carts, which I was the first to introduce into the Mátalé district, are probably to this day known there as "caerts," and the small bullocks that draw them as "beasties."

guages, and performed a valuable service in arranging and publishing the first Cingalese and English grammar. At the time I now speak of, viz. 1827, he had three churches, thirteen schools, and upwards of five hundred scholars, under his superintendence; and all these institutions were maintained at a wonderfully small expense, less than 150*l.* per annum to the parent society in England. He had many followers in the neighbourhood of Hangwellé, and received great assistance and support from an old gentleman, the Modeliar, or native magistrate of this district.

Previous to meeting with Mr. Chayter, I was little inclined to consider favourably, or estimate highly, the success of European missionaries in the East; but as regards Ceylon, although I cannot but regret the numerous and perplexing divisions of the Christian community, yet from my first acquaintance with their proceedings, until I left the island, it is bare justice to them to record my opinion that they have been zealous without bigotry, and have done much, and worked judiciously, for the introduction of real Christianity, by educating, from early youth, young natives in the English language and Christian religion.

At Hangwellé, I was delighted with the sharp feeling of the evening air, so different from the moist atmosphere of the sea-coast, on the south-west side of the island; and not less so with the softness of the scene, and the wondrous blaze of the fire-flies, as the breeze shook them from the dark foliage, and they again strove to regain the shelter of the surrounding trees. Nothing can be imagined more enchanting than the refreshing coolness and beauty of the nights as you approach the mountains in the interior of Ceylon; for, even if the surpassing lustre of the moon and stars be obscured by clouds, the innumerable fire-flies (with brilliancy only inferior to the lights of heaven) serve to realise all those ideas which wildering fancy forms of Fairyland.

The brilliancy of the fire-fly was on one occasion the cause of an accident to a gentleman, who, on emerging from the heat of a mess-room, imagined a fire-fly, which started before him, to be a lantern borne by a servant: the eccentric motions of the insect were set down by the master as vagaries of the domestic, until a volley of oaths, and a rush at the refractory bearer, was cut short by a headlong plunge into the cold lake of Kandy.

Although it was late at night when we retired, we were again on our way before daylight the next morning. Mr. S—— and Mr. H—— rode; while Colonel L—— and myself, who had put our faith on erroneous advice and inland navigation, were glad to mount ourselves on two arm-chairs, over which were placed talipot leaves to protect us from the sun; and underneath the seat two long flexible bamboos were strapped, the projecting ends of which rested on the shoulders of four natives, who bore us along easily and merrily. I occasionally descended from my perch to shoot snipe in the rice-fields, or jungle-fowl in thickets: the latter are continually announcing their position by a shrill double-call, which is somewhat like the cry of the partridge, but has no resemblance to the crowing of a cock. This call, when commenced by one jungle-cock, is answered by any other within hearing; then, with hostile intent and alternate sounds of defiance, they gradually advance to their morning combat: they are even more pugnacious than their domestic brethren; and I have seen jungle-cocks, when replied to (apparently in a very different dialect) from the fowl-yard, advance within its precincts, and give battle to its champions. In taste, their flesh resembles that of the pheasant: in appearance, the male is like the common red dunghill cock, only with more glossy plumage, and a yellow spot in the centre of the red upright comb; the female is much smaller in proportion, and in colour resembles the heath-hen of the moors.

Between Hangwellé and Avisavellé, the ground is very uneven, and much of the country is covered with bamboo, which forms one of the most impenetrable kinds of low-sized jungle. At a little distance a bamboo brush-wood resembles gigantic rushes, each of which, on a nearer approach, proves to be of the size and shape of a common fishing-rod; and those which are higher than the mass, or grow on the outside, hang over in the most graceful bends.

After advancing about four miles, we saw the Kandian mountains and Adam's Peak appearing through a wooded valley, and forming a superb termination to the rocky banks and heavy forest scenery into which we were entering. As we proceeded, we fell in with troops both of the Wandurá and Rilawá monkeys. The former are of a large size, very dark grey colour, almost black, and with long white beards; this, with their sedate looks, grave habits, and hoarse voices, gives them a most patriarchal appearance. The Rilawás, on the contrary, are of a reddish fawn-colour, with the hair on the top of their heads spreading from a centre, and projecting far over their faces; this causes them to appear as if surmounted with a broad Scotch bonnet, but their manners do not correspond with their sober aspect and covenanter-looking head-dress: they are small-sized, restless, wonderfully active, singularly inquisitive, and unconquerably mischievous.

White birds, in shape resembling herons, and of many different sizes, we met with in numbers; by Europeans they are all called paddy-birds, as they are generally found in the paddy (rice) fields: along with them we saw, but did not get a shot at, a species of curlew as large as a duck, with white plumage, and black legs and beak. We also saw several of the birds called by the Cingalese kaendatta, which I do not recollect to have seen described: they have a long serrated bill, on the upper mandible of which rises a large horny crest, giving to the head the general appearance of a long helmet, and so large as to be quite out of proportion to the size of the body, which is not larger than that of a duck. The kaendatta feeds entirely on fruit, and so seldom quits the trees, that natives assert it never alights on the ground, as from the shortness of its legs it would be unable to raise itself again upon the wing: its flesh is dark-coloured and well flavoured; its plumage is black, with a few white feathers in the wing.

On our arrival at Avisavellé, the Modeliar informed us that the large herds were at some distance off, and in a very dense jungle; but that he had certain information of a hora-alia (rogue elephant) that was little more than a mile from the rest-house. Against this one we determined immediately to proceed. Natives believe a rogue elephant to be a turbulent member expelled by the unanimous consent and assistance of a whole herd; also, that he is destructive to crops and dangerous to people, and is alike dreaded by his own kindred and by the inhabitants in the neighbourhood of his haunts: he seldom ranges beyond ten or fifteen miles, and is generally to be found in the same forest. Some rogue elephants have killed many people; for, having once overcome their dread of man, and made a successful essay, homicide seems to become to them a favourite amusement: they have been known repeatedly to remain quiet near some jungle-path (contrary to their usual habit, which is to be always in motion) until a victim came within their reach. I afterwards knew an instance of a rogue elephant in mid-day coming into an open field, killing a woman by trampling her to death, and then leisurely returning to the forest; neither irritation in the animal, nor any inducement to the act, could be perceived by a number of persons who were near the unfortunate victim. It is more easy to account for rogue elephants attacking natives carrying loads of rice; this often happened during the Kandian rebellion, although many of those Coolies (baggage porters) who were missing, and supposed to have been killed, merely kept out of the way, and concealed themselves until a change of circumstances should free them from the compulsory execution of a most arduous, fatiguing, and dangerous service.

From Avisavellé we passed down the bank of the Seetawaka river, through scenery which closely resembled an English park; fine glades of green turf, with clumps, thickets, and forest-trees of enormous size, gave beauty to this woodland scene, until we arrived at a thick bamboo jungle. Into this we entered, and filed along a narrow, damp, dark buffalo track: here the fallen leaves seemed to be alive, from the innumerable land-leeches that moved amongst them; and it required the excitement of a wild elephant in the thicket to prevent me from stopping to pluck these ferocious vermin from my feet, hands, and neck. In passing along, our guide stopped, and, reaching up his hand, pointed to a tree, the trunk of which was coated with mud at least as far as nine feet from the ground: this showed us the height of the elephant of which we were in pursuit, and who had been lately using this tree as a scratching-post. A little farther on, and the native, who was leading, suddenly stopped, and, bending his head almost to the ground, pointed to a small open swamp, at the same time drawing in his breath, and repeating rapidly in a whisper, *Onna! onna! onna!* (There! there! look there!) Kneeling down amongst legions of leeches, I was just in time to see a huge elephant slowly raising himself from his luxurious mud-bath in a shady quagmire: for a moment I hoped he was about to charge at us; and I was the more impressed with this opinion from the instantaneous shifting of our guide from the front to the rear of our party, in which position he would no doubt have been equally ready to lead the retreat, as, to do him justice, he had been forward in heading the advance. The animal, still but indistinctly seen, paused for a second, then blew sharp through his trunk, curled it close up, wheeled round, and tore through the thick-set bamboos, which appeared to yield before and close behind his ponderous figure. It was impossible to follow into such a jungle; we therefore sought the open ground, and commenced shooting pigeons, which we found in considerable numbers and variety. On two different occasions, this day, large snakes glided from before me, and disappeared amongst the decayed leaves of the jungle. Whether they belonged to the class of the harmless garindi (rat-snake), or to the poisonous nága (hooded snake), I could not decide, as I had not as yet learned to distinguish between these serpents, which are as similar in appearance as they are different in character.

I cannot sufficiently account for the wondrous few accidents that occur from snakes in Ceylon; that desire, common to all animals, to shun the path of man, appears to me the only reason of much force which I have heard advanced. From experience I can assert that snakes, even poisonous ones, are very numerous,* and the few deaths which they cause is to me quite incomprehensible; therefore, the timidity of new-comers on this head is not only a natural impulse, but a rational feeling, and only gives way gradually before long habit and continued impunity. Elephant shots get much sooner rid of their fears on this subject than other people do, as the excitement of the sport absorbs all minor feelings, and snakes are not thought of when elephants are to be pursued.

* At Mátalai, a place by no means remarkable for the number of snakes in its vicinity, I had killed in four years, and in a space not exceeding twenty acres, ten venomous snakes, viz. five cobra-capels, two polongas, and three karawalas: four of these cobra-capels were upwards of five feet in length, and one of the la-polongas measured four feet and a half.

On our way back to Avisavelle we shot pigeons of four different kinds, called by the Cingalese Maílagoya, Batagoya, Kurulugoya, and Kobaiya. The maílagoya, in size, appearance, and habits when alive, and in flavour when cooked, is the same as the common wood-pigeon. The batagoya is a small dark-green pigeon, with shining plumage like the bright part of a mallard's wing: this bird is never seen in flocks, and very generally is found solitary, picking insects amongst the fallen leaves on jungle footpaths; the flesh of the batagoya has a strong bitter taste. The kurulugoya is commonly found in flocks, and perched on the highest trees; their colour is a very light green, with a pink tinge on the breast and part of the wings The natives say that neither the batagoya nor kurulugoya will live in confinement. The kobaiya is like the ground turtle-dove, of a grey colour tinged with pink: they are very abundant in most parts of the island.

On our return to the rest-house, we commenced divesting ourselves of the leeches, and then tried to staunch the bleeding of their wounds: we had been warned against plucking off these creatures forcibly and suddenly, as tending to irritate the wound; but we found that touching them with brandy instantly made them drop off; salt, gunpowder, or lime-juice produced the same effect, but not quite so quickly. The Ceylon land-leech is incredibly numerous on the hills, and such parts of the interior as are exempt from a long continuance of dry weather: they are of a brown colour; their usual size is about three-fourths of an inch in length, and one-tenth of an inch in diameter; they can, however, stretch themselves to two inches in length, and then are sufficiently small to be able to pass through the stitches of a stocking. They move quickly, are difficult to kill, and it is impossible to divert them from their bloody purpose; for, in pulling them from your legs, they stick to your hands, and fix immediately on touching the skin, as they are free from the scruples and caprice which is sometimes so annoying in their medicinal brethren. They draw a great deal of blood; and this, with considerable itching, and sometimes slight inflammation, is the extent of annoyance which their bites give to a man in good health; but animals suffer more severely from their attacks, and sheep will not thrive in pastures where there are leeches.

We have the authority of Dr. Davy to show that, in persons of a bad habit of body, leech-bites fester, become sores, and degenerate into extensive ulcers, "that in too many cases have occasioned the loss of limb and even of life." Dr. Davy's experience of those effects was during the rebellion of 1818, at which time the troops were exposed to so many hardships and privations that their constitutions were grievously impaired. From longer experience I should be inclined, even in the extreme cases laid to their charge, to exonerate the leeches from any graver accusation than their having inflicted punctures on persons of debilitated constitutions, and their having taken blood from those who could not afford to lose it.

Lime-juice, vinegar, most acids, or stimulants, soon cause the itching of leech-bites to abate, and prevent their ulceration; the best way to frustrate the attacks of these insects on the nether man, is to case one's-self in nankeen pantaloons with feet attached: this dress should be made with well-joined seams, and to tie round the waist.

Having detached the leeches from our persons, bathing after the native method was our next employment: this is a simple process; nothing more being required than a few earthenware vessels (water-chatties), which are easily procured. The invariable shape of these vessels is that of a broad depressed bulb, with a short neck about three inches in width; they contain a gallon and a half or two gallons of water; and as many as the bather requires being filled and placed within his reach, he raises them one by one with both hands until he can overturn and decant their contents on the top of his head.

By the time we were dressed, dinner was ready; and this day, as on most such occasions, our bill of fare consisted of game furnished by our guns; fowls, which in all inhabited parts of Ceylon are to be procured in abundance, and at very moderate prices: tongue, and a salt hump of beef, were the only part of our feast which had accompanied us from Colombo; the table was completed by the never to be despised, but ever present, curry and rice. and chicken cutlets. In all parts of the island beer and wines are cooled by immersing the bottles in water in which saltpetre is dissolving. Oranges, plantains, pines, and rambukans formed our dessert: the ubiquity of the first three as component parts of a Cingalese dessert is only to be matched by the curries, which are to be found placed at every breakfast, lunch, or dinner.

It is well to have smokers in the party if you have taken up your quarters in a place where moschettos abound, as these troublesome insects abscond from the poisonous fumes of tobacco.

> "So bees with smoke, and doves with noisome stench,
> Are from their hives and houses driven away."

And here I shall anticipate and state my opinion, founded on eleven years' experience, that the habit of smoking tobacco is extremely injurious to the health of Europeans* in Ceylon: why it has been encouraged and sanctioned in any part of the world is to me a matter of surprise, considering what I have seen of its evil effects, and how little I have ever heard or seen deliberately advanced in favour of this practice.

* This habit as yet has not become general, nor is it practised to great excess by the Cingalese; but it is unfortunately spreading rapidly, and may be expected to keep pace with the increase of drunkenness, with which it is so naturally allied.

From the description I have already given of a Ceylon rest-house, I have only to say of Avisavellé that it afforded shelter, and the country around offered a succession of beautiful landscapes. Whatever the traveller might require in the way of furniture and cooking-apparatus had to be carried on men's shoulders, and of course were procured of the most portable kind. A small bed with moschetto curtains was an invariable accompaniment whenever I started on any expedition, unless I travelled in a palanquin: this conveyance may be described as a box, which serves for a house or for a bed; the top of a palanquin may also be used as a table. Moschetto curtains are extremely useful; they are made of the thinnest muslin: yet I believe them to be equally effectual in excluding malaria as they are in preventing the intrusion of moschettos. While I am on the subject of the preservation of health in the jungles of Ceylon, or in travelling through the country, I may mention that a cup of strong coffee is a sure protection from the effects of morning dews or the heavy drizzling fogs which are most prevalent in the Kandian valleys, but in some seasons are to be met with in all parts of the island. These fogs, which are frequently extremely

The masticatory called Betel, hitherto in general use by the natives, is, I believe, much more wholesome than the use of tobacco in any shape; moreover, instead of being an excitement to drinking, it has the effect of appeasing hunger and thirst.

dense, do not seem to be in any way prejudicial to health beyond the effects produced on the human frame by exposure to moisture when fasting and thinly clothed.

The guns having been cleaned, and our ammunition arranged, we betook ourselves to rest, in hopes that the elephants would not move off during the night, and thus escape from our meditated attack. Soon after daylight we were relieved from our anxiety on this, the only point on which we had fear or doubt, by the information that several herds had joined, that their united numbers were between twenty and thirty, and that they were still in the same forest; I now anticipated nothing less than a speedy return to Colombo in the character of a successful elephant shot.

By the time we had finished our breakfast, a sufficient number of persons and tom-toms (native drums) had been collected; and we started under the guidance of the Modeliar, who conducted us back two miles on the Hangwellé road. Here we halted; and, while loading our guns, he dispatched the people and tom-toms to encircle the herd, and to await his signal to commence driving. We were now directed into a narrow path in a bamboo jungle, and, after proceeding along it for about half a mile, the Modeliar placed Mr. S—— and myself at the foot of a rising ground; Colonel L—— and Mr. H—— he placed a little farther up the ascent, where the forest was more open. The bamboos everywhere around us, except on the winding path in which we stood, grew as closely together, and were five times the size of common osiers; so that from our position it was only by stooping and peering through two or three small openings that we could discern objects even at a distance of five yards. There was now a dead silence for a few minutes, until loud calls, proceeding from persons stationed in trees, were passed along to a considerable distance, and proved to be the signal for the beaters to commence operations. Soon after this, we could just distinguish a very distant shout swell upon the breeze, and again all was silent for a considerable time; it was in these quiet intervals that the beaters were cautiously advancing and taking up new positions on the ground from which the elephants had receded. After this, shouts arose somewhat nearer, and the short pattering sound* of tom-toms could be distinguished. At this distance the general effect produced by the long-continued shouts of the people, combined with the noise of the advancing

* All the various kinds of native drums are usually called by Europeans tom-toms, but they have different Cingalese names, and have even less resemblance to each other in shape than in sound: some are large, some small, and formed like the drums used by European regiments; others are long and narrow, wide in the middle, and small at either end; while another kind is exactly the reverse, being very wide at the ends, and so narrow in the middle as to resemble an hour-glass: there is also a kind resembling kettle-drums.

elephants, was that of the rushing sound and heavy fall of a great body of water; but, as the mass approached, the breaking of branches, the beating of tom-toms, the wild shouts of the people, and the crash of decayed and falling trees, could be distinguished from the ponderous tread of the advancing herds as they pressed through the yielding forest.

In our position, the heat and want of air was most oppressive, for no thick foliage shaded us from a vertical sun; and, although the bamboos were insufficient for shade, they effectually excluded the very slight breeze which occasionally murmured over our heads, and shook the withered leaves.

With heavy tread and noisy tumult the elephants came on, and rested, as far as we could judge from the sound, within twenty yards of us; and then again succeeded an interval of dead silence. To us they were still invisible, and the utmost straining of my eye-sight was unable to gain me a glimpse of any of them: at this time, anxiety and excitement made my senses so acute, that not only did I feel the pulses thump with unwonted violence, but the ticking of my watch sounded on my ear as if a church-clock had located itself in my pocket; neither could I turn my head without feeling and fancying I heard the joints of my neck creak on their pivots. The beaters in the mean time had advanced, and, from a short distance behind and around the elephants, arose loud shouts of people and the rolling of tom-toms: immediately the jungle in front of us seemed heaving forward, and a second or two only elapsed before the heads of the two leaders of the mass were distinct and bearing directly on us. I fired at the one immediately opposite to me, and not more than ten feet distant: he stopped, and was in the act of turning when I fired again. Mr. S—— had also fired twice at the other leader, and with the same want of success; for the whole herd tore back through the brushwood, and rushed towards the hill.

Ere we could load again, double shots from both our friends on the rising ground announced the direction which the elephants had taken, and caused some of them to turn down; and these we heard tearing through, and at length stationing themselves in the bamboos behind the place where we stood. Having re-loaded, we cut into something like a buffalo track, leading towards the spot where we imagined the elephants to be; but were soon overtaken by a native, who endeavoured by signs to persuade us to turn back and follow him. Tolerably sure of the position of our game, and not dreaming of any accident having occurred, we were pushing on, when another native came after us, and in broken English said, "One gentleman plenty sick." The close jungle and suffocating heat naturally suggesting itself to us as the cause of his malady, we handed to the messenger a specific in the shape of a brandy-flask, and were about to proceed on our path, notwithstanding the deprecative shakes of his head, and unintelligible sounds intended for English, his stock of which seemed to have been exhausted in the announcement above quoted. At this time the noise of elephants near us induced silence, and we distinctly heard Colonel L—— calling to us that H—— had been seized by an elephant: on this we hastened to the spot, and found H—— perfectly collected, but bearing evident marks of his recent encounter. That one of his arms and one collar-bone were broken we soon ascertained; but were afraid, from marks which showed that he had been rolled over on the ground, that he might have received more serious injuries. From what I heard at the time and on my return here a few weeks afterwards, I believe that Colonel L—— and H—— each fired both barrels at elephants advancing on them. After the discharge, as the one at which H—— fired rushed forwards, he turned to receive his spare gun; but the native who held it had fled: H—— then endeavoured to escape, but fell; and the animal, coming up, knelt down, and with its head attempted to crush him against the ground, and in doing so rolled him over. In perfect ignorance of the perilous situation of his friend, Colonel L——, observing the elephant apparently butting against the ground, concluded it was a wounded one, and went up for the purpose of giving a finishing shot. On seeing him quite near, the animal suddenly raised itself and rushed into the jungle; while, to the utter astonishment of Colonel L——, H—— got up from apparently the very spot which the elephant had just quitted. Had Colonel L—— been a few seconds later in running up, H—— would probably have been sacrificed; or, had Colonel L—— fired and killed the elephant it must have fallen upon and crushed H——, who in every way had a narrow escape.

The active and energetic Modeliar soon caused a temporary litter to be prepared by some of his followers, while others cut down such bamboos as might obstruct its carriage through the path: this done, we soon reached the road, and afterwards met the Modeliar's palanquin, into which we transferred our disabled friend, and proceeded towards Hangwellé; our dinner unfortunately lying in the opposite direction. On reaching Hangwellé we found a boat ready, in which without loss of time we embarked; and the stream, that in the height of our spirits, and when flushed with anticipated sport, had defied our utmost exertions to proceed on our upward voyage, now bore us swiftly along, baffled, discomfited, and dinnerless. We reached the bridge of boats at midnight; and, in an hour after, H—— was in the fort of Colombo, attended by the medical men, who ascertained that the only very severe injuries he had received were those we had already remarked.

After placing our disabled friend in the hands

of the surgeon, I accompanied Colonel L—— to his house on the Galle road, and there we bethought us how eighteen hours of fatigue and fasting might best be repaired. As a preliminary to something more substantial, a glass of liqueur was proposed; and, seeing it both rich and clear, I willingly consented to make it a bumper. Had I been able to control my feelings for a few seconds after swallowing it, my kind host would also have taken as a cordial what my premature exclamation enabled him to shun as an odious drug: "fine cold-drawn castor-oil" was found printed on the label!

H—— recovered rapidly from the effects of his accident; but it was a warning which, combined with our most unwelcome fast and signal failure in elephant shooting, was a sufficient reason for my commencing to acquire more minute information regarding the interior arrangement of an elephant's head before I should again run the risk of facing a herd at close quarters. The Colombo Medical Museum afforded me the opportunity of examining the skeletons and sections of the skulls of these animals; by which I at once perceived that the real information I had picked up on this subject was very limited, the instructions I had received extremely incorrect, and that my conclusions were proportionably erroneous. I found that the brain of an elephant occupies but a small space, perhaps not more than one-eighth part of the head, the bones of which were very thin and particularly light. The fore part of the head (in front of the brain) for a thickness of eight inches is formed of cells separated by thin plates of bone: this, with the muscles necessary to move their trunks and support their enormous heads, is a satisfactory explanation why those persons who have attempted to shoot elephants without being close to their game have invariably proved unsuccessful. Having been made aware of this fact, our want of success was owing, not to firing at too great a distance, but to our ignorance of the small size and peculiar position of the brain of an elephant.

CHAPTER VI.

ELEPHANT SHOOTING NEAR HANGWELLÉ.

Peaceful, beneath primeval trees, that cast
Their ample shade o'er Niger's yellow stream;
And where the Ganges rolls his sacred wave;
Or mid the central depth of blackening woods,
High-rais'd in solemn theatre around,
Leans the huge elephant.—THOMSON.

A Second Start for Elephant Shooting. — Modeliar of Hangwellé. — Rambukan.—Native Garden.—Porcupines.—Porky.—Following Two Elephants. — The Country near Hangwellé. — Unceasing Harvest. — Excessive Heat. — Elephant shot. — Brandy and Water. — Elephant Charge. — Fatal Accident. — Return to Hangwellé. — Deaths by Elephants. — Major Haddock.—Mr. Wallett.—Extraordinary Escape.—Accident.

In December 1826, only a few weeks after the unsuccessful attempt at elephant shooting already related, having received a report from the Modeliar that two elephants had appeared in his neighbourhood, Mr. S—— and I lost no time in availing ourselves of the information, and despatching our guns and supplies; but, before they arrived, we presented ourselves on horseback, and were kindly welcomed by the Modeliar to his place near Hangwellé. His house, which was large, and built on the plan of those inhabited by Europeans in Colombo, stood in a beautiful situation, commanding a view of Adam's Peak, and was surrounded by thriving plantations and an extensive garden of young cocoa-nut trees. Amongst other fruit-trees, I here for the first time saw the rambukan in full bearing. The outer rind of this fruit (a very rough skin) is first green, but when ripe changes to a dark scarlet colour; this being removed, the inside presents a clear, cool, mucilaginous substance, adhering to a hard, unpalatable kernel: there is, therefore, little to eat in the rambukan; but it possesses refreshing properties and an agreeable flavour. The rambukan was, I believe, originally brought from China; but in Ceylon it grows without trouble, and bears fruit in seven or eight years. On learning that the whole of this plantation, as well as the ground on which the buildings stood, had been cleared from jungle only a few years previously, I was astonished that a speculation so evidently successful, and so much in accordance with the habits of the people, seemed to find few or no imitators. I had yet to learn, and did not then discover, how completely every improvement of men, manners, and the soil, was checked, even prevented, by the system of compulsory labour and services, with their concomitant abuses, which then prevailed, as it always had done under Cingalese, Portuguese, and Dutch rulers.

Soon after our arrival two men appeared before the Modeliar to ask his advice, and to explain their inability to pay certain taxes, in consequence of the extensive damage done to their garden of young cocoa-nut trees by porcupines, which, during the absence of the proprietors on Government service, had entirely destroyed a promising plantation, the joint labour of these men for several years. The favourite food of the porcupine is the heart of young cocoa-nut trees, which it is often difficult to guard from their attacks; as, even if surrounded with stones or a wall, these creatures will burrow under and destroy the plant. They are also very destructive to fences, through which they easily gnaw a passage; and this serves to admit hares and the meeminna* into the cultivated grounds and gardens. If disturbed in their path, (and they are the most capricious of all created animals,) porcupines will frequently cut a new gap every succeeding night for a week before hitting on one that will serve them for a permanent approach. At a later period of my stay in Ceylon, one of these animals, caught young, and brought up as a pet about my house, became so familiar as to accompany the person who usually fed it to a considerable distance: it occasionally absented itself for two or three days at a time, but always returned, generally making its first appearance after its wanderings in the dinner-room, to

* A very small, nimble, and beautiful species of deer common in Ceylon.

which it might be heard snuffing its way soon after the meat was put on the table. It was particular in examining (principally by smelling, a sense it possessed very acutely) all corners of the house for crickets, and in remarking any change in the position of the furniture. One night, having pushed open the door of a room in which a gentleman was sleeping, it immediately proceeded to the work of demolishing a dressing-case; the noise it made in this operation having awakened the proprietor, he flew to the rescue, but had no little difficulty in wresting his property from Porky, who left the room in very bad humour, and continued snuffing and bustling about the outside of the house for the remainder of the night. Shakspeare has admirably characterized the porcupine; it is essentially fretful: even this one, after it had attained its full size, although tame, fearless, and enjoying perfect liberty, was seldom five minutes in one's presence without exhibiting some sudden act of caprice, pettishness, or passion.

Our intelligent host, the Modeliar, seemed perfectly aware of the advantages of education, and had proved his sincerity of conviction on this head by sending one of his sons to be educated at the Calcutta college. This young man, from his acquirements and character, was one of the first native gentlemen who benefited by the liberal and enlightened policy embodied in the royal charter granted to Ceylon in 1833.

The report brought in by the natives who had

been sent to watch the elephants was very unsatisfactory. The only two that had appeared in the neighbourhood had moved off, and were last seen near a village six or seven miles from Hangwellé. Being determined to follow them, we started two hours before daylight next morning; and proceeded across the country, through narrow jungle paths, to the place where it was expected they had taken up their free quarters. This was in a swampy jungle, beyond which rose a rocky hill about three hundred feet in height, partly covered with trees and thickets, and joined by a narrow neck to a bare black rock shaped like a haycock. These hills appeared like outposts to the line of low-sized mountains along which formerly ran the boundary line between the Kandian country and the British territory. Here we found ourselves at fault; but, while our followers were scanning the jungle, a man arrived, and, through the Modeliar, earnestly besought us to push on and destroy the two elephants, that had stationed themselves in his cocoa-nut and coffee garden, and had torn down and destroyed a number of his trees. We had already travelled six miles, and now advanced five more; and then breakfasted close to a small and very thick bamboo jungle, into which the elephants had retired.

In the direction we had come, I was surprised at the small proportion which the cleared and cultivated land bore to that which was still in a state of nature. The extent of connected woods, the height of the trees, the prodigious size, length, and regular spiral form of the creeping plants that scaled the loftiest stems and then extended themselves over the surrounding thicket, the "unpierced shade" of the forest, the blaze of light on the field, combined to produce an indescribable richness of effect, marred only by the profuse oppressive luxuriance of vegetation, from which the eye had no escape.

Embosomed in wood, a few small rice-fields occasionally presented themselves; and the cultivators, who had been on the alert all night to protect their crops from wild animals, were now emerging from watch-huts (perched in trees and on rocks), and straggling home to their morning meal: none of the houses were to be seen, they are always in shade; but their locality is easily ascertained (in the interior) by the evidence of cocoa-nut trees.

On one side might be seen portions of the rice-field in every stage of preparation, from those but partly abandoned by the reaper, yet already under the hands of the ploughman, up to the level bed of mud ready to receive the already sprouted grain; here, in short, appeared endless spring and ceaseless summer. On the other side might be traced grain in every part of its progress, from the first scattering of the seed until its produce was again trodden out under the feet of buffaloes on a threshing-floor, which was merely a space cleared and levelled from the adjoining bank of the field. All this gave proof of an everlasting summer bordering upon autumn. In this part of Ceylon "seed-time and harvest" never cease; cold and winter are alike unknown.

The arrangements for driving out the elephants having been completed, we were stationed on an extensive slope facing the semicircular jungle, which the beaters had surrounded. Our position was on a buffalo track, perfectly without shelter from the sun, and with no other screen for our persons than a bush about four feet high, behind which we sat, and through which we could distinctly see the progress of the people employed in driving. As the animals showed evident signs of maintaining their position, the people were obliged to be cautious in advancing, and their proceedings appeared to us to be painfully tedious. Our impatience arose from two circumstances; viz. our anxiety to encounter the elephants, and a desire to escape from the fierce sun that darted directly upon us. Full two hours we continued in this position; at last the elephants broke from the jungle, and bore directly towards the place where we remained concealed. We allowed them to approach until one was within ten or twelve feet (the other being partly behind): we then stood up, and they slightly turned to the right, by which one was effectually screened by the other as they attempted to rush past. Mr. S—— and I both fired at the nearest, which fell over at our feet; while we dashed up the steep slope, expecting to overtake the other, or that he would turn on us when he gained the verge of the forest. In this we were disappointed, and only fired two random shots as he disappeared through the closing jungle. The great excitement was now over, and I began to feel the effects of the burning sun to which we had been so long exposed in a bare field: my skin was tight, dry, and burning hot; my face flushed, my head dizzy, and my frame weak. In deference to the opinion of others, and contrary to my own theory — that brandy or any other stimulant (even in this climate and under violent exercise) was unnecessary and hurtful,—I was accompanied by a person carrying brandy and water. A tumbler of this restorative I hastily filled, and eagerly swallowed. Little did I expect the instantaneous and beneficial change which it produced: the disagreeable symptoms vanished; and I, who one minute before was weak and helpless, now felt perfectly able for any fatigue. The greatest relief I experienced was the skin again becoming moist, an effect the more readily produced by the water becoming tepid from exposure to the sun.

From this digression those who read may be inclined to think, as I did, that our day's work was over; and that to retrace our steps after taking off our elephant's tail (the elephant's tail, like the fox's brush, is the signal of victory), was all that remained for us to do. On the contrary, the elephant kept possession of his tail, and we lost one of our followers, — thus. Mr. S—— and I were leisurely descending the hill, and approaching the bulky mass,—a dead elephant, as we for the last twenty minutes supposed it to be; and around the carcass fifty or sixty people had assembled, and were squatted on their haunches, chewing betel. Suddenly we saw them spring to their feet, and the assembly appeared to be rapidly diverging from the late centre of attraction: we could now distinguish the elephant moving on the ground; then heard him blowing shrilly through his trunk, and perceived that he was attempting to rise. We had discharged our good guns, and they were not reloaded; so that three cut-down muskets were all we had left, except one single barrel, which had been given to a young boy to carry, and he was still far behind. The elephant was already on his knees; no time was to be lost: we rushed forward, and discharged the three muskets close to his head.* Luckily for us, he moved off in the opposite direction from where we stood. At this moment the gallant little native boy came up, and thrust the single barrel into my hand. I fired; the elephant dropped on his knees, and in that situation remained full half a minute; then recovered himself, and dashed into the jungle near to where he first broke cover.

* Those who know what utterly worthless and unserviceable firelocks pass under this name, and are issued to the working portion of the British army, may not be prepared to hear that all the three muskets went off; certainly they will not be surprised to learn, that, although fired within three feet of the animal's head, they had no effect in retarding his motions.

While we were loading our guns the beaters again surrounded the jungle. This was only completed when we saw the elephant dash through the bamboo thicket, which yielded before his furious charge and weighty body as if it was but a field of water-reeds. His trunk was now erect; and, emitting a loud and long-continued squeal, he directed his headlong force against a withered tree which grew on a rocky bank. The tree was broken, and hurled to the ground. The day was now far spent, and the animal appeared so furious that the beaters were recalled: the last of the party which had accompanied us from Hangwellé was seen to emerge from the jungle, and we were about to proceed homewards, when the man ran up to inform the Modeliar that he had seen the mangled body of a man lying near the tree which the elephant had cast down. We were not long in getting a path cleared to the place, and in having the unfortunate man removed to the outside of the jungle; he was still alive, but insensible and dreadfully mangled. One native asserted that he was near when the accident happened, and saw the elephant strike the man as he was falling from the tree; but, from the nature of the wounds, I believe they were occasioned by the man being pitched from a considerable height, and alighting headforemost amongst broken rocks. The person who thus lost his life was the owner of the ground, and the same who had called us in the morning in hopes we would have rid him of the animals which had ravaged his plantations. The man survived for three days; the elephant died the same night, after making his way to a neighbouring stream.

Having conveyed the man to his own house, and rendered every assistance in our power, we started on our return to Hangwellé, although the sun was already set; and, from the indistinct and winding nature of our path, we did not reach the Modeliar's house until eleven o'clock P.M., and nineteen hours after we started in the morning. The Modeliar, although an elderly man, bore the fatigue well, and acted the landlord with much hospitality; but his sense of propriety was evidently severely tried when for some time he strove to resist joining in the mirth which was excited by one of the party falling fast asleep in the middle of dinner, with an arm snugly deposited in a huge oval dish of rice pudding.

The two elephants we had been in pursuit of this day were larger than those I had seen on a former occasion; but altogether their size was not so great as I was prepared to expect, and they had a reddish colour, which I could not account for. Their size, I presume, did not produce its full effect in consequence of the gigantic portions of forest vegetation with which they were in contact; but I afterwards discovered that wild elephants are very rarely so large as tame ones: the red colour of their skins was that of the earth in this neighbourhood; for elephants in the heat of the day employ a great portion of their time in picking up dust with their trunks, and scattering it over their bodies. To these accidents from elephants in this neighbourhood I may add the melancholy death of Major Haddock of the 97th regiment, which occurred some time after, within a mile of Ruanwellé;* at which place his family resided, he being

* Ruanwellé on the Kellania-ganga, and nine miles beyond Avisavellé

the commandant and agent of Government for the surrounding district. The elephant he was in pursuit of, after being severely wounded and driven back into the forest, reappeared close to Major Haddock, who fired and immediately moved to one side; his servant, who had stood behind him, then fired; and the animal turned off towards Major Haddock, whom he seized, threw down, and trampled to death. This was the work of a moment; for the servant flew to the spot, and, while he was raising the mangled remains of his gallant master, the elephant walked slowly off. Sir Robert Wilmot Horton, Governor of Ceylon, has erected a stone pillar, with an inscription, to mark the precise spot where this melancholy catastrophe occurred.

Elephant shooting, in exciting interest, as far exceeds any other sport in Ceylon, as does the animal itself compared with the lesser tenants of the forest. From the strength of all, and the fierceness of some elephants, prompt measures and presence of mind are absolutely necessary to the sportsman's safety; yet Major Haddock was the only European gentleman killed by an elephant during my residence in Ceylon, and I believe he was quite inexperienced, and moreover had entrusted his spare gun to a native, who fled when the animal first rushed out from the jungle. That this was the only fatal accident to an elephant-shot may be considered astonishing, when I recollect how few of those that followed the sport but had been on various occasions in imminent danger, and narrowly escaped (some not altogether unhurt) from the encounter.

It was only a few months after I had written the above remark on the numerous and narrow escapes of elephant-shots, that I received intelligence of the melancholy death of another acquaintance, a most promising young man, whose untimely fate is thus described in the Ceylon newspapers:—

"Mr. Wallett (only son of Brevet-major Wallett, C.R.R. commandant of Jaffna) was killed by an elephant on Thursday last, near Ruanwellé. It appears that, having heard of a tusker,* Mr. Wallett, attended by two native boys, went in pursuit, and met it in a herd of three. He fired one barrel, and is said to have hit the animal; but the second barrel of his gun missed fire, and the elephant rushed upon him before he could get another gun from his terrified attendants. It immediately crushed him to death, and went off for a few minutes; but, returning, thrust his tusks through the body, and tore all the clothes off it. It is a curious coincidence that Mr. Wallett lost his life not far distant from the place where Major Haddock was killed by an elephant seven years ago."—*Colombo Observer*, 1st October 1838.

* An elephant with tusks is commonly called by Cingalese sportsmen a "Tusker."

"Lieutenant Gallwey, 90th Light Infantry, and Ensign Scroggs, of the 18th Royal Irish Regiment, proceeded last Thursday to the place where Mr. Wallett was killed by the elephant, in expectation of finding the animal, and being revenged for the loss of their deceased friend.

"The following are the particulars of the encounter in which Messrs. Scroggs and Gallwey destroyed the elephant to whose fury Mr. Wallett recently fell a victim; from which it will be seen that these gentlemen, or one of them at least, narrowly escaped the fate of their lamented friend:—

"The elephant having been constantly watched since Mr. Wallett's death, no delay took place in pointing out his position; but, owing to heavy rain, it was not till four in the afternoon that Messrs. Scroggs and Gallwey could venture to go in search of him. Very shortly after entering a dense bamboo jungle, they discovered him slowly approaching them; and, having allowed him to come pretty close, both gentlemen fired together at his head. The atmosphere being so exceedingly damp and heavy, the smoke hung around for some seconds, during which they were in the most anxious suspense, not knowing the position of the elephant; till, on its clearing a little, they saw him still advancing on them, when, on receiving the contents of their two remaining barrels, he turned round and fell on his knees. Quickly recovering himself, however, he retreated rapidly through the jungle, closely followed by his pursuers, who again fired three shots at him without any apparent effect, his position rendering it exceedingly difficult to see a vulnerable spot. The fourth shot, however, fired by Mr. Scroggs, as the elephant turned half round, took effect somewhere in the side of his head, and again brought him to his knees.

"A halt now took place to load the guns, and, this being accomplished, both gentlemen ran on the elephant's track for nearly half a mile at the top of their speed without getting a sight of him; till at last, on reaching the commencement of a slight descent, he was discovered about twenty yards off, still retreating; but, on seeing his pursuers, he wheeled round and rushed furiously at them. Mr. Gallwey, who was in front, fired both barrels deliberately into his head, but without stopping him for an instant; and had barely time to throw himself to one side out of the path of the infuriated animal, whose trunk, as Mr. Gallwey turned round to escape, was within six feet of him. At this instant, Mr. Scroggs, who was about six yards behind Mr. Gallwey, fired at the right temple of the elephant; and the next moment had to crouch to one side to allow the brute to pass him, which he did, almost touching Mr. Scroggs, and without appearing to notice him. Directly he had passed, Mr. Scroggs ran for a yard or two across the jungle, hoping to get a side-shot at his head;

and in this he succeeded, for, the moment he crossed the path so as to come on the left side of the elephant, the brute wheeled round to get at him, and, as he was in the act of doing so, Mr. Scroggs fired his last barrel, which, taking effect immediately behind the left ear, produced instant death.

"On examining the head, it appeared that the shot which Mr. Scroggs fired at the right temple just as Mr. Gallwey jumped to one side, had providentially knocked out the elephant's right eye; and, as both gentlemen fortunately took to their own left in getting out of the brute's path, this circumstance accounted for their escape. Had they taken the other side, one, if not both, must have perished. The elephant was the largest ever seen by Mr. Gallwey, who has killed nearly one hundred with his own gun, but we are unable to state his exact dimensions."—*Colombo Observer*, 22nd October 1838.

The following adventure, relating to one of the gentlemen who killed the elephant, is copied from a published letter, dated in January 1837.

"We had excellent sport, having 'bagged' one hundred and six elephants among four of us in three days; but I had a narrow escape from shooting my friend G——. We had all followed three elephants into a thick bit of jungle, and came up with them at an opening of perhaps twenty feet square. G—— and I went at the same 'bird,' which, after taking some shots from both of us, and one or two from our companions, got into the cover, but suddenly burst out again almost upon G——, who was close behind it, and who, being unloaded, bolted back, and stumbled over the trunk of a dead elephant, sufficiently within reach of the live one. In the mean time, a Cooly had put a fresh gun into my hand; and, as I fired, G——, in rising from his stumble, brought the top of his cap on the line of sight. I saw the cap jerk and open, and the elephant drop at the same instant. The cap was of wicker-work, covered with blue nankeen, and in shape a hunting-cap, fitting close to the head: the ball had opened full four inches of it; his hair was not cut, but still it was a frightfully close shave."

This was not the only accident to the same daring and successful sportsman, who, only a few days after this adventure, escaped with life, but not unscathed, having received a very severe contusion from the blow of a wounded elephant.

CHAPTER VII.

JOURNEY TO ADAM'S PEAK.

Not vainly did the early Persian make
His altar the high places and the peak
Of earth-o'ergazing mountains, and thus take
A fit and unwall'd temple, there to seek
The spirit in whose honour shrines are weak
Uprear'd of human hands. Come and compare
Columns and idol-dwellings, Goth and Greek,
With Nature's realms of worship, earth and air;
Nor fix on fond abodes to circumscribe thy prayer!

BYRON.

Set out for Adam's Peak. — Ancient Temple at Kellania. — Visited by Gautama Buddha. — Queen of Kellania Tissa. — Her Death. — Fate of the High-priest. — Submerging of the West Coast of Ceylon. — Wihari Dewi. — Native Potters. — King of Kandy defeated at Hangwellé. — Cowardice and Cruelty. — Seetawaka. — Raja Singha the Apostate. — Longevity. — Ceylon Bird of Paradise. — Mountain Scenery. — Chules. — Ratnapoora.

HAVING, from my first landing in the autumn of 1826, been eager to visit the mountains of the interior, I only waited for the season most free from clouds and rain, and started in February 1827 for Samanala (Adam's Peak). This mountain, from the earliest ages, has been an object of veneration to the inhabitants of the East, and was for centuries a theme of interest and mystery to those of the West, until the conquest of the Kandian country opened the way to this sacred citadel of ancient religions.

The route by which I proceeded to Adam's Peak lay for some distance along the left bank of the Kellania-ganga, having diverged from the great Kandy road at the bridge of boats across that river. The Kellania-ganga derives its name from a village situated on the right bank, and possessing, as a memorial of its antiquity, a dágoba, which, B.C. 280, was extended by the tributary King Yatálatissa over one built on the same spot by the Nága King Mahódara, B.C. 580. Kellania was probably the capital, and has for ages been the chief place for the worship of Weebeesana, a hero of the Ramayan, grandson of Pulastyia,* friend of Rama, the traitorous brother and deified successor of Rawena on the throne of Lanka.† At the time of Gautama Buddha's appearance,‡ Kellania would seem to have been the capital of a division of the island called Nága-Diwayina; and that its inhabitants, called Nágas, were easily converted, and afterwards zealously adhered to the Buddhistical doctrines, for which they were rewarded by various relics and a second visit

* Vishravas, called Pulastyia (Ramayan).

† The Rajawallia states this to have happened 1844 years before Buddha, or B.C. 2387.

‡ B.C. 588.

of the Buddha. In his first visit to Ceylon, Gautama converted the Nágas, and settled a dispute between two of their Princes, Chulódara and Mahódara, who made an offering to him of the throne composed of gold, inlaid with precious stones, which had been the original cause of their quarrel: over this throne a dágoba was built, and is encased in the one now standing. At the request of Miniasa, uncle of the Nága King Mahódara, Gautama made his third visit to Ceylon, and left the impression of his foot beneath the waters of the river: a deep eddy in the stream is now pointed out as the spot; it is near the temple, and the natives say that the circling of the current here is the Kellania-ganga descending in homage to this sacred memorial. Having arranged the disputes of the Nágas and confirmed their faith, the prophet departed for Samanala, Díggánakhya,* and the other places which had been sanctified by the presence of former Buddhas.

The following romantic legend, connected with

* Digganakhya. The principal buildings at this place were erected by Saidatissa in the second century before Christ, and there is little doubt that their ruins form the subject of the following note of Bertolacci's work on Ceylon:—

"There is a pagoda, forty miles south of Batticaloa, in the centre of a very thick forest. It was unknown to Europeans until discovered by Mr. Sawyers, collector of Batticaloa, in the year 1810. I should be at a loss in what era to class it. The size of the building is gigantic; and the prejudiced natives report that it was erected many thousand years ago by giants ten cubits tall. The cone, forming the pagoda, is entirely

Kellania, is to be found in Cingalese histories; the period is about 200 B.C.

The beautiful Queen of Tissa, King of Kellania, having been seduced by his brother Uttiya and their intercourse detected, he fled to Gampola; from thence he soon after sent an emissary disguised as a priest. This person was instructed to mix in the crowd of priests, who, along with their chief, daily attended at the palace to receive their alms; at which time it was expected the messenger might find an opportunity of safely delivering a letter with which he was entrusted to the Queen, who always assisted at the distribution of alms. The disguised messenger entered the palace along with a multitude of priests, and, having caught the eye of the Queen, dropped the letter: the sound of its fall was heard by the King, who immediately turned round and seized it. The King, having

covered with brick and mortar; its basis is about one quarter of a mile in circumference, and the top and sides are now planted with large trees that have fixed their roots in the ruins, and, elevating their heads fifty or sixty feet high, shade this little hill. * * * *

"The pagoda which I am describing is surrounded by a square enclosure, a mile in circumference, consisting of a broad wall made of bricks and mortar, and having within it a number of cells. The entrance to this enclosure is through a colonnade of stone pillars about ten feet high.

"Near the pagoda are seen the ruins of another large building of the same materials. Some of the natives report that it was the palace of a king, erected many years after the pagoda."

perused the guilty communication, in the height of his fury decided that the High-priest must be cognizant of the intrigue; for not only had the messenger come as a priest in his train, but the letter appeared to the King to have been written by the High-priest. He was forthwith thrown into a cauldron of boiling oil; at the same time, the Queen was bound and cast into the river, and the messenger was hewn in pieces. The real writer was afterwards ascertained, and it was then remembered that Uttiya had been a pupil of the unfortunate High-priest, and had acquired exactly the same method of writing.

Not long after these events, the sea began to encroach rapidly on the west coast of Ceylon, and the King became persuaded that this calamity was a judgment against him for the cruel and unjust sentence he had executed on the High-priest. In hopes of preventing the onward progress of the waves, and to appease the wrath of those gods who control the waters, Tissa determined to sacrifice his virgin daughter Sudhádéwi; and, having secured her in a covered golden canoe, on which was inscribed "a royal maiden," he caused it to be launched into the ocean. The flood continued to increase; and the monarch, mounted on his elephant, had proceeded to view the destructive effects of the raging waters: while thus engaged, the earth opened, and the King disappeared amidst flames which burst from the sinking wreck of his richest provinces. Before the waves ceased to encroach upon the land, six hundred and forty villages (four hundred and seventy of which were principally inhabited by divers for pearls) had been overwhelmed, and the distance between Kellania and the sea-coast had been reduced from twenty-five to four miles.

The vessel in which the young Princess was immolated, having been drifted to the south-west, was discovered and brought to land by some fishermen in the Mâgam district, which was at that time a separate kingdom, under the control of Kawantissa Raja. He, having heard of the mysterious appearance of the golden canoe, proceeded to the coast at Totalu Ferry; and, after reading the inscription, released the Princess, whose name he changed to Wihari Dewi, and whom he afterwards married.

Wihari Dewi became the mother of Dootoogaimoonoo, a prince who restored the Cingalese power, and expelled the Malabars, to whom both Kellania Tissa and Kawantissa had been tributaries. Many Buddhists believe that her merits and good fortune are so great, that, in a future transmigration, she will become the mother of Mytrée, the expected Buddha.

The path, as I proceeded, lay very much through cocoa-nut tree plantations; and, when it emerged from them, it was either to enter on some swampy plain of levelled rice-fields, or to cross some low ridge covered with brushwood. These rising grounds are only cleared and cultivated periodically, after a lapse of seven, eight, or ten years, according to the circumstances of the people and quality of the soil. When the proper time arrives, the brushwood is cut down, and in a few days is sufficiently dry to admit of being burned on the ground ; the ashes are then scattered, and form the only stimulant or manure which the land receives; this simple form of tillage is completed by slightly hoeing the surface preparatory to sowing the grain. Various kinds of corn which do not require irrigation are usually raised ; but in the moist parts of the Kandian provinces a particular species of rice is cultivated, on high grounds which have been ploughed, or turned over with a large hoe: although a precarious crop, this species of rice, in favourable seasons, yields a most abundant return. After the ground is prepared, there is still a material work to perform in fencing around the field ; and for this purpose sticks enough have been spared from the conflagration: these, stuck in endways close together, and tied with creeping plants, form a sufficient fence against small animals; but, to protect the crop from hogs, buffaloes, and elephants, numerous watch-huts are erected, and are always occupied during the night by the cultivators.

The villages on the road to Hangwellé are principally occupied by potters, and I was much struck with the elegant form of the common earthenware vessels which they were employed in making. They commenced by placing the prepared clay on a flat stone two feet in diameter, moving horizontally on a pivot; and the manner of working is exactly described in the two lines of Homer:

> "Fleet as the wheel whose use the potter tries,
> When, whirl'd beneath his hand, its axle flies."

In the manufacture of earthenware, if elegance of form alone were to be consulted, without regard to utility or convenience, the Cingalese potters are certainly much superior to their brethren of the trade in Europe; but, besides that the small base and great height of some of their vessels render them more liable to accidents, long narrow necks prevent the eye from detecting the existence of impurity within, nor can the hand be introduced for the purpose of having them cleaned.

The village of Hangwellé, on the banks of the Kellania-ganga, had a small fort, which is now unoccupied and in ruins, but was at one time a post of some consequence, as commanding the principal routes both by land and water which led from the interior of the island to Colombo. In 1803, the garrison of this place, amounting only to one hundred men, principally invalids, under Captain Pollock, 51st regiment, gave a signal defeat to the last King of Kandy and the multitude of his rabble army. This occurred at the time when, flushed with the butchery he had perpetrated on a sickly detachment of troops under Major Davie, the King and his councillors, mistaking falsehood and treachery for policy and courage, imagined themselves capable of overthrowing the British power in Ceylon, and had advanced thus far on their way to attack Colombo. The King was amongst the first who fled, and, during the rout, having been overtaken by two of his chiefs,* he attempted to screen his own cowardice and satisfy his cruelty by accusing them of want of energy, and ordering their immediate execution: other victims would have shared their fate, had not an accidental and trifling noise renewed the personal fears of the royal monster, and induced him to resume his flight.

"Captain Pollock destroyed a richly ornamented bungaloe, erected not far from Hangwellé for the reception of the King. In front of it stood two stakes, on which it was intended to impale the English prisoners; they exactly agree with the description of those barbarous instruments given by Knox in his historical relation of Ceylon, published in the year 1681."†

From Hangwellé to Avisavellé the scenery gradually improves, and the situation of the rest-house and village at the latter place is particularly pretty; but, before reaching Avisavellé, a sudden halt, and continued shouts from the palanquin bearers, announced that the road was occupied by elephants, and had the effect of making them retire into the jungle. It was close to this spot that I had my

* Called Leuké and Pahalapané.

† Cordiner's Ceylon.

first adventure in elephant shooting, which has been already described.

From Avisavellé I crossed the small but navigable river, a tributary stream of the Kellania-ganga, for the purpose of examining the ruins of Seetawaka, once the residence of the longest-lived, if not the bloodiest tyrant in modern history, Raja Singha of Seetawaka, surnamed by Buddhists the Apostate. During a dangerous illness, Raja Singha, enraged at the discouraging replies made to him by Buddhist priests when he wished to receive consolatory promises, caused many of them to be put to death, their sacred and historical books to be burned, and gave the custody of the Sree Pada (sacred footstep on Adam's Peak) to some Fakirs, whose assurances were more consonant to his wishes. From that sickness the King recovered, and died (after being defeated in battle by Don Juan), partly from chagrin, partly from an accident, — a thorn which ran into his foot,—at the great age of one hundred and twenty years. In his later years Raja Singha added impiety and apostacy to the long and otherwise complete catalogue of his crimes. The age of Raja Singha is mentioned by the Portuguese historian, who had good opportunities of acquiring correct information on this point; for the tyrant was not only the inveterate enemy, but also the near neighbour to the Portuguese in Colombo.

Instances of great longevity are by no means rare in the Kandian country: in Matalé, I knew several persons upwards of one hundred years of age; and, immediately before leaving that place in 1837, I had the satisfaction of seeing one of them reap an excellent crop of rice, on ground which he had himself, in the previous year, cleared from a thick forest, and then prepared with the hoe; he had also watched his field in an open hut, and protected it from the inroad of wild animals.

Seetawaka is said formerly to have been called Seetawadé, and to have obtained that name from its being the spot, according to Hindu tradition, where Indrajit caused a figure resembling the captive Seeta to be beheaded, in order that Rama, giving up all hopes of regaining his consort, might abandon the war he was then waging against Rawena for her recovery. Seetawaka stands on an angular piece of ground, formed by a bend of the river and a ravine; and here, within several quadrilateral enclosures, is situated the remains of the Bairaindé Kowilla, erected for demon worship by Raja Singha about the middle of the sixteenth century. The thickness of the jungle, which grew luxuriantly, and spread from the interstices of its well-laid pavement, prevented me from obtaining a correct measurement of its size, or knowledge of its peculiar architecture; but, so far as I could discern, it appeared to have occupied the centre of an elevated stone platform of eighty feet square, and to have been about thirty feet in length, formed of handsome carved pillars supporting a cornice. The plan of the pillars of this building appeared to be as if eight ornamented pilasters projected, two on each side, from a plain square pillar. This building was overthrown when Seetawaka was taken and burnt by the Portuguese in the latter part of the sixteenth century; and the foundations and part of the walls of one of their forts, which commanded the site of this town, still remain on the elevated bank and opposite side of the river.

A bird, called the Ceylon Bird of Paradise by Europeans, although it is merely a long-tailed fly-catcher, is very common in this part of the island, and may be seen flitting about in the thick copses and dark ravines. It is about the size of a sparrow, with a black head, and a tail five times its own length, composed of very flexible feathers of pure white: the disproportioned length of this bird's tail gives it the appearance of having a narrow piece of cloth attached to it, and is the origin of the Cingalese name Redi-hora (cloth-stealer).

From Avisavellé the road was almost level, passing along a delightful valley, on one side of which arose a variety of abrupt rocks and peaked hills covered with wood, while on the other and more inland side the range of mountains was continuous; but the highest ridges were obscured by a dense mass of vapour. After our arrival at Nacondellé, the evening cleared up, and disclosed Adam's Peak opposite to us, and beyond the square pillar-like mountain of rock called Uno-Dhia-Parawatia, which towered over ridges of nearer hills, its perpendicular sides reflecting the setting sun, and contrasting powerfully with the verdant covering and deep shadows that darkened the valleys.

In advancing from Nacondellé to Ratnapoora, I was occasionally surprised to observe how firmly the bearers kept their feet, and supported the palanquins, in passing along some single slight elastic tree, or bamboo, which acted as a bridge to a ravine of considerable depth. As we travelled this stage during the night, we required the light of chules, which are bunches of dried cocoa-nut leaves or bamboos: the glare of light which these throw around, and the noise of the persons who carry them, are effectual protections against elephants, and have a grand effect in passing through a stately forest or rocky pass.

Ratnapoora is a small fort, occupying the summit of a rocky hillock, which rises in a long narrow valley bounded on all sides by high and thickly wooded hills. The fort, although a place of no military strength, is sufficient protection against natives; and, in the time of the rebellion, gave security to a considerable village which lies under its walls. The Kalu-ganga, which even here is little more than fifty feet above the level of the sea, runs near the fort, and affords to this part of the country the advantage of water-carriage to Caltura and Colombo; but it frequently overflows the whole valley around Ratnapoora, only leaving visible the fort, and a little rising ground on which is situated the residence of the agent of Government for the district of Saffragam. In looking up the gap through which the Kalu-ganga issues from the great mountain range, three summits (apparently of equal height) presented themselves; for the very moist atmosphere at this place prevented me from distinguishing (unless for a few minutes immediately after sunrise) that two of these peaks are much nearer than Samanala, and inferior in elevation.

CHAPTER VIII.

ASCENT OF THE PEAK.

Majestic woods, of every vigorous green,
Stage above stage, high waving o'er the hills,
Or to the far horizon wide diffus'd,—
A boundless deep immensity of shade.—THOMSON.

Mr. Turnour. — Start from Ratnapoora to ascend the Peak. — Morning. — Gillemallé. — Bo-trees. — Cingalese Forest. — Palabadoolla. — Metal Frame of the Sacred Footstep. — Mohammedan and Hindu Pilgrims. — Scenery.—Echo.—Mountain Torrents.—Diabetme.—Ascent from Diabetme.—Legends. — Seetla-ganga. — Pilgrims bathing. — Summit of the Ridge. — Mohammedan Traditions. — Ascent of the Cone. — Iron Chains. — Ladies ascend the Peak. — Description of the Summit. — The Sacred Footstep. — View from Adam's Peak. — Deiya Guhawa. — Resting-place of Buddha. — Extraordinary Night Scene. — Traditions of the Peak. — Thermometer. — Descent. — Temple of Saman. — Saman. — From Ratnapoora to Caltura. — The Kalu-ganga.—Kobberagoya.— Kalamander Wood. — Caltura to Colombo.

AT Ratnapoora I spent some days with Mr. Turnour, who has since done so much in restoring Cingalese history, in developing that of India, and in examining the primitive religion of Gautama Buddha.

At four o'clock in the morning, Mr. B—— and I set out on foot from Ratnapoora to ascend the

Peak, but did not reach Gillemallé until near eight, although the distance is only seven miles: the road, which was very uneven, kept generally near the bank of the river, passed under the shade of some rocks surmounted by a Buddhist temple, and crossed a considerable stream near its junction with the Kalu-ganga.

We felt the coolness of the approaching morning become more chilly immediately before and at the time of sunrise; and the heavy fogs, common in the mountainous parts of the interior, began to descend first like mist, and then as drizzling rain: this, however, was soon dispelled; and

> "Morn, her rosy steps in the eastern clime advancing,
> Sow'd the earth with Orient pearl."

We now heard at no great distance from us the screaming of peacocks, and the call of the jungle-fowl; but were unable to approach them in consequence of the tangled thorns and thick underwood of the forest. At the same time we discovered that our clothes were soaked in blood from the bites of leeches; these had either introduced themselves through flaws in our raiment, or, having ascended until they found no obstruction from dress, had fixed themselves on our necks.

> "Now gentle gales,
> Fanning their odoriferous wings, dispense
> Native perfumes."

From the many jessamines, from the various orange-flowers, from the citron and lime, from the areka, from innumerable plants and flowering trees, arose their divers perfumes; these, blended in the morning dew, and wafted on the early breeze, afforded the most delicate and exquisite fragrance.

Gillemallé is situated on a gentle elevation, round which the river flows; before it lies a rich cultivated plain, interspersed with gigantic forest-trees, and bounded on all sides by wooded hills, which rise into stupendous mountains towards the Peak. From Gillemallé, in passing along the plain, we saw many comfortable native houses situated in gardens amidst cocoa-nut, areka, jack,* shaddock, plantain, and other fruit-trees; also the talipot with its immensely large fan-shaped leaves, and the bo-tree, which is sacred to Gautama Buddha, and in consequence generally to be found protected by a stone wall. Some of these venerated trees were

* The jack-tree grows to a very large size, and is not only the most useful, but also the most beautiful of the Ceylon forest-trees, from the great size of its spreading top, and the deep shade of its dark-green leaves. It produces an extraordinary quantity of fruit from its branches, its trunk, and even from its roots. I have seen upwards of one hundred and fifty on a tree at once. The fruit has a rough green covering, and contains a great number of kernels about half the size of a pigeon's egg: these, when the fruit is ripe, are contained in a luscious yellow covering, which is too strong-tasted for Europeans; but, before it ripens, the kernels, when cooked, form a good vegetable, and are very commonly the foundation of the curries used by the labouring Cingalese. The size and weight of the fruit varies from one to fifty pounds' weight. The wood of the jack-tree is generally used in making furniture, and much resembles the commonest kinds of mahogany.

surrounded by several platforms, on which were erected little altars; and at these the natives might be seen offering flowers to the sylvan emblem of the object of their devotion. At the extremity of the plain we crossed another stream; and immediately beyond this the path becomes very steep, and ascends through a continued forest. The great size and regularity of form in many of the creeping plants were amongst the first wonders which attracted my notice in the Cingalese forests; and I soon discovered that the existence, continuance, and extinction of trees in Ceylon is very different from the parallel stages of those which grow in climates so cold that winter renders them torpid through half their duration. To-day a seed, to-morrow a sapling; then but a few years more, and the soil and climate of Ceylon have raised it to be a tree of great height, goodly size, and far-extending shade: its decline once commenced is proportionately hastened by the creepers that twine around its stem, the air-plants that corrode its bark, the white ants that mine into its vitals; and even the heavy rains and fierce heats that fostered its early growth now forward its rapid decay. In Ceylon hurricanes are unknown, and in its far-extending forests trees may be seen leafless and dead, yet with all their branches, even the twigs, perfect, and appearing as if they only awaited a change of season to call them into life; yet such is their state of internal decay, that even the hand of man might hurl to the ground those mummy monarchs of primeval forests.

Four and a half miles from Gillemallé we reached Palabadoolla, the last inhabited spot on this track. It possesses a comfortable rest-house, and a wiharé (temple of Buddha): here we saw and examined the metal frame which is usually placed over the Sree Pada (sacred footstep) on Adam's Peak; it was undergoing repair, and the yellow metal of which it is composed appeared to correspond in value to the gems (plain and coloured glass) with which it is profusely ornamented. At this place we saw a cheerful party of respectably dressed Mohammedan pilgrims of both sexes; they were on their way to worship at the place of penance of the progenitor of their race, the first of their prophets.* This civil and comfortable group were scowled upon from a corner by two men, apparently ill-fed, and certainly ill-favoured, sinister-looking persons, in the dress of Hindus: these were also bound to the same spot to worship a different name; but whom it was their religion pointed to, and had brought them so far to honour, I had no person capable of interpreting, nor did they seem anxious to explain.

* "God here promises Adam that his will should be revealed to him and his posterity; which promise the Mohammedans believe was fulfilled at several times by the ministry of several prophets, from Adam himself, who was the first, to Mohammed, who was the last. The number of books revealed unto Adam, they say, was ten."—*Note to Chapter II. Al Koran of Sale.*

Leaving Palabadoolla, we continued to ascend, and often approached the edge of a precipice whose terrors were hid by the close foliage and thick underwood, until arriving at the rock called Nihila-hellagalla: then the great depth of the valley under our feet, the precipitous mountain opposite, and the country through which we had passed, burst at once upon our view. While stopping at this place to listen to an echo, and to various fables of the guides, we began to feel the great difference of temperature, and perceived that the creeping plants were gradually giving place to the mosses. The path by which we had come did not improve as we advanced, and was evidently more frequently occupied as the bed of a torrent than as a highway, so that pilgrims during the heavy rains must have great difficulty in striving against the steep ascent and rapid stream. At the season when the great concourse of people make their pilgrimage (April and May), there are generally heavy rains, which, by causing a sudden rise in the mountain torrents, often occasion the loss of lives; and great hardships are endured by many, who are detained without food or shelter, alike unable to advance to their destination, or to return for supplies, until the waters subside. Immediately after our arrival at Diabetme, which proved an uninhabited and scarcely habitable rest-house, the clearing up of some clouds, which had partially obscured the mountains, enabled us to distinguish the full extent of the magnificent scene. The view from this spot is unimpeded for three-fourths of the circle, and, excepting water, presented every variety of the grand and beautiful in forest landscape. The prevailing tints of the forest were the richest reds and browns of every shade; these (where so great a proportion of the trees are evergreen) are produced by the young shoots and leaves, which generally appear in these colours or exhibit the palest green. The most striking views were, on the east, Samanala, (the Peak,) of a remarkably regular bell-shape, rising on a long ridge of mountains; it was about four miles distant, and the small temple on the summit was barely visible. On the west, the sun, setting on the level country, and nearly behind the stupendous rock mountain of Uno-Dhia, was more attractive to the eye than the object of our excursion. In so far as awe is a component part in sublimity of effect produced by the grandest features of nature, the views in Ceylon are often deficient; for a general softness is diffused over its scenes by an exuberant vegetation, which screens the greatest cataracts, festoons the steepest rocks, and clothes the summits of the highest mountains with majestic forests.

Diabetme is four miles from Palabadoolla, and nearly the same distance from the Peak: here the fowls were killed that we might require during our stay at the holy footstep, as no follower of Buddha would break his first commandment and destroy life within the hallowed precincts, which with to-morrow's dawn we were about to enter, and to which Diabetme was the nearest outpost. Several of my followers, who had been "of master's religion" in Colombo, openly avowed themselves Buddhists here; and, in honour of the place and its memorial of their teacher, they had preserved their best dresses to put on after purifying themselves in a sacred stream which lay in our route. At Diabetme the thermometer at nine o'clock P.M. stood at 60°, and at five o'clock A.M. next morning it was as low as 49°.

After having despatched an early breakfast, we sent forward our servants and supplies, and then started; we soon came to a ravine from which the ascent proceeds by one hundred and thirty rude steps cut in an immense face of smooth rock. On the left-hand side, and about half-way up, there is the figure of a man, and an inscription cut in Cingalese characters. The figure is a wretched attempt in outline; and the inscription, which may be considered as modern, relates to the execution of the work. The wild areka-tree was seen in a few parts of the jungle through which we had this morning passed; and the tall white stems and graceful form of this palm produced a pleasing variety in the heavy shade and sullen forest which everywhere presented itself, and generally limited our view to the abrupt path (sometimes facilitated by rough ladders) which rose before us, or the thick jungle that hemmed us in on every side. Ill-defined as the path was, and in some places less distinct than the elephant-tracks which crossed it, yet it is the principal approach by which many thousands of pilgrims annually reach the Peak; it was the principal route even before the earliest dates which record or tradition has preserved; and every remarkable stone or peculiar bank we came to had its appropriate name, usually connected with some wild legend of the early gods, airy ghosts, or malignant demons of this region of mystery and romance. Soon after ascending the steps, we arrived at the torrent of the Seetla-ganga (cold river); in which, conforming ourselves to the example of our attendants, we bathed, and like them dipped our heads under water three or four times. I performed this ceremony as quickly as possible, but suffered for several hours severe pain in my ears, in consequence of the sudden chill I had received. The stream of the Seetla-ganga precipitated itself over a ridge of rock; and amongst the detached masses below were various pools, in which the natives were performing their ablutions before daring to draw near to the object of their reverence. The sides of the torrent at this place were formed of steep rocks, with large trees whose branches closed across the stream. Of the people who accompanied us, some were bathing; others, having put on their best attire, were in various positions and separate parties reclining on the rocks:

altogether I doubt if any imagination could have combined a scene so wild with groups more suitable.

As we passed under the rock called Diwiyagalla, the guides attempted to point out the marks of a tiger's foot of gigantic proportions, to which, as usual, a fabulous legend was attached; but my want of faith or imagination was so great, that I was quite unable to figure it as the likeness of any part of any living creature. For a mile after we left this spot, the forest was so thick that we never saw the Peak, although it rose immediately above our path, until we reached a clear space of ground at the base of the cone, and on the summit of the continued ridge. Here we saw the grave of a Mohammedan saint who probably, considered himself fortunate in closing his pilgrimage, and resting in peace, so near the place at which the father of mankind, and the first of Mohammedan prophets, had been obliged to stand in penance so long and so uncomfortably. The Mohammedans believe that Adam, whose height was equal to a tall palm-tree, after having been thrown down from Paradise, which was in the seventh heaven,* alighted on this

* "But Satan caused them to forfeit Paradise, and turned them out of the state of happiness wherein they had been: whereupon we said, Get ye down,† the one of you an enemy unto the other; and there shall be a dwelling-place for you on earth, and a provision for a season."—*Al Koran, Chap. II.*

† "The Mohammedans say, that, when they were cast down from Paradise, Adam fell on the isle of Ceylon, or Serendib,

peak, and remained standing on one foot until years of penitence and suffering had expiated his offence and formed the footstep.

From the pilgrim's grave we could perceive our guides carrying carpet-bags and necessary supplies, without availing themselves, even at the steepest places, of the assistance of the chains: this they are enabled to do from early habit; being without shoes is also in their favour in this part of the journey, particularly as the region of leeches does not extend to so great an elevation.

Pursuing our way, the path was steep, and two or three chains afforded assistance, which, although useful, might have been dispensed with; until we came suddenly to a point where it was necessary to turn to the left on the brink of a tremendous precipice. My feelings at this place may have been sublime, of which it has been asserted that terror is one great source; they certainly were not pleasant: but, repressing them, and firmly grasping the iron chains, a few minutes brought me to the summit. Accidents to those who are scaling this steep acclivity are by no means so common as might be expected; this is much owing to the active intrepidity of the guides, by whose assistance several

and Eve near Joddah (the port of Mecca) in Arabia; and that, after a separation of two hundred years, Adam was, on his repentance, conducted by the angel Gabriel to a mountain near Mecca, where he found and knew his wife, the mountain being thence named Arafát; and that he afterwards retired with her to Ceylon, where they continued to propagate their species."—*Note to Chap. II. of Sale's Al Koran.*

ladies have accomplished the ascent, and an aged priest was conveyed up in a light palanquin. The height of the Peak is seven thousand four hundred and twenty feet above the level of the sea; and its summit, of an elliptic form, seventy feet in length by thirty in breadth, is surrounded by a wall five feet high: immediately within this, a level space of irregular breadth runs all the way round, and the centre is occupied by the apex of the mountain, a solid granite rock, about nine feet high at the highest part; on this is the Sree Pada (sacred footstep).

Probably Saman,* whose name the Peak and mountain bear, may have a prior claim; but the Sree Pada † is now held by the Buddhists as a memorial of Gautama Buddha, by the Mohammedans it is claimed for Adam,‡ and the Malabars and other Hindus assert that it was Siva § who imprinted this faint exaggeration of a footstep. This venerated memorial is five feet seven inches in length, two feet seven inches in breadth, and the very slight resemblance which it has to the shape of a foot is given by a margin of plaster coloured to resemble the rock; it is upon this moulding that the metal case which we had seen at Palabadoolla is fitted, before the usual time

* Thence called Samantakuta and Samanala.

† Sacred footstep (of Buddha).

‡ And by Mohammedans called Baba-Aadamalei.

§ By Malabars called Sivanolipadam.

when pilgrims are expected to arrive. A temple, built of wood, surmounts the rock; and is retained in its exalted situation by many strong iron chains fastened to the stone, and also to the trees which grow on the steep sides of the cone. A wooden temple, three feet in height, dedicated to Saman; a pansola (priest's house), six feet square, built of mud (and occupied by us, the priest being absent); one large and one small bell (the former cracked), completed the catalogue of valuables in this sanctuary of the heathen.

The view from Adam's Peak is essentially grand; in every direction are seen mountains clad in eternal forests, with bare rocks and precipices of such huge size, that even the luxuriant vegetation in this "Eden of the Eastern wave" has been unable to conceal their stern beauty. Over two of these poured small cascades, shining like streams of light; flashes of which also attracted the eye to the course of the Mahawelli-ganga, and several streams which would not otherwise have been discerned. A peak, on one side overhanging its base, rises at a short distance to the south of Samanala, and appears but little inferior to it in height; it is called Deiya Guhawa (cave of the god), and by natives its summit is believed as yet to remain unpolluted by human footsteps. A priest, confident in his sacred character, is said to have ascended so far, that the light was observed which he had kindled at night beneath the overhanging summit of this haunted mountain; next day he returned a confirmed maniac, and unable to give any account of what he had seen. There is nothing incredible in this story, for the dreaded mountain is apparently easier of ascent than Samanala; and we need not be surprised at the melancholy fate of the priest, if we take into consideration how strongly the mind of a native (nurtured in the belief of demons) would naturally be acted on when alone in an untrodden solitude, haunted by the vague terrors of superstition, and the just dread of savage animals.

Beyond the higher mountains a few cultivated valleys, distant and indistinct, appeared amidst hills gradually decreasing to the sea, which might be distinguished melting into the humid blue haze in which all distant objects were confounded. The general impression of the scene was dreary; and this feeling is increased by the recollection that these vast forests have in some places encroached on cultivated districts, and even extended themselves over cities, temples, and tanks, — works of vanity, devotion, and utility, scarcely exceeded in magnitude by those of the greatest nations of antiquity.

We descended for some distance by the Kandy road, the only other approach to the Peak than the one by which we had arrived; and, so far as we saw, this path is not only free from dangerous precipices, but could scarcely be called difficult. It would be a task of easy accomplishment to join the Diabetme with the Kandy path before it reaches the cone; but I suppose increased facility of communication, by diminishing the dangers, might decrease the merits of the pilgrimage. On several of the rocks without the wall there are inscriptions in different languages; those in Cingalese, which I procured, are only records of the death or of the pious visit of some unknown devotees. While scrambling on the eastern side, I came by accident upon the Bhagawa-Lenna, an overhanging rock under which all the Buddhas are said to have reposed during their visits to the Peak. The mountain on this side is covered with large rhododendron trees, whose branches, extending into the sacred enclosure, there offer their superb crimson flowers close to the shrine of Saman, their guardian god.

As soon as the fire, which we had kindled close to the door of the priest's hut, began to sink, I was awakened by the cold wind which whistled through numerous holes in our "mud edifice," and was compelled to resort to exercise to keep myself warm for the remainder of the night. My vigils, however, were amply rewarded by the varied and extraordinary scenes of earth and air which I witnessed. At first the moon, shining bright, made the features of the nearer mountains appear distinct; while the deep valleys looked fathomless, from the dark shadows that fell on some, and the cold grey mists that lay in others: from these, small clouds occasionally detached themselves and ascended, creating a chilling damp for the few seconds that they hung around the sacred pinnacle ere they slowly floated onward, or sank again upon the mountain. A breeze then stirred, and clouds that had hitherto lain in repose were at once in wild commotion, passing, enveloping, or pressing in tumultuous masses along the mountains, which, overspreading, they seemed to engulph. When these "airy billows" rolled and heaved around the Peak, I felt as if the rock on which I stood was sinking in the abyss; another second overwhelmed me in a sea of vapour:

"All that expands the spirit, yet appals,
Gathers around these summits, as to show
How earth may pierce to heaven, yet leave vain man below.

Standing on this "landmark in the sea of time," every circumstance conspired to recal the native legends,—that here the spirits, from unrecorded ages to the present, hover in clouds and darkness near their sacred fane and native forests. The wind fell, and morning dawned on a smooth lake of matchless beauty, from the number of abrupt and richly wooded islands which it contained: this, far from being a creation of fancy, was a deception of nature, and required the aid of reflection and memory to recal the true features of the scene, and to assure me that it was but the troubled vapour of the night which had subsided into the calm expanse, and that I had previously admired these islands in their true form of rocks, woods, and mountains.

Cingalese history records that the four Buddhas of the present era have successively visited the Peak, and left the impression of their feet (on which are the mystical symbols) as seals of their successful exertions, and proofs of their superhuman power.

The first of these, Kakusanda, must have appeared about 3001* years B.C. He found the Peak, called

* Elsewhere I have given my reasons and the authorities from which I have derived or deduced the dates of the appearance of these four Buddhas. The date of Kakusanda, B.C. 3001, and Konagamma, B.C. 2099, have not the same convincing proofs as the eras of Kasyapa and Gautama; nor is it likely, from the remote ages in which the two former must have flourished, that sufficient data exist by which their eras can now be satisfactorily ascertained.

Deiwakuta (Peak of the God), and memorials of the Buddhas of a former era existing on its summit; it was their example he followed, and their doctrines he came to renew.

The second Buddha, Konagamma, appeared about 2099 B.C.; and the Peak had even then acquired the name, which, with little variety, it has since retained, viz. Samantakuta (Peak of Saman), probably named from Saman,* the brother and companion in arms of Rama, when he conquered Lanka (Ceylon): this, according to a Cingalese account, happened 2386 B.C.

The third Buddha, Kásyapa, followed at an interval of 1100 years, or about 1014 B.C.

The fourth and last Buddha, Gautama, having arrived at Kellania from the continent of India, passed on to the Peak, rested in Bhagawa-Lenna, and from thence proceeded to Diggánakhya, 577 B.C.

The Buddhas appear to have selected for their worship situations pleasing by their beauty or remarkable for natural grandeur. On Samanala's Peak we feel the reason, and must admire the policy of that choice; for who could stand on this throne of clouds, overlooking the fairest portion of the earth, and fail to acknowledge a mysterious and beneficent power? The most permanent and splendid temple that mortal ever raised can be overthrown by man, may fall by accident, and must yield to age; it cannot, therefore, inspire those

* Called in the Ramayan, and by Hindus, Lakshman.

overwhelming sensations of space and time which we associate with this eternal altar of an Almighty Creator.

The visits of several Kings of Ceylon, their pompous processions and various offerings, fill up the history of Samanala in more modern times.

The thermometer during our stay on the Peak was never below 49°, and at this point it only remained for a very few minutes immediately before and at the time of sunrise. At seven o'clock A. M. we commenced our descent, and I now remarked that the chains, all of which rest upon and lie along the rock, are only attached to it at their upper ends; and this accounted for the circumstance which I had heard, that, twelve years before our visit, several natives were blown over the precipice, and yet continued clinging to one of the chains, during a heavy gust of wind; but in such a situation no assistance could be rendered, and they all perished. Dr. Davy mentions being informed that, only a fortnight before his visit to the Peak, (in April 1817,) two natives looking down the precipice "became giddy and frightened, fell, and were dashed to pieces." These chains are in general of very clumsy workmanship, and with links of many different sizes; on some, inscriptions may be found, stating who had placed or repaired them (which few will stop to read): but, no doubt, those who made and fixed these chains deserve the gratitude of pilgrims, and merit the favour of their gods; yet those few who pass this way, and prefer walking to crawling, cannot forgive them for not raising the chains from the ground, so that they might be used as a rail; and the catastrophe abovementioned shows how much these offerings would have been enhanced in utility by fastening each chain at both ends to the rock.

At eight A. M. after a fatiguing walk of twenty miles, and a descent of more than seven thousand feet, I returned to my comfortable quarters at the collector's house; and there heard from Mr. Turnour with surprise, that, notwithstanding the assertions of English writers to the contrary, there existed very ancient and connected native histories of Ceylon; that he had himself so far verified their accounts of extensive cities of the olden time by visiting the vast remains of the most ancient capital, Anurádhapoora. He also informed me that several places of note mentioned in their histories were as yet unknown or unnoticed by Europeans; these I determined, if possible, to discover, and my notes of future excursions will show with what success.

From Ratnapoora we returned to Colombo by descending the Kalu-ganga to Caltura in a boat of the same construction as that in which I had vainly attempted to ascend the Kellania-ganga on my way to Hangwellé; but I now found a great difference in the accommodation, for this boat was new and clean, and we had the stream in our favour.

Two miles below Ratnapoora we passed the principal temple of Saman, who may be considered the tutelar deity of this portion of the island; and in the sanctum of this building is contained what is called by courtesy the golden bow and arrow of the god. The figure of Saman is always painted yellow; he is the same as Lackshman (the brother of Rama), and is said in Cingalese traditions to have retained the sovereignty of the western and southern parts of Ceylon after the death of Rawena, and to have greatly improved the laws. From him the Peak has received its name, and to him is dedicated a grove of scarlet rhododendron trees, which forms the gorgeous mantle from the rocky summit to the eastern base of Samanala. The accounts of Saman seem to be involved in more than common obscurity and confusion, arising from a convert and follower of Buddha bearing the same name. This disciple of Gautama appears to have retired to the Peak, and from thence impressed on the multitude the precepts of wisdom by the power of superstition.

When staying at Ratnapoora, I had visited this temple of Saman; and found nothing there to attract attention except the situation, the large bo-trees, and the pair of elephant's tusks which graced the entrance. The earliest mention I have seen made of the Saffragam temple of Saman (which is either this or the one on the Peak) is, that in the reign of Dappoola, A.D. 795, a statue of Ramachandra,* formed of red sandal-wood, was sent from Dondera to be placed in the temple of Saman at Saffragam.

The Kalu-ganga, although without any bold scenery, presents numberless pretty river-scenes, with rugged banks, wooded hills, rocks, and rapids. In the over-hanging trees we saw troops of monkeys and a few pea-fowls, and on the banks of the river some very large kobberagoyas: these are a species of lizard, which are prettily marked, indolent, harmless except to fowls, and sometimes they attain to a great size. I killed one seven feet in length. In the district of Saffragam, the kalamander-tree was, until about this time, to be found in considerable quantities; but, from the beauty of the wood, and the consequent demand for furniture made of it, it has now become almost extinct, and a large tree is never met with. There are great varieties of wood in Ceylon,—I have seen one hundred and seventy specimens; but kalamander, with its alternate shades of black and light-brown, is much the prettiest.

Within fourteen hours after we went into the boat at Ratnapoora, we landed at Caltura, where our palanquins were in waiting, and in them we proceeded to Colombo by a flat monotonous road which passes through a continued forest of cocoa-nut trees.

* An incarnation of Vishnu.

CHAPTER IX.

THE ANCIENT CITIES OF KURUNAIGALLA AND ANURADHAPOORA.

Long have thy tributary hills around
With labor'd art and vivid culture glowed,
As up their sides the rising terrace wound,
And o'er their surface genial currents flowed;
Then, when the sun his ripening beams display'd,
Of many dazzling rays a gorgeous train,
Their fruitful slopes in blooming grace arrayed,
Shone a wide amphitheatre of golden grain.

Hon. W. Granville.

Road to Kurunaigalla. — Flowering Forest-trees. — Hattanagalla. — King Sirisangabo. — Terraced Rice-fields. — Watch-huts. — Allow. — Ruins at Kurunaigalla — a Capital of the Island. — Story of Vasthimi. — Unicorn. — Cane Bridge. — Pertinacity of Elephants. — Yapahoo. — Native Attendants — their Habits — their Character. — Ancient Stone Bridges. — Great Stones riven from the Rock by Wedges — shaped by Chisels. — Butterflies. — Nuverakalawia. — Customs in that Province. — Arrival at the ancient and long-abandoned Capital of Anurádhapoora.

In March 1828, I set out for Kurunaigalla, with the intention of examining its remains of former days, then of proceeding to the ancient capital of

Anuradhapoora, and from thence to the pearl fishery of Manár.

Again I enjoyed the delightful change of scenery which presents itself in passing from the maritime provinces near Colombo, into the Kandian country. There the imbul * and murata † trees, covered with scarlet and pink flowers, or the blaze of white blossoms on the nágaha ‡ trees, form a beautiful variety to the heavy green of continuous forests; and cocoa-nut trees are only seen in plume-like tufts near villages, of which they are the valuable ornament and certain index. At the Hattanagalla-oya,§ the road approaches one of the low ranges of hills which diverge in all directions from the mountainous centre of the island; and four miles off to the right is situated the rock of Hattanagalla, surmounted by religious buildings. The principal of these were erected about A.D. 248 by Goloo Abhaa, to the memory of the King Sirisangabo, who had abandoned his throne, and retired in disguise to this place, where he was killed by a peasant in order to obtain the reward offered for the head of the King by his successful competitor for the throne. Sirisangabo appears to have been a weak monarch, but is lauded as a worthy Buddhist, and munificent patron of the priesthood; and his successor, Goloo Abhaa, in his attempts to con-

* Imbul, thorny cotton-tree.

† Murata, lagerstroemia reginae

‡ Nágaha, iron-wood tree.

§ Oya, small river.

ciliate that body, erected a dagoba * and endowed a wihare † near the spot where the victim of his ambition was slain. A Cingalese history of the buildings on this rock details the merits of the devout Sirisangabo, the wonders worked at his tomb, the offerings made to the priests, and the royal grants or individual gifts bestowed on the establishment at Hattanagalla.

It appears, by an inscription recorded about the year A.D. 262 on the rock of Mehintalai, that King Sirisangabo was son of the Prince Abhaha-Sala-Mewan and the Princess Dewoogon, both of whom were of the royal race (which in this inscription is called the Cshettrya race of the dynasty of Okaaka).

From Turnour's remarks on Cingalese inscriptions, I find that three princes "repaired to the court of the reigning sovereign, Wija-Indoo, in A.D. 241. They were received into favour, and appointed to the highest offices of the state; of which they availed themselves, in the course of a few months, to conspire against their benefactor, and to put him to death. One of these princes, Sangatissa, ascended the throne, and retained the other two, Sirisangabo and Goloo Abhaa, in their high stations. Sangatissa was carried off within four years by poison, which was secretly administered to him in a jambo-fruit by the inhabitants of the western

* Dagoba, a monument enclosing a relic of Buddha.

† Wihare, a temple of Buddha.

villages, to which the King was in the habit of making excursions, when he probably subjected these people to the extortions inseparable from the royal progresses of the olden times. Sirisàngabo succeeded him in A.D. 246, who was a rigid devotee, and had taken the vows of the order 'Atta-Sill;' the ordinances of which, together with the observance of many rules of devotion and acts of self-denial, totally prohibited the destruction of animal life. It may readily be conceived that the feebleness of a government administered by so bigoted an enthusiast soon led to anarchy. Crimes of the greatest enormity, committed with impunity, rapidly increased in all parts of the kingdom. When the malefactors were brought to the prison of the capital, as the King's vows precluded the possibility of their being executed, they were secretly released at night after condemnation, and the corpses furnished by the usual casualties of a populous city were exhibited at the place of execution, on gibbets and impaling poles, as the victims of the violated laws. By these means, says the Buddhist historian, a pious King successfully repressed crime, and yet gave the criminal time and opportunity to reform. The result, however, as might have been expected, was precisely the reverse of that representation. The whole frame of society was disorganised; and a famine, with its usual concomitant, a pestilence, combining with these public disorders, Goloo Abhaa, who then held the office of treasurer, easily wrested the sceptre from the weak hands which then swayed it. Sirisangabo offered no resistance. He privately left the city, taking with him nothing but his 'pirankada' (water-strainer), which is used by devotees to prevent the destruction of the lives of the animalculæ which they would otherwise imperceptibly swallow in drinking unstrained water, and met his fate while wandering as a hermit at this rock of Hattanagalla."

The streams, as you proceed into the Kandian country, move more briskly; the clearness of their waters, and the noise of their ripples, being in strong contrast with the sluggish progress of the rivers, whose greasy waters creep through the level districts saturated with slime and mud from the rice-fields. Not only the lower part of the irrigated valleys, but also the sides of every rivulet as it descends from the hills, however steep they may be, are formed into terraces; and, when these are cultivated, the brilliant green of the rice crops serves to diversify the general olive tint of Kandian landscape. The watch-huts, from whence the natives protect their fields, are often highly picturesque; particularly when perched on overhanging crags, or amongst the branches of some huge forest-tree, from which the watchmen can command a view of any intruding elephant, and to which they can flee if their discordant yells and lighted brands prove insufficient to repel their powerful enemy, or, as sometimes happens, should only tend to provoke his attack.

Having diverged from the great Kandy road at Ambapusse, I crossed the Maha-oya at the Ferry of Allow, a beautiful spot on the side of a clear rapid river, but, like most such places in the immediate vicinity of running water in the interior of the island, it has a capricious and occasionally a pestilential climate. From Ambapusse, which is thirty-six miles from Colombo, to Allow, five miles farther, I was obliged to be on the alert, as a herd of elephants had been patrolling the road, and had damaged some of the temporary bridges; but, as it was still early when I passed, they had not left the shade of the jungle, to which elephants generally retire as soon as the sun becomes powerful. This piece of road, although much frequented, and having carts continually passing and repassing, also pioneers at work improving the bridges, was for years after this infested with elephants. Passing a large Government granary at Hondelle, eight miles farther brought me to Kurunaigalla, fifty-eight miles from Colombo. Kurunaigalla is situated near the base of a rocky mountain, about six hundred feet in height, called Aetagalla,* from its striking resemblance to a tusk elephant; this is the last of a range which is named from the likeness of different portions of it to various animals, — beginning at Andagalla

* Aeta, tusk elephant.

(eel rock), Ibhagalla (tortoise rock), Kurunaikigalla (elephant leader rock), and Aetagalla (tusk elephant rock), where the range abruptly terminates. Near to where the agent of Government's house is now placed, the palace of the Kings of Ceylon formerly stood; and from thence a path, with occasional stone steps, leads up the rock to the top of the mountain, and passes by a dagoba and wihare, in which is modelled the footstep of Buddha, copied from that on Adam's Peak, Samanala. Still farther on, we found the remains of a wall, built across a hollow, and protecting a path, which was the only other approach to the summit, except the one from the lower palace. Near this place are some small stone pillars, and a pond in the rock, partly natural, but improved by steps of masonry descending to the water. On the bare rock above are the remains of buildings, which must have been intended to contain either penitents or prisoners; for nothing less than fanaticism or compulsion could have furnished tenants to houses situated where the rock gets so heated during the day that its proper temperature is not regained until long after sunset, and is then succeeded by chill blasts, or damp exhalations from the flat country beneath. On the very summit are the remains of the building which contained the Dalada * relic during the reigns of four pious and powerless Kings who held their

* The Dalada, tooth of Buddha; a relic esteemed by Kandians as the palladium of the country.

court at Kurunaigalla, in Pali history called Hasti-saila-poora; it was the first of these four, Bhuwaneka Bahoo the Second, who removed the Dalada to this place from the more ancient capital of Polannanna A.D. 1319.

From the time that Kurunaigalla became the capital, and even for hundreds of years after it was abandoned, the rocks of Aetagalla and Andagalla were used in royal grants as symbols of duration: thus, "So long as the sun and moon, so long as Aetagalla and Andagalla endure, this grant is made; and, should any one violate the injunctions contained in this perpetual edict, he will be born as a dog or a crow." These dreaded forms of transmigration seem to have been a common threat or anathema denounced against those who should disturb grantees in their gifted rights. To one patent, sculptured in stone in the deserted city of Pollannarua, is prefixed the figure of a man standing between these two abhorred and carrion-eating animals.

There is a tradition preserved in this part of the country, that a natural son of one of these Kings succeeded in seizing the throne, and for some time made himself popular; but afterwards, having offended the priesthood, they assembled on the summit of the rock to celebrate a religious ceremony, and invited the King to honour it with his presence. On his arrival, assassins, who lay in wait, rushed on the usurper and hurled him headlong from the precipice. Casi Chitty, in his Ceylon

Gazetteer, says the usurper's name was Vasthimi, that he was the son of a Mohammedan woman, and that he had offended the Buddhist priesthood by showing a predilection for the faith of his mother, Vasthimi Kumaraya.

From the ruins on the summit of Aetagalla the Peak of Samanala is visible, and to it our attention was attracted by the priest who had accompanied us, and who, after repeating some religious exercises, concluded his devotions by first kneeling and then prostrating himself with his eyes still fixed on the sacred mountain. He informed us that the imitation of the impression of Buddha's foot in his temple had been modelled at the time Kurunaigalla was a royal residence, that a princess, who was unable to undertake a pilgrimage to the real Sree Pada, might here make offerings to a copy.

In the neighbourhood of Kurunaigalla I found sculptures of elephants, lions, and an animal resembling the heraldic unicorn, having the legs and body of a horse, and a horn shaped like the tusk of an elephant. If the unicorn (called Kangawena by the Cingalese) ever existed, it is extraordinary that no remains of it should have been discovered; if it never did exist, the general belief of such an animal, and the near identity of its form in the sculpture and description of different countries, is equally unaccountable, for the light figure of a unicorn could never have been derived from the clumsy carcass of a rhinoceros.

From Kurunaigalla I went six miles upon the Trinkomalee road to see a native suspension-bridge over the Dederoo-oya. It was formed of the mahawai-waela, (cable-rattan,) which is occasionally found three hundred yards in length, and with little difference in thickness at any part: this circumstance, combined with its light weight and extreme toughness, renders it particularly well adapted for the purpose to which it was here applied. A

suspension-bridge of this construction is commenced by fixing a cane round two large trees growing on opposite sides of the river, the diameter of their stems determining the breadth of the bridge: when a sufficient number of canes have been fixed in this way, small slips of the same material are placed across to complete the roadway. A cane is then tied at the proper height to form the hand-rails, which are united to the bridge by small sticks that form a mutual support, and retain the rails in their proper position. The work is then completed by fastenings let down from all the branches which project in the direction of the bridge across the river; for by this means the vibration is diminished, and the strength rendered sufficient. From the length of this bridge, and its height above a rapid stream and rocky channel, it formed a pleasing object to those who were not under the necessity of trusting themselves on such an aerial structure. The approach to this bridge (which, as may be supposed from its construction, was only for foot-passengers) suited well with its position and materials; being by ladders tied together in the same way as the rest of the work, viz. with jungle creeping-plants, which are everywhere to be found in abundance, and supply the places of both rope and nails in Kandian edifices.

The arrangements for building sheds for ourselves, horses, and followers, in the jungle, having been completed by orders from Mr. C——, the agent of Government in the district, (with whom we travelled,) we started at day-break on our way to the ancient capital of Anurádhapoora, and had not proceeded a mile when the tom-toms disturbed a large elephant that had been luxuriating during the night in a rice-field. Kurunaigalla is one of those places which lie in the track of elephants in passing across the country, and, although no obvious reason can be seen to justify their preference of this particular line, yet they continue to adhere to it with uncommon perseverance: the formation of seven or eight roads converging at this place, which owes its existence of late years to the military station and head-quarters of the revenue and judicial offices of the district being established here, is insufficient to induce the elephants to abandon their former route, and they continue to pass through this large village, to the great annoyance of its inhabitants. Their pertinacity does not abate, although their numbers have considerably diminished; for the late agent, Mr. B——, (who had only been promoted a few months before,) as well as some of his predecessors, was a keen and successful elephant-shot. He had killed nine in one forenoon, which was the greatest number at this time known to have been bagged in one day by a single sportsman.

From Kurunaigalla to Anurádhapoora our route lay nearly north, and the foot-path on which we travelled was either through rice-fields or over gentle elevations covered with brushwood. This continued during the first day's journey; but, as we advanced, the country became more level, fewer villages were seen, and less cultivation, with more extensive jungles, marked the difference between that part of the country which has a constant supply of river water, and the more northern districts, which depend upon rain to fill the tanks and irrigate the fields. The distance to Anurádhapoora, although only eighty miles, occupied us three days: this slow progress was in consequence of the number of persons who accompanied us, to carry our supplies and their own when we should pass on beyond the cultivated and inhabited portion of the district.

We slept at Koombakalawia, Madawatchy, and Neelicolom; and rested during the heat of the days at Hierapitia, Kattapittia-weva, and Epauella. The rock of Ununugalla, near Hierapitia, Yakdessagalla (which is seen from Kurunaigalla), and Galgiria-kande were the most prominent features on those ridges of hills, which gradually descend into the plains and jungles which surround the ancient capital of the island. Near Koombakalawia are situated the remains of Yapahoo, which was for some time the residence of a branch of the Cingalese royal race, one of whom succeeded to the throne A.D. 1303, and made this place the capital; but it only remained so for eleven years, when it was taken possession of by an army sent by the King of Pándi (Madura), which destroyed the town and carried off the Dalada relic.

Our native attendants, even those who had been carrying baggage during the whole day, seemed little inclined to sleep at night; and never retired while any of the tom-tom beaters or singers who accompanied the agent's party were exercising their uncouth instruments or croaking voices. That a singer amongst Kandians did not require a musical voice I soon discovered, and found that this, as well as all other occupations amongst them, was hereditary: that the son of a singer must of necessity sing; as the son of a dancer, however deficient in agility, was still condemned to caper to the sound of tom-toms. As a consequence of this absurd system, the most gaunt and awkward Kandian I ever saw hobbled as chief dancer, in honour of the Dalada (Buddha's tooth), on a pair of legs scarcely more pliable, and very little thicker, than ordinary crutches. It was not uncommon for two of the professional singers to commence and maintain a dialogue, which they continued to invent and pour out in a sort of recitative monotony: during this performance they practised such wit as they possessed, levelled at all those whom they disliked and dared to lampoon; they also made frequent allusions to public grievances, as well as to the private and current scandal of the district. Any sly hit against Raja Karia (King's duties, compulsory labour) was sure to be received with unusual satisfaction, although at this period the people never dreamt of seeing it abolished,—still less could they have anticipated that within five years they were to be entirely emancipated from Raja Karia, and every restriction that checked their prosperity, hindered their improvement, or prevented them from indulging a proper ambition.

Every native carried the sheath of an areka-nut flower, a light tough substance, which served them for a plate on which to pile their rice; they had, also, a manner of folding it up in the form of a square vessel, and in this shape it served to carry water in those stages where it was scarce or unwholesome.

Besides those who carried our baggage, and the usual allowance of grass-cutters, horse-keepers, and servants, a great number of official persons of all ranks, and their followers, were in attendance upon the agent; and my observations upon them only more confirmed my opinion of the acuteness as well as the veracity of Robert Knox, although it is upwards of one hundred and fifty years since he published his account of the Kandians. During his long captivity and unrestricted commerce with them he enjoyed the best opportunities of forming a deliberate opinion of their character. Such as he described them in 1680, they were found to be in 1815, when the last of their despot Kings was driven from the throne; and such, with little alteration, they continued until made free by the charter of 1833. Knox says, "In carriage and behaviour they are very grave and stately, like unto the Portugals; in understanding quick and apprehensive; in design subtle and crafty; in discourse courteous, but full of flatteries; naturally inclined to temperance, both in meat and drink, but not to chastity; near and provident in their families, commending good husbandry; in their dispositions not passionate, neither hard to be reconciled again when angry; in their promises very unfaithful, approving lying in themselves, but misliking it in others; delighting in sloth, deferring labour until urgent necessity constrain them; neat in apparel, nice in eating, and not given to much sleep."

The streams we crossed on our way from Kurunaigalla were the Dederoo-oya, Kimboola-oya, Meeoya, and Kalawia-oya: near the place where we crossed the latter river we discovered and examined the remains of an ancient stone bridge, consisting of a pier of considerable length projecting into and contracting the stream, which was both broad and rapid. The stones used in constructing this pier vary from eight to fourteen feet in length; they are laid in regular lines, and some are jointed into one another: each course also recedes a few inches from the edge of the one underneath; and this form, while it offers less direct resistance to the current, gives additional strength to the building. In the rocks which form the bed of the river we could distinguish square holes, in which stone pillars had been placed; and the bridge had been completed by laying long stones or beams of wood on these so as to connect the different parts of the structure, which, there is reason to believe, was built by the King Mahasen, and that the rapid river has fretted and plunged against this artificial barrier for full fifteen hundred years. At a short distance farther down the stream, the site of another bridge can be traced, which appears to have been constructed on the same plan, but either at an earlier period, or of less durable materials. At these ruins I first remarked that the large stones had been riven from the adjacent rocks by means of wedges, and that any farther shaping or ornament had been done by chisels. On my arrival at Anurádhapoora, this manner of working quarries and splitting stones was everywhere observable, and satisfied me that the natives of Ceylon, two thousand years ago, used those expedients for procuring large granite pillars, and shaping their ornaments, which have only been introduced into Britain in the nineteenth century. In conformity with the wild tradition of the natives, that the King Mahasen could compel even the demons to work for him, and that this bridge is a specimen of their masonry, the ruins here are known by the name of Yakka-Bendi-palam (bridge built by devils). A stone was pointed out to us (in the upper row), on the under side of which it is said the figure of the architect is cut.

Here, as in several other parts of the country, we saw myriads of butterflies passing in a continued stream in the same direction. I have observed these flights to continue for days together in different parts of the country, and that it sometimes consisted of various-coloured butterflies, but generally proceeding in a direction towards the centre of the island. The natives believe that their destination is Adam's Peak, and from this circumstance I presume it is that the Cingalese name for a butterfly is derived, viz. Samanaliya.

Having crossed the Kalawa-oya, we entered the Nuwara-Kalawia district, and perceived a marked difference in the customs, manners, and appearance of the inhabitants, who were taller, and with more regular features, but neither so healthy-looking nor so robust as those of the mountainous districts. Instead of the usual dress of Kandians, viz. a coloured handkerchief bound round the head, they wore a peculiar sort of turban, fastened so that in the middle and on the top of the head a peak projected upwards somewhat resembling the crest of a helmet. In entering the house prepared for our reception we had to pass between two elegantly formed earthenware lamps, about three feet high; these were ornamented with cocoa-nut flowers, and were burning, although it was mid-day. As we were stepping across the threshold a cocoa-nut was broken; and this completed the ceremony of receiving us, and dismissing evil spirits from our temporary abode.

After crossing the Kalawia-oya there was little worthy of observation until we reached the artificial lake called Tissa-weva, and perceived on the opposite side, and rising far above the ancient forest by which they were surrounded, Buddhist monuments, like hills covered with wood, and surmounted by the remains of spires. As we proceeded on our way, the scattered materials of ancient buildings, and numberless stone pillars, assured us that we had arrived within the limits of the ancient capital of Ceylon, Anurádhapoora.

CHAPTER X.

ANCIENT CAPITAL OF ANURADHAPOORA.

Remnants of things that have passed away,
Fragments of stone reared by creatures of clay.—BYRON.

Situation of Anurádhapoora. — Founded B.C. 500. — *Relics of Gautama Buddha.— Walls of the City.—Its Extent* 256 *square Miles. —Known to Ptolemy. — Knox visits it in* 1679. — *Account of Knox.—Court of the Sacred Tree. — The Brazen Palace. — Sixteen Hundred Stone Pillars. — Kandian Punctilio. — Place of the Royal Funeral-piles of Ancient Kings. — Game. — Chewing Betel. — Dágobas. — Monumental Tombs of Buddha's Relics. — Ruanwelli-saye. — King Dootoogaimoonoo's Death. — Batiyatissa-Raja. — Glass Pinnacle on a Spire. — Glass known in Ceylon as a Protection against Lightning prior to* A.D. 246. — *High-priest. — Ruins of Toopharama. — Beautiful Columns. — Lankarama. — Abhayagiri built* B.C. 76. — *Its Height then* 405 *feet. — Jaitawanarama. —Contents of its Dome* 456·071 *cubic yards of Masonry. — Ancient Native Families. — Ruins of the Palace. — Escape of King Elloona. — Death of King Elala. — Curious Injunction regarding his Tomb. — Pilame Taláwe. — Tanks. — Cells for Priests. — Wells. — Stone Vessel. — Ancient Native Account of Anurádhapoora. — Prince Sali. — Former Population of Ceylon. — Second Visit to Anurádhapoora. — Cairns. — Native seized by a Crocodile. — Scene at Nuwarawewa. — Pea-fowl. — View of the Forest-covered City.*

IN ages of impenetrable antiquity, the plain on which Anurádhapoora was afterwards built had acquired a sacred character; for it is recorded, that, when the first Buddha of the present era visited this place, he found it already hallowed as a scene of the ancient religious rites of preceding generations, and consecrated by Buddhas of a former era. The position of Anurádhapoora has nothing to recommend it for the capital of Ceylon; and the site, if not chosen from caprice, was probably dictated by superstition. It would not, therefore, be difficult to account for its final desertion, consequent decay, and present desolation, even if history had not preserved a record of the feuds, famines, wars, and pestilence, which at various times oppressed the country, and reduced the number of inhabitants so as to render the remainder incapable of maintaining the great embankments of their artificial lakes. These having burst, their waters spread over the country as their channels were neglected, and this made its unhealthiness permanent by forming noxious swamps and nourishing unwholesome forests. The warm and damp nature of the Ceylon climate excites an activity of vegetation, which the indolence and apathy of the native character are not calculated to struggle against; and the present population is inadequate either in number or energy to do more than resist the incessant effort of the vegetable kingdom, stimulated by an eternal spring, to extend its beautiful but baneful luxuriance over that portion of the surrounding districts which man still retains in precarious subjection.* Anurádhapoora is first mentioned by that name about five hundred years before Christ; it was then a village, and the residence of a prince who took the name of Anurádha on his settling at this place, which the King Pánduwása had assigned to him when he came to visit his sister the Queen Bhadda-kachána. They were grandchildren of Amitódama, the paternal uncle of Gautama Buddha. It was chosen for the capital by the King Pádukábhya, B.C. 437; and in the reign of Dewenipiatissa, which commenced B.C. 307, it received the collar-bone of Gautama Buddha, his begging-dish filled with relics, and a branch of the bo-tree under which he had reclined. Anurádhapoora had been sanctified by the presence of former Buddhas, and these memorials of Gautama increased its sacred character; additional relics were subsequently brought, for which temples were reared by successive sovereigns; and Wahapp, who commenced his reign A.D. 62, finished the walls of the city, which were sixty-four miles in extent, each side being sixteen miles, and thus enclosed a space

* Six years after the time of which I am now writing, Government formed a road to Aripo, and established an European officer at Anurádhapoora as revenue and judicial agent for the district, in order, if possible, to hasten the developement of its resources. When I left the island it was considered an unhealthy station, but, by perseverance, there is little doubt that it will improve. Had this district been formerly unhealthy, Anurádhapoora would not so long have remained the capital of the island.

of two hundred and fifty-six square miles. Anuradhapoora is mentioned, or rather is laid down in the map of Ptolemy in its proper position, and by the name of Anurogrammum.*

For upwards of twelve hundred years Anuradhapoora remained as the capital of the island, with the exception of one reign, when a parricide and usurper transferred the insignia of royalty to the impregnable rock-fort of Sigiri. In the eighth century Polannarua was chosen as the capital in preference to Anurádhapoora; at which place the fame of wealth had survived its possession, and too often attracted the spoiler. The religious edifices were occasionally repaired by pious sovereigns until the time of Mágha, a successful invader, who held sway in Ceylon from A.D. 1219 until 1240; during which time he completed the destruction of many temples, and endeavoured to destroy the Cingalese records.

Knox, speaking of Anurádhapoora, which he passed in making his escape from captivity in A.D. 1679, says, "It is become a place of solemn worship, in consequence of the bo-tree under which Buddha sat." He adds, "They report ninety Kings† have reigned there successively, where, by the ruins

* Gráma, or Gramya, is used for a town; so also is Poora, but the latter generally means city.

† It is the general belief of uneducated natives that the name of the city is derived from Anu-Rajah (ninety Kings); but it was from the name of the constellation Anurádha, under which it was founded.

that still remain, it appears they spared not for pains and labour to build temples and high monuments to the honour of this god, as if they had been born only to hew rocks and great stones, and lay them up in heaps: these Kings are now happy spirits, having merited it by these their labours." In making his escape along the bed of the Malwatte-oya,* Knox passed another part of the ruins, but does not seem to have been aware that they were part of Anurádhapoora. He says, "Here and there, by the side of this river, is a world of hewn stone pillars, and other heaps of hewn stones, which I suppose formerly were buildings; and in three or four places are the ruins of bridges built of stone, some remains of them yet standing upon stone pillars."

The above extracts are taken from "An Historical Relation of the Island of Ceylon in the East Indies, by Robert Knox, a captive there for nearly twenty years." This is a work of great interest, and was originally published in London in 1681. Nothing can be more admirable than the extent of memory, acute observation, and inflexible veracity exhibited in his account of the country and people; nor can anything be more interesting than the simple narrative of his own sufferings. His perseverance, fortitude, and firm religious belief enabled him to overcome misfortunes, to rescue himself from a tedious captivity, and finally to

* Malwatte-oya, flower-garden river.

regain his station as commander of a ship under the East India Company.

The father of Robert Knox was also named Robert: he commanded the Ann frigate in the service of the East India Company, and sailed on the 21st of January 1657 from the Downs; the vessel was dismasted in a storm on the Coromandel coast on the 19th of November 1659, and proceeded to the bay of Cotiar (opposite to Trinkomalee) to refit, and with permission to trade there. For about twenty days the crew of the ship were allowed to land and return without any interruption; but, after that, a native chief, by order of the Kandian King, contrived by falsehood and treachery to seize the captain and seven of his men; then, by the same devices, he got hold of another boat and her crew of eleven men. He next attempted to gain possession of the ship, by inducing the captain to send an order to the officer on board, directing him to bring the vessel up the river; the captain sent his own son, but it was to warn the officer, and direct him to proceed without loss of time to Porto Novo. Young Knox, however, returned to share his father's captivity; and the whole of those taken prisoners were removed into the interior of the country. The captain and his son (Robert) were sent to the village of Bandar Koswatte, and there were soon attacked by severe fever and ague, which carried off the father, February the 9th, 1661. Young Knox was then very ill, and it was not without much difficulty that he managed to get his father's body buried; and for many months he suffered severely from the effects of the same disease. It was not long after the loss of his father that he accidentally had an opportunity of purchasing an English Bible at a price sufficiently moderate for his means. Never for a moment laying aside his design of escape, yet behaving with such discretion as never to incur suspicion from the jealous tyrant who then ruled in Kandy, Knox acquired a character for prudence, industry, and honesty, which is even yet preserved by tradition in the neighbourhood of the place where he resided, and where a spot is still known as the white man's garden.* After a captivity of nearly twenty years' duration he contrived to accomplish his escape, not without great danger from the numerous wild animals and alligators that are to be found near the course of the Malwatte-oya, which flows through a dense forest and a country void of population. Knox reached the Dutch fort of Aripo on the 18th of October 1679; afterwards having been sent to Batavia, he from thence returned to England in September 1680, and was soon after made captain of the Tarquin in the East India Company's service.

All the ruins at Anurádhapoora, even the lofty monuments which contain the relics of the Buddha, are either entirely covered with jungle, or partly

* Between Kandy and Gampola.

obscured by forests; these the imagination of natives has peopled with unholy phantoms, spirits of the unrighteous, doomed to wander near the mouldering walls which were witnesses of their guilt, and are partakers of their desolation.

Although simplicity is the most distinguishing characteristic of the ancient architectural remains of the Cingalese, yet some of the carving in granite might compete with the best modern workmanship of Europe (in the same material) both as to depth and sharpness of cutting; and the sculptures at Anurádhapoora, and places built in remote ages, are distinguished from any attempts of modern natives, not less by the more animated action of the figures, than by greater correctness of proportion.

The only place clear of jungle was in front of the Maha-wiharé (great temple), where a shady tree occupied the centre of a square, and a stone pillar, fourteen feet high, stood beside the figure of a bull cut in granite, and revolving on a pivot. In the entrance from this square into the Maha-wiharé are a few steps admirably carved with laborious devices, and still in perfect preservation. Ascending these, and passing through a mean building of modern construction, you enter an enclosure three hundred and forty-five feet in length, by two hundred and sixteen in breadth, which surrounds the Court of the Bo-tree, designated by Buddhists as Jaya-Sri-maha-Bodinwahawai (the great, famous, and triumphant fig-tree).* Within the walls are perceived the remains of several small temples; and the centre is occupied by the sacred tree, and the buildings in which it is contained or supported. This tree is the principal object of veneration to the numerous pilgrims who annually visit Anurádhapoora: they believe what their teachers assert, and their histories record, that it is a branch of the tree under which Gautama sat the day he became a Buddha, and that it was sent from Patálipoora by the King Dharmasoka, who gave it in charge to his daughter Sanghamitta; this priestess had been preceded by her brother, Mihindoo, who, B.C. 307, was successful in re-establishing in Ceylon the purity of the Buddhist religion.

No one of the several stems or branches of the tree is more than two feet in diameter; and several of the largest project through the sides of the terraced building in which it is growing. This structure consists of four platforms, decreasing in size as you ascend, and giving room for a broad walk round each of them.† From the self-renovating properties of the bo-tree, it is not at all impossible that this one might possess the great antiquity

* Ficus religiosa, generally called by natives Bo-gaha, bo-tree, the name generally used by Europeans.

† The spot on which the tree stands is believed to have at former periods been the position where the emblematic trees of former Buddhas grew, viz. Kakusanda Buddha's, the mahari tree; Konagamma Buddha's, the atika tree (ficus glomerata); and Kaseyapa's, the nigrodi (baniayan).

claimed for it by the sacred guardians:* if so, the forbearance of Malabar conquerors must be accounted for by their considering this tree sacred to other gods; the profits derived from pilgrims may also have induced them to give full weight to the alleged partiality of Brahma for this beautiful tree.

One side of the square in front of the Maha-wihare is occupied by the ruins of the Lowa-Maha-Päya, called also (from the materials with which it was covered) the Brazen Palace. The remains of this building consist of sixteen hundred stone

* Buddhists assert that the sacred tree at Buddha Gya in Bahar "was planted by Dugdha-Kamini, King of Singhal-Dwipa 414 years before the birth of our Saviour." —*Hamilton's E. I. Gazetteer.* Dootoogaimoonoo, King of Ceylon, and a most

pillars placed in forty parallel lines, forty pillars in each, and occupying a square space, each side of which is two hundred and thirty-four feet in length. The pillars in the middle of this ruin are still eleven and a half feet above the ground, and measure two feet in breadth by one foot and a half in thickness; the middle pillars are slightly ornamented, but those in the outer lines are plain, and only half their thickness, having been split by means of wedges, the marks of which operation they still retain. The Lowa-Maha-Pâya was erected by the King Dootoogaimoonoo B.C. 142: its height was two hundred and seventy feet; it contained one thousand apartments for priests, and was covered with one sheet of metal. This edifice seems soon to have fallen into decay; and was rebuilt by Dootoogaimoonoo's successor, who reduced its height, making it seven instead of nine stories, which it was at its original formation. It underwent many repairs, and was varied in height by several different Kings, until A.D. 286, at which time it was thrown down by Mahasen during the period of his temporary apostacy: so completely did this monarch execute his work of destruction on this and several other religious buildings, that

zealous Buddhist, reigned from B.C. 164 until B.C. 140; and if the tree at Gya was planted by him, as above mentioned, not only the original one there, but also one planted by Dharmasoka, King of India, in the fourth century before Christ, at the same city, must have been destroyed by the votaries of an adverse faith.

their sites were ploughed up and sown with grain. Having returned to his former faith, Mahasen commenced rebuilding the Maha-Páya, but died before it was finished; and it was completed by his son and successor, Kitsiri Maiwan, soon after his accession in A.D. 302. It was then that the original pillars were split, to supply the places of those which had been broken. Amongst the sacred occupants of this building, the priests most eminent for their piety were exalted to the uppermost story, whilst those who had fewest claims to sanctity were lodged nearest to the earth. As native stairs only differ in name from ladders, the ascent of nine stories must have been a severe trial to the bodily infirmities of the elder priests; but one of the strongest prejudices of the natives, and about which they continue to be exceedingly jealous, was, not allowing an equal or inferior to sit on any seat or remain in any place more elevated than themselves. From adherence to punctilio on this subject, there was a ludicrous scene at Colombo in 1802, when the Kandian ambassadors remonstrated against entering the carriage sent to convey them to an audience with Governor North, because the coachman was placed on a more elevated seat than the one which they were to occupy. This weighty matter was happily adjusted to their satisfaction, and they entered the carriage; but positively refused to allow the doors to be shut, fearing they should appear as prisoners.

On the left of the road leading from the Maha-wiharé towards the dágoba of Ruwanwelli, and in thick jungle, six carved stones define the limits of a small mound. This is the spot where a grateful people and a zealous priesthood performed the last duties to the remains of Dootoogaimoonoo; a King whose valour and piety had restored the supremacy of the Cingalese race and Buddhist religion, and who had not only repaired the injuries which the capital had sustained from foreign invaders of an adverse faith, but had ornamented it with many of those buildings which even now attract attention and excite wonder after having endured for two thousand years.

The quantity of game in the immediate neighbourhood of the ruins was astonishing, and in no part of the island are elephants more numerous; for within the precincts of this hallowed city, at the time I speak of, 1828, no native would have ventured to transgress the first commandment of the Buddha, viz. from the meanest insect up to man, thou shalt not kill. As if aware of their right of sanctuary, whole herds of spotted deer and flocks of pea-fowl allowed us to approach very near to them; and while employed in examining the ruins, in the presence and with the assistance of the priests, I deemed it advisable to commit no murder on the denizens of the forest; but on the last day of our stay we left the gentlemen of the long yellow robe behind, and proceeded to hunt deer with Mr. C.——'s dogs in a plain about three miles from the place of our temporary residence.

When not employed in speaking, our followers seemed to be eternally occupied in chewing betel, a custom almost universal at this time with all ranks of natives; and although the name of the leaf of a creeping-plant resembling pepper is used as a general term, three component parts are necessary for this masticatory; viz. areka-nut, which is used in very thin slices; fine powdered lime, made into a paste; and, a small portion of these two being rolled up in a betel-leaf, the whole is put in the mouth. This preparation tinges the saliva, the lips, and even the teeth of a dark-red colour; but I believe it to be perfectly wholesome, and to have some useful properties, such as soothing nervous excitement, and acting as a stimulant, without any of the evil effects produced by the use of spirits, which nevertheless is, I am afraid, too often superseding the use of betel. Those who could afford it, mixed up cardamom seeds and the leaves of various aromatic plants with the areka-nut; and the value of the instruments for preparing the betel gave one a pretty good idea of the wealth and rank of the possessor: a pair of nippers for slicing the areka-nut, a small box for holding the lime, and a straw case to contain betel leaves, might, I believe, have been found tucked in the waist-cloth of every one of the several hundred natives who accompanied us. Night and day they were chewing betel, and when they were awake they seemed to talk of nothing else exchanging leaves and the contents of their lime-boxes seemed like the old Scotch custom of exchanging snuff-mulls.

Amongst the ruins of this city, the dágobas,* or monumental tombs of the relics of Buddha, the mode in which they are constructed, the object for which they are intended, above all, their magnitude, demand particular notice. The characteristic form of all monumental Buddhistical buildings is that of a bell-shaped tomb surmounted by a spire, and is the same in all countries which have had Buddha for their prophet, lawgiver, or god. Whether in the outline of the cumbrous mount, or in miniature within the laboured excavation, this peculiar shape (although variously modified) is general, and enables us to recognise the neglected and unhonoured shrines of Buddha in countries where his religion no longer exists, and his very name is unknown. The gaudy Shoemadoo of Pegu, the elegant Toopharama of Anuradhapoora, the more modern masonry of Boro Budor in Java, are but varieties of the same general form; and in the desolate caves of Carli, as in the gaudy excavations and busy scenes of Dambool, there is still extant the sign of Buddha—the tomb of his relics. Dagobas may be referred to the first stage of architectural adventure, although I cannot agree with

* Dágoba, from Dhatu-garba (womb, or receptacle of a relic).

those writers who assert that the character and form of Buddhist buildings betray evident marks of having been borrowed from the figure of a tent; for in my opinion their progress may clearly be traced from the humble heap of earth which covers the ashes or urn of the dead, up to the stupendous mount of masonry which we see piled above some shrunken atom of mortality. These monuments in Ceylon are built around a small cell, or hollow stone, containing the relic; along with which a few ornaments and emblems of Buddhist worship were usually deposited, such as pearls, precious stones, and figures of Buddha: the number and value of these depended on the importance attached to the relic, or the wealth of the person who reared the monument.

The description given in Cingalese histories of the rich offerings and rare gems deposited with some of the relics is very splendid, but the existence of wealth and wonders which cannot be reached may well be doubted; the accounts of the external decorations and ornaments of these dágobas are also magnificent, and probably more correct. In a sohona, or Cingalese cemetery, may be perceived a variety of miniature dágobas: if the little earthen mound raised over the ashes of the dead be encircled with a row of stones, we see the origin of the projecting basement; if the tomb be that of a headman or high-priest, we may find it cased with stone, and perhaps surrounded with a row of pillars: on all these we find an aewaria branch planted; which, after taking root and shooting out its cluster of leaves, gives the semblance of the spire and its spreading termination.* In short, the monumental tombs of Buddha's relics only differ in size, and in the durability of their materials, from the humble heap which covers the ashes of an obscure priest or village chief. The tomb of Alyattes, as described by Herodotus, and which he informs us as a monument of art was only second to the remains in Egypt and Babylon, appears to have been of the same form as the sepulchral mounds of the Buddhists. In materials and construction the dágobas of Anuradhapoora far exceed the tomb of Alyattes, and fully equal it in size. All the dágobas at Anurádhapoora were built of brick, and incrusted with a preparation of lime, cocoa-nut water, and the glutinous juice of a fruit which grows on a tree called by the natives Paragaha. This preparation is of a pure white; it receives a polish nearly equal to marble, and is extremely durable. The Ruwanwelli-saye, one of these monuments of peculiar sanctity, was built by the King Dootoogaimoonoo; but the spire being unfinished at the time of his death, B.C. 140, it was completed by his brother and successor, Saidatissa. It stands in the centre of an elevated square platform, which is paved with large stones of dressed granite, each side being about five hundred

* Called Kot by the Cingalese, and Tee by the Siamese.

feet in length, and surrounded by a fosse seventy feet in breadth; the scarp, or sides of the platform, is sculptured to represent the fore-parts and heads of elephants, projecting and appearing to support the massive superstructure to which they form so appropriate an ornament. In the embankment surrounding the fosse, a pillar, deep sunk in the earth, still projects sixteen feet above the surface, and is four feet in diameter; this stone is believed to have been removed from the spot where the dágoba now stands, and that it once bore an inscription and prophecy, which in a superstitious age no doubt caused its own fulfilment. The prediction ran, that, at the place where this stone stood, a superb dágoba of one hundred and twenty cubits* in height would be reared by a fortunate and pious monarch.

Dootoogaimoonoo, during his last illness, caused himself to be conveyed near to this monument of his piety; and, when all hopes of completing the spire during his lifetime were at an end, his brother had the model of it made of light timber: this placed on the dome, and covered with cloth, satisfied the anxious wish of the expiring King. The place to which Dootoogaimoonoo was conveyed is a large granite slab surrounded with pillars; near this a stone, hollowed out in the shape of a man's body, is shown as the bath which he used when suffering from the bite of a venomous snake.

* Carpenter's cubit, two feet three inches.

On the stone pavement which surrounds the Ruwanwelli-saye lies the broken statue of the King Batiyatissa, who reigned from B.C. 19 until A.D. 9, and appears to have been one of those persevering zealots who "hope to merit heaven by making earth a hell:" the marks of his knees worn in the granite pavement are pointed out as memorials of superior piety, and certainly, if authentic, bear lasting testimony to the importunity of his prayers or the sincerity of his devotions. It is recorded of this King that by supplication he obtained divine assistance to enable him to open the under-ground entrance into the interior cell of this temple; and that he succeeded in entering and worshipping the many relics of Buddha which it contained. In the thirteenth century Mága, a foreign invader, instead of faith, employed force: he broke into the sanctum, plundered its treasures, pulled down the temples around Ruwanwelli, and ruined its dágoba, which was originally two hundred and seventy feet in height, but is now a conical mass of bricks overgrown with brushwood, and one hundred and eighty-nine feet high. Sanghatissa placed a pinnacle of glass on the spire of Ruwanwelli, as the author of the Mahawanso says, "to serve as a protection against lightning." Sanghatissa reigned four years, and was poisoned in A.D. 246. The Mahawanso was written between A.D. 459 and 477, and shows that the non-conducting property of glass with regard to the electric fluid had been remarked previous to that period.

At a considerable distance from the outer enclosure of the dágoba the priest pointed out to me a stone slab twelve and a half feet long by nine and a half feet broad, which is supposed to cover the secret entrance by which the pious King, as well as the ruthless invader, gained admittance to the interior of the Ruwanwelli-saye. A few weeks previously to our visit, the late high-priest, an albino, had died at a very advanced age: he had been long known by the appellation of the White Priest of Anurádhapoora; and his senior pupil, who accompanied me in exploring the ruins, aspired to succeed his master. I was then along with the agent of the district, through whose recommendation he expected to be appointed; therefore no spot was so sacred, and no secret so precious, but that it might be communicated to me. The aspirant became high-priest, and ever after denied to European visitors all knowledge of the secret entrance to this monument, as well as several other places of peculiar sanctity; neither could it be brought to his unwilling remembrance that he had ever known them himself, or pointed them out to any one. The history of this building, its traditions, the list of offerings made to the relics enshrined within it, and the splendour of its external appearance, are recorded at length; but its chronicle contains so much exaggeration in regard to the number of the offerings, and so little variety of events, that the specimen already given may perhaps be considered more than sufficient, and will be my excuse for not dilating on the history of other buildings, of which only similar facts are written, and similar dull details have been preserved.

Toophárámaya, although inferior to many in size, yet far exceeds any dágoba in Ceylon, both in elegance and unity of design, and in the beauty of the minute sculptures on its tall, slender, and graceful columns; this dágoba is low, broad at the top, and surrounded by four lines of pillars, twenty-seven in each line, fixed in the elevated granite platform so as to form radii of a circle of which the monument is the centre. These pillars are twenty-four feet in height, with square bases, octagonal shafts, and circular capitals; the base and shafts, fourteen inches in thickness, and twenty-two feet in length, are each of one stone; the capitals are much broader than the base, and are highly ornamented. Toophárámaya was built over the collar-bone of Gautama, when it was brought from Maghada in the reign of Dewenepeatissa, B.C. 307; and the ruins of a building which adjoins it received the Dalada relic when it arrived in Ceylon, A.D. 309.

Lankarámaya was erected in the reign of Mahasen, between A.D. 276 and A.D. 302; it is in better preservation, but much inferior in effect to the Toophárámaya, from which the design of the building is copied.

The Abháyagiri dágoba, built by the King Walagam Bahoo, between the period of his restoration to the throne B.C. 88, and his death B.C. 76, was the largest ever erected in Ceylon: it was four hundred and five feet* in height; and the platform on which it stands, as well as the fosse and surrounding wall, are proportionately extensive. The height of this ruin now is two hundred and thirty feet, and the length of the outer wall one mile and three quarters; the whole of the building, except a few patches near the summit, is covered with thick jungle and high trees, even where the inter-

* One hundred and eighty Cingalese carpenter's cubits.

stices of the pavement, composed of large granite slabs, were all that yielded nourishment to the trees or secured their roots.

The Jaitawanarámaya was commenced by the King Mahasen, and completed by his successor, Kitsiri Maiwan, A.D. 310: its height was originally three hundred and fifteen feet,* and its ruins are still two hundred and sixty-nine feet above the surrounding plain. A gentleman, who visited Anurádhapoora in 1832, calculated the cubic contents of this temple at four hundred and fifty-six thousand and seventy-one cubic yards; and remarked, that a brick wall, twelve feet in height, two feet in breadth, and upwards of ninety-seven miles in length, might be constructed with the still remaining materials. Even to the highest pinnacle the Jaitawanarámaya is encompassed and overspread by trees and brushwood; these are the most active agents of ruin to the ancient buildings of Ceylon, as their increasing roots and towering stems, shaken by the wind, overturn and displace what has long resisted, and would have slowly yielded before time and the elements.

During our stay at Anurádhapoora, a Kandian lady presented a petition to the agent of Government, requesting his interference on behalf of her son, who was detained as a state prisoner for having been implicated in the rebellion of 1817-18. She stated that he was her only son, and that the large

* One hundred and forty carpenter's cubits.

family estates were now ravaged and laid waste by wild animals; that in this remote district, for want of his superintendence, the tanks for irrigation were neglected, and cultivation was rapidly decreasing; moreover, that he was the hereditary guardian of the sacred edifices of this ancient capital, and that in his absence the buildings and temples were neither protected nor repaired, the revenues being either misapplied by the priests, or appropriated to their own use. The old lady also alluded to the antiquity of their family, whose ancestor, she said, had accompanied the branch of the sacred tree from Patalipoora,* B.C. 307. On inquiring, I found that the very remote antiquity of this family was acknowledged by the jealous chiefs of the mountain districts; and I could not help feeling an interest in the last scion of a race, whose admitted ancestry reached far beyond the lineage of Courtenay, or the descent of Howard.

This chief soon afterwards obtained permission to visit his estates; and at a subsequent period, having assisted in securing the pretender to the Kandian throne, (who had been secreted since 1818 in this part of the country,) he was not only permitted to return to his estate, but was reinstated in office as chief of the district. Although not a clever man, his appearance and manners were dignified and gentlemanlike: he died in 1837, leaving a family to continue the race, and bear the digni-

* The modern Patna.

fied appellation of Surya Kumara Singha (descended from a prince of the solar and the lion race).

The system of adoption in the Kandian law renders the continuation of a particular family much more probable than in any country where such a proceeding is unknown, or unsanctioned by fixed institutions or all-powerful custom. In Kandian law, a child adopted in infancy (and born to parents of equal rank with the person who adopted the infant) had the same right of inheritance both to titles and estates as if the actual child of the person who had become its guardian, and who, after a public adoption, was called and considered the father. In general, the children adopted were selected from the nearest relations of the person, who determined through this means to prevent all risk of being without children to watch his declining years, and inherit his family estates. Several of the highest rank of Kandian chiefs pretend to trace the descent of their families from those natives of Maghada who accompanied Mihindoo and the relics of Buddha from the continent in the fourth century before Christ. Two families claim descent from Upatissa, a minister of state, and *interim* King for one year, B.C. 505; and one of these, who maintained his right by inheritance to the name which he bore (Upatissa), produced to me a box containing a quantity of dust, and some minute frail shreds of tissue, which, he said, were the remains of a dress worn by his royal and somewhat remote ancestor.

I have only seen a few written genealogies of Cingalese chiefs, and, in following them, found wider and more startling gaps than any I had been accustomed to leap over in a backward trace to the progenitor of some individuals who figure in the modern British peerage.

Amidst the ruins of the palace stand six square pillars supporting some remains of a cornice; each of these pillars is formed of a single stone, eighteen feet in length, and three in breadth. There, also, is the stone canoe made by order of King Dootoogaimoonoo in the second century before Christ, to hold the liquid prepared for the réfection of the priests; it measures sixty-three feet in length, three and a half feet in breadth, and two feet ten inches in depth. Within the precincts of the royal buildings, projecting from the mould, and half covered by the roots of a tree, a stone trough, from which the state elephants drank, recalled to mind the history of King Elloona, and the busy turbulent scenes enacted in by-gone ages within those walls; where now the growl of the elephant, the startling rush of wild hog and deer, the harsh screams of peacock and toucan, increase the solemn but cheerless feelings inspired by a gloomy forest waving o'er a buried city.

Elloona having murdered his cousin, the Queen Singha Wallee, became King of Ceylon, A.D. 38, and was soon after imprisoned by his rebellious subjects: the Queen, in despair, caused her infant son to be dressed in his most costly robes, and ordered the nurse to place him at the feet of the state elephant, that the child might be killed, and escape the indignities inflicted on the monarch. The nurse did as she was commanded; but the elephant (without hurting the young Prince) broke his chain, rushed through the guards, threw down the gates, and forced his way to the royal captive, who got on his back, and, rushing through the streets of the capital, escaped in safety to the sea-coast. From thence he embarked for the Malaya country: having raised an army there, he returned to Ceylon, and regained his kingdom after an absence of three years. Elloona recognised with affectionate joy the animal that had been the means of saving his life; and several villages were appointed to furnish food and attendants to the royal elephant during the remainder of his life.

The Isuramuni Wihare, (a temple partly cut in the rock,) the Saila Chytia, (a small monument built on a spot where Buddha had rested himself,) and the tomb of Elala, are amongst the ruins visited by the pious pilgrims. Elala was a successful invader, who conquered Ceylon, B.C. 204, by means of an army which he led from Sollee (Tanjore). The Cingalese princes who possessed the southern and the mountainous parts of the island as tributaries becoming powerful, Elala built thirty-two forts to protect the level country on the south against their incursions; these forts were taken in succession by the Prince Dootoogaimoonoo, who finally encountered his rival in single combat, and slew him with a javelin. They were each mounted on an elephant, and, as the battle was preceded by a challenge, both the leaders fought under the insignia of royalty: on the spot where Elala fell, Dootoogaimoonoo erected a monument and pillar, on which there was inscribed a prohibition against any one passing this tomb in any conveyance, or with beating of drums. Elala is described, even by the Buddhist historians, as being a good ruler and valiant warrior; he must have been an old man when he encountered Dootoogaimoonoo, having reigned for forty-four years after completing the conquest of Ceylon: his death occurred B.C. 161. Time has hallowed the monument which it has failed to obscure, and the ruined tomb of an infidel is now looked upon by many Buddhist pilgrims as the remnant of a sacred edifice: although twenty centuries have elapsed since the death of Elala, I do not believe that the injunction of his conqueror has ever been disregarded by a native. In 1818, Pilamé Talawé, the head of the oldest Kandian family, when attempting to escape, after the suppression of the rebellion in which he had been engaged, alighted from his litter, although weary and almost incapable of exertion; and, not knowing the precise spot, walked on, until assured that he had passed far beyond this ancient memorial.

Pilamé Talawé was apprehended in this district,

and transported to the Isle of France; from whence he was allowed to return in 1830, and soon after died from the effects of intemperance. He had narrowly escaped death in 1812 for treason to the King of Kandy; as sentence had been passed, and his father and cousin had already suffered before he was brought prisoner to the city. The commencement of a religious festival was the reason assigned at that time for sparing his life; although his slender abilities and slothful habits are supposed to have been more powerful arguments in favour of the King's granting mercy, than the supplication of friends, or the intercession of the priests, to whom it was apparently conceded. Pilamé Talawé was the last of the direct branch of that family which exercised the privilege of girding on the royal sword at the inauguration of the Kandian monarchs.

Besides eight large tanks at Anurádhapoora, there are several of a smaller size built round with hewn stone; and in the side of one of these a priest pointed out apartments, cells, which he said had been occupied by priests as places for contemplation when religion flourished and the tanks were full: one of these cells, which we examined, proved to be formed of five slabs, and its dimensions were twelve feet in length, eight feet in breadth, and five feet in height; the lowest stone, or floor of the cell, must have been nearly on a level with the water in the tank. We also saw many wells built round with stone; one very large one near the Ruwanwelli-saye is circular, and the size diminishes with each course of masonry, so as to form steps for descending to the bottom in any direction.

Near the footpath leading to the Jaitawanarámaya, lies a vessel ornamented with pilasters cut in relievo; it is formed out of a single granite stone, and is ten feet long, six feet wide, and two feet deep. It was used to contain food for the priests.

The following is translated from an ancient native account of Anurádhapoora.

" The magnificent city of Anurádhapoora is refulgent from the numerous temples and palaces whose golden pinnacles glitter in the sky. The sides of its streets are strewed with black sand, and the middle is sprinkled with white sand; they are spanned by arches * bearing flags of gold and silver; on either side are vessels of the same precious metals, containing flowers; and in niches are statues holding lamps of great value. In the streets are multitudes of people armed with bows and arrows; also men powerful as gods, who with their huge swords could cut in sunder a tusk elephant at one blow. Elephants, horses, carts, and myriads of people are constantly passing and

* Arches formed of areka-trees split and bent, or of some other pliable wood, were always used in decorating entrances and public buildings on days of ceremony or rejoicing; but I have never seen an arch of masonry in any Cingalese building of great antiquity.

repassing: there are jugglers, dancers, and musicians of various nations, whose chanque shells and other musical instruments are ornamented with gold. The distance from the principal gate to the south gate is four gaws (sixteen miles); and from the north gate to the south gate four gaws: the principal streets are Chandrawakka-widiya,* Raja-maha-widiya,† Hinguruwak-widiya, and Mahawelli-widiya.‡ In Chandrawakka-widiya are eleven thousand houses, many of them being two stories in height; the smaller streets are innumerable. The palace has immense ranges of building, some of two, others of three stories in height; and its subterranean apartments are of great extent."

With the exception of the four principal streets, the others were built of perishable materials, and were named from the separate classes which inhabited them. The Chandalas (scavengers and corpse-bearers) resided beyond the limits of the city; yet it was a girl of this caste that Prince Sáli, only son of Dootoogaimoonoo, married, and chose rather to resign all chance of succession to the throne than to part from his beauteous bride. The detailed account of Prince Sáli's romantic attachment to Asoka Malla is probably less correct than a tradition preserved in Kotmalia, viz. that Sáli's mother was not of the royal race, but a woman of the Goyawanza (cultivator class), with

* Moon street. † Great King street.

‡ Great Sandy street, or from the river Mahawelli-ganga.

whom Dootoogaimoonoo formed a connection at the time he was a fugitive in the mountainous district of Kotmalia, to which place he had fled to avoid the effects of his father's anger, and by which act he acquired the epithet of Dootoo, or the Disobedient, prefixed to his own name of Gaimoonoo. Dootoogaimoonoo forgave his son, and admired the bride; but appointed his brother, Saidatissa, as successor to the throne, that the Mahawanzae (great solar dynasty) might be preserved in all its purity.

The great extent of Anurádhapoora, covering within its walls a space of two hundred and fifty-six square miles, will not give any just grounds on which to estimate the extent of its population; as tanks, fields, and even forests are mentioned as being within its limits. The number and magnitude of the tanks and temples constructed by the Kings Dootoogaimoonoo, who reigned from B.C. 164 to B.C. 140, Walagam-bahoo, who reigned from B.C. 89 to B.C. 77, and Mahasen, who reigned from A.D. 275 to A.D. 302, are the best vouchers for the numerous population which at these periods existed in Ceylon; yet, as the tanks at least were formed by forced labour, we cannot rate the wealth of the nation by the extent of its monuments. The public works of Prakrama-bahoo the First, who reigned from A.D. 1153 to 1186, prove that even then Ceylon had a much more numerous population than it now possesses; and Cingalese accounts of that period state the number of males, exclusive of children, as amounting to three million four hundred and twenty thousand. This number may be, and probably is, overrated: but let those who doubt that an immense population formerly existed in Ceylon, compare the prodigious bulk of the ancient monuments of Anurádhapoora, Mágam, and Polannarrua, with those erected by later Kings of the island; then let them compare singly the remains of the Kalaa tank,* the Kaudela tank,† or many others, with any or all the public works accomplished in Ceylon for the last five hundred years. In constructing the immense embankments of these artificial lakes, labour has been profusely, often, from want of science, uselessly expended; as I believe many of these great tanks, which are now in ruins, would, if repaired, be found inapplicable to the purposes of irrigation for which they were designed: that is, the extent of plain which could be cultivated by means of these reservoirs would be of less value than the sums which it would be requisite to expend in repairing and maintaining the embankments.

In Anurádhapoora, the only sacred buildings of modern date are a few small temples erected on the foundations, and from the materials, of former structures; they are supported by wooden pillars,

* The Kalaa tank was completed before A.D. 477.

† The Kaudela tank is now an extensive plain between Minirie and Kandely.

which, even in the same building, present a great variety of capitals, and perfect defiance of proportion. These mean temples, with their walls of clay and paltry supports, form a striking contrast to the granite columns, massive foundations, and stone pillars which still stand, or lie scattered in endless profusion amidst the ruined heaps and proud remains of former ages. They serve to prove that Buddhism only clings with loosening grasp, where it once held sovereign sway over mind and matter.

In September 1832, I again proceeded to Anurádhapoora, through Dambool, Manawewa, Kágamma, near which are the ruins of the Nakha (finger-nail) dágoba, and Tirapan. In several places, when we approached within twenty miles of the city, we perceived great heaps of stones on the road-side: they were intended to commemorate events which are long since forgotten; but, nevertheless, every pilgrim adds a stone to these nameless cairns. About ten miles from Anurádhapoora, I sat down on the rocky bank of a very small pond, in the Colon-oya forest: soon after, a native trader came up, and pointed to a spot near me, from whence, he said, his companion, only a few days before, had been dragged by an alligator; the unfortunate man, while resting here during the heat of the day, had fallen asleep close to the water, and in this state was seized by the reptile. My informant, having procured assistance from a village some miles off, had attempted to recover the body of his companion;

but was unsuccessful, as it was found that the pond communicated with an underground cavern. I emerged from this forest upon the plains around the Nuwarawewa (city lake), which at this time contained but a little water in detached pools; these were surrounded, almost covered, by a wondrous assemblage of creatures, from the elephant and buffalo, pelican, flamingo, and peacock, alligator and cobragoya, down through innumerable varieties of the animated creation: in the back-ground, the crumbling spires of Anurádhapoora appeared over the wooded embankment of this artificial lake. I had supplied myself and my followers with abundance of pea-fowl, which were to be met with in numbers at every open space where water was to be found; and, on first entering one of these glades, I have seen twenty of them within a space of one hundred yards in diameter. Pea-fowl are naturally wary; and, if it is a place where they have been occasionally disturbed, it requires great caution to ensure getting near enough to shoot them. The morning is the best time for pea-fowl shooting, as in the evening they keep near the edge of the jungle, and in the forenoon they retire to some thick dark copse, generally overhanging water, and there rest during the heat of the day; it is at this time that the natives, who never throw away a shot, usually kill them at roost.

Since my former visit in 1828, all the dágobas had suffered some diminution, in consequence of the heavy rains which had fallen in January 1829; and the whole of the Abháyagiri had been cleared from jungle by a priest, whose zeal in the difficult and dangerous task had been nearly recompensed with martyrdom, a fragment of the spire having fallen on, and severely injured, this pious desecrater of the picturesque. The season had been particularly dry, and the foliage of those trees which grew on rocky ground presented all the variety of an English autumn; however, the change of the monsoon was approaching, and heavy rain fell during the night of my arrival. At daybreak next morning I ascended on the ruins of Mirisiwettiya, and found the forest plains of this district shrouded by mist and rising clouds; but,

> "Though the loitering vapour braved
> The gentle breeze, yet oft it waved
> Its mantle's dewy fold,"

and magnified forms of mount-like sepulchres were shadowed on the drear expanse. As the sun arose behind the rock of Mehintalai, the "silver mist" was dissipated in small clouds, or fell in glittering drops: all was damp, vast, and silent, as if the waves of oblivion had only now rolled back from the tombs of antediluvian giants; and the half-formed rainbow, which glanced amid these monuments, was the first which had brightened the earth, or gladdened the remnants of a perished race.

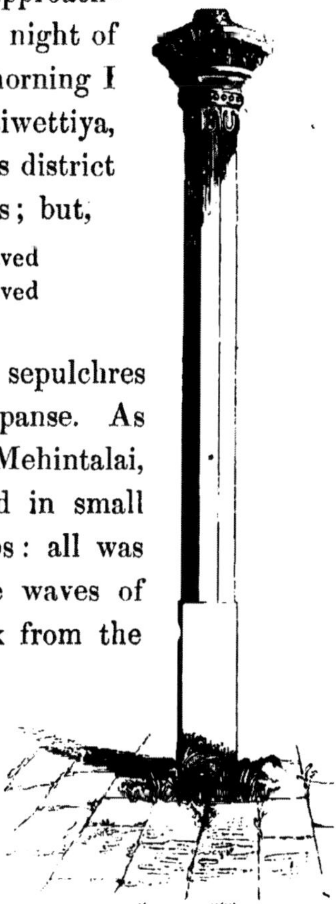

See page 226.

CHAPTER XI.

FROM ANURÁDHAPOORA TO MANAR PEARL FISHERY.

See how at once the bright-effulgent sun
Rising direct, swift chases from the sky
The short-lived twilight; and with ardent blaze
Looks gaily fierce through all the dazzling air;
He mounts his throne; but kind before him sends
The general breeze, to mitigate his fire,
And breathe refreshment on a fainting world.—THOMSON.

Desólate Country. — Devil Dancer. — Curious Ceremonies. — Wild Scene.—Tank of Tamenawillé.—Surgical Operation.— Kondátchie. — The Doric. — Natives assembled for a Pearl Fishery. — Theories in Europe regarding Ancient Trade of Ceylon, and the Paumban Passage. — Objections to these Theories.—Embassy to Rome from Ceylon.—Palaesimundo.— Malabars and Mohammedans. — Ceylon connected with the Continent. — The Ramayan. — Price of Pearls. — Kudra-Malai. — Native Canoes.

IN proceeding from Anurádhapoora to Aripo in March 1828, we slept at Oyamadoe, Payamadoe, and Tamenawillé, having previously sent people forward to clear the path and to prepare leaf huts for our accommodation: the persons who had been despatched on this employment had been much annoyed by wild animals, and the huts which they built were repeatedly injured by elephants. On our way through the long-continued jungles of this dreary route, we saw very few birds; and those we met with were invariably in the neighbourhood of some pond or open space; but the noise of our followers frequently excited the attention of elephants, who, after a few low growls, might be heard moving off from the unwonted tumult. To the villages once existing on this line of road, and still figuring in maps of Ceylon, the word Palu (desolate) for a distance of forty miles was an invariable addition to the name of the place. Extensive rice grounds, but partially covered with grass, proved that some of these villages had been recently deserted, for the ever encroaching jungle had not as yet cast over them that verdant shroud which will consign them to oblivion, until a great increase of population can force back the mighty power of useless vegetation.

At Payamadoe one human being remained; he was a Kapua (devil-dancer), and gained a livelihood by predicting events and prescribing medicine to those who conveyed salt into the interior by this dreary route. His small hut of frail materials also served for a Kowila (inferior temple to gods or devils); it was situated on the bank of a sluggish stream, and shaded by an immense banyan tree. Under its branches, an open space levelled and strewed with sand, served the Kapua for a theatre on which to exhibit the various attitudes and violent contortions which apparently constituted the whole of his devotions; and certainly his performance had the effect of riveting the attention and exciting the liberality of our numerous followers. At night we crossed the stream to witness the ancient Yaka ceremonies:* these rites belong to a superstition which may dispute priority if it were not conjoined with the Bali (planetary) worship; like it this superstition is alluded to in the earliest traditions, and, like it, has maintained its hold over the minds of the natives through every change in the government or variety in the religion of Ceylon. The Kapua, an athletic and very active man, danced to the noise of the tom-toms which had accompanied our party, and kept excellent time with his feet and hands; on which, as well as on his neck, arms, and ankles, he wore large hollow metal rings called Salamba. Occasionally he appeared in the highest state of bodily and mental excitement; his flesh quivering and his eyes fixed as if straining to distinguish forms in the gloom of the surrounding forest. In this mood, advancing towards the person for whom his incantations were performed, and while continuing one long respiration, he predicted the fate, or prescribed for the complaint of the demon worshiper. I examined several of the Kapua's small packets of medicine; they were

* Demon offerings mentioned in the Ramayan.

leaves folded up, and containing plain ginger in powder; this was, however, to be taken mixed in very warm water, and with some peculiar ceremonies. As the water in this part of the country is notoriously unwholesome, it is probable the people benefited by his nostrum. The firm belief in its efficacy conjoined with the ceremonies no doubt contributed to the successful result; for all the invalids declared themselves to be perfectly cured, and the Kapua was continuing his laborious rites, with untired energy, when at midnight I left him in the full career of his medical and prophetic duties. The scene I had just witnessed was impressive from its mysterious wildness; the banian tree, which stretched its huge branches on one side above the frail temple and three hundred natives of different ranks, on the other side extended far over the stream; while the Yakadupha torch (formed of resin and nitre) of the exorcist, threw over the scene an indistinct light and livid colouring, in which his wild figure, long dishevelled hair, and frantic gestures, could be discerned and contrasted with the mute and motionless body of the spectators, or the intensely anxious look of the one who stepped forward to hear of "coming events," and pry into his future fate. Anon the torch blazed for an instant, then sank into a dull blue flame, which blonded with the halo formed around it by the dank fog that rested on the slimy stream. With such a light, and in such a chilling stagnant atmosphere, the gigantic trees, even the people amongst whom we stood, had an unearthly semblance, as if the spirits of past ages were shadowed forth—those who had known these woods and wilds ere death had gained exclusive dominion over man, or the face of nature had been obscured by forests. It is strange, but true, that here there has been more change in nature than in mankind; a populous district has become a noxious wilderness; its villages and temples are overwhelmed by jungle; while the manners and religion of the Cingalese, the rich dresses of the chiefs, and scanty covering of the lower classes as they now stood before us, have remained for upwards of two thousand years comparatively unchanged.*

At Tamenawillé our quarters were near a small lake, which seemed to have attracted to its vicinity every kind of living creature; these combined at night in imposing upon us a most villainous concert of flapping, chirping, buzzing, drumming, humming, creaking, squeaking, croaking, ticking, scratching, scraping, barking, howling, growling, roaring — earth, air, and water contributing their share of performers to the wearying dissonance. From every part of the interior of our hut sounded the bassoon of the frog and "shrill clarion" of the cricket; while on the outside the elk snorted trombone to the serpent bass of the elephant. In Ceylon, from man

* The antiquity of the Kandian dresses is mentioned in their history, and authenticated by existing sculptures.

down to the minutest atom endowed with life, there is one continued system of oppression; each preying on those that are inferior in power or courage. Amongst many animals, and most insects, there is a continued war of extermination in progress; which, alone, from the rank vegetation and general climate, prevents their overturning the order of nature, and remaining undisputed lords of earth and air. Often whilst resting in the jungle during the noon-day heat, I have found extreme interest in observing the sagacious manœuvres employed by some insects, particularly those of the ant kind, in carrying on their interminable feuds and furious wars.

Between Payamadoe and Tamenawillé we had an opportunity of witnessing a curious specimen of native surgery,—the putting in an ankle joint which had been dislocated: the poor man who had met with the accident seemed to be suffering great pain; when a head-man, who practised the healing art, set to work with peculiar gravity, promising to repair the damaged limb. He first secured the unlucky man's shoulders to one tree, and the foot of the injured limb was made fast to another by a double rope; through this double the head-man passed a short stick, which he afterwards twisted round and round until he had tightened the cord and stretched the limb. In doing this, the practioner twisted coolly, while the patient bawled lustily; then suddenly the stick was withdrawn, allowing the cord to untwist itself, and the ankle was found to be perfectly reinstated.

A few granite pillars, ancient landmarks, and the ruined embankments of very extensive tanks, were the only traces of man or his labours which we saw until, having passed the Kandian limits, which reach to within six miles of Aripo, we bade farewell for the present to the gloomy jungle, hailed the refreshing sea breeze, perceived the British flag flying, and soon found ourselves involved in the busy crowds and insufferable stench of the wretched village of Kondátchie. This place is the station of the boats employed in the pearl fishery, and gives name to the bay in which the principal oyster banks are situated, although the fishery is generally called "of Manár," from the island and district of that name; or "of Aripo," from an old fort situated near the mouth of the river,* which, after passing by Anurádhapoora, makes a bend to the north-east, before meeting the Curundu-oya and directing its course due west to the sea, which it reaches four miles to the north of Kondátchie. The ground here is low, and consists of sand and clay covered with stunted prickly jungle; a few tattered cocoa-nut trees looked like exiles in an uncongenial clime; yet even in their drooping state, they were less annoying to the eye than the unvarying stiffness of the palmyra-palm, and struck me as retaining over them that advantage of appearance which

* The Malwatte-oya, flower-garden river.

the dishevelled ringlets of a mop, if planted on its handle, would possess over a furze broom in the same predicament. A very large house, built by Governor North, at a great expense, is called the Doric, from the style of its architecture, which may be correct, but its plan and situation are so ill suited to the place, as to make it appear one of the most prominent features of the ugliest landscape I had seen in Ceylon. Having heard that the concourse of people assembled at the fishery, caused a large town, with long streets and valuable shops, to start up as if by magic from the barren plain, my disappointment was great to find that natives sitting near, or sleeping under two or three palmyra leaves, supported on one side to the height of three feet, procured for such a shelter the appellation of a house, and that lines of the same were miscalled streets: as to the valuables exposed for sale, during the week I remained, they consisted of a few coarse cloths, and the commonest earthenware vessels in which the natives cook their rice. Very few of the multitude seemed to possess much property; but every one speculated as far as he could command money or credit; and even this excitement appeared insufficient, as many might be seen employed in other kinds of gambling, besides that of purchasing pearl oysters. Two or three natives who had come from the continent of India were reputed to be rich, the outward and visible signs of which were gaudy palanquins, and one of them, moreover, had a gorgeous umbrella, covered with purple velvet, and embroidered with gold.

The arrangements for each day's fishing commenced at midnight, at which time a gun was fired as a signal, and all the boats started, having the land breeze to waft them to the fishing-bank, on reaching which, they anchored until the day was sufficiently advanced, and the water smooth, in which state it remains during the interval between the land and sea breezes. The diving then commenced, and continued with wonderful exertion and perseverance until the sea breeze set in; then a signal gun was fired, and the boats, returning with the Government vessel, formed an animated and pleasing scene, which was succeeded by the bustle of selling the oysters by auction, and distributing the shares to several temples, various subordinate officers, the boat-owners, and shark-charmers.

The manner of diving is well described by Cordiner, from whom I have copied the following account:—

"About half-past six or seven o'clock, when the rays of the sun begin to emit some degree of warmth, the diving commences. A kind of open scaffolding, formed of oars, and other pieces of wood, is projected from each side of the boat, and from it the diving tackle is suspended, three stones on one side, and two on the other. The diving-stone hangs from an oar by a light country rope and slip knot, and descends about five feet into the water. It is a stone of fifty-six pounds weight, of the shape of a sugar-loaf. The rope passes through a hole in the top of the stone, above which a strong loop is formed resembling a stirrup-iron to receive the foot of the diver. The diver wears no clothes, except a slip of calico about his loins; swimming in the water, he takes hold of the rope, and puts one foot into the loop or stirrup on the top of the stone. He remains in this perpendicular position for a little time, supporting himself by the motion of one arm. Then a basket, formed of a wooden hoop and network, suspended by a rope, is thrown into the water to him, and into it he places his other foot. Both the ropes of the stone and basket he holds for a little while in one hand; when he feels himself properly prepared, and ready to go down, he grasps his nostrils with one hand to prevent the water from rushing in, with the other, gives a sudden pull to the running knot suspending the stone, and instantly descends; the remainder of the rope fixed to the basket is thrown into the water after him at the same moment; the rope attached to the stone is in such a position as to follow him of itself. As soon as he touches the bottom, he disengages his foot from the stone, which is immediately drawn up, and suspended again to the projecting oar in the same manner as before, to be in readiness for the next diver. The diver, in the bottom of the sea, throws himself as much as possible upon his face, and collects everything he can get hold of into the basket. When he is ready to ascend, he gives a jerk to the rope, and the person who holds the other end of it, hauls it up as speedily as possible. The diver, at the same time, free of every incumbrance, warps up by the rope, and always gets above water a considerable time before the basket. He presently comes up at a distance from the boat, and swims about, or takes hold of an oar or rope, until his turn comes to descend again; but he seldom comes into the boat until the labour of the day is over. The basket is often extremely heavy, and requires more than one man to haul it up, containing besides oysters, pieces of rock, trees of coral, and other marine productions.

"The manner of diving strikes a spectator as extremely simple and perfect. There is no reason to believe that any addition has been made to the system by Europeans; nor, indeed, does there seem the smallest room for improvement.

"The superstition of the divers renders the shark-charmers a necessary part of the establishment of the pearl fishery. All these impostors belong to one family; and no person who does not form a branch of it, can aspire to that office. The natives have firm confidence in their power over the monsters of the sea, nor would they descend to the bottom of the deep without knowing that one of those enchanters was present in the fleet. Two of them are constantly employed. One goes out regularly in the head pilot's boat, the other performs certain ceremonies on shore. He is stripped naked and shut up in a room, where no person sees him from the period of the sailing of the boats until their return. He has before him a brass bason full of water, containing one male and one female fish made of silver. If any accident should happen from a shark at sea, it is believed that one of these fishes is seen to bite the other. The shark-charmer is called in the Malabar language, *cadalcutti,* and in the Hindostanee, *hybanda;* each of which signifies a binder of sharks. The divers likewise believe, that if the conjuror should be dissatisfied, he has the power of making the sharks attack them, on which account he is sure of receiving liberal presents from all quarters. Sharks are often seen from the boats, and by the divers when they are at the bottom of the sea, but an accident rarely occurs. Many fisheries have been completed without one diver being hurt; and perhaps not more than one instance is to be found in the course of twenty years.

"The prejudices of the natives, however, are not to be combated with impunity, and any infringement on their established customs would be impolitic, if it were practicable. Their superstition in this particular is favourable to the interests of Government, as from their terror at diving, without the protection of the charms, it prevents any attempts being made to plunder the oyster-banks."

The boats in use for the pearl-fishery are roughly built; they are about one ton burthen, draw little water, and have only one sail; each boat contained ten divers, and ten others to assist, besides a soldier to prevent thefts, as the banks at the time I visited the fishery, were fished by Government, contrary to the usual practice, which had been to rent the fishery. Those oysters which were not sold immediately on the arrival of the boats were thrown into enclosures, which were paved, the floors having a slope towards a shallow reservoir. Some of these places were also occupied by the most extensive purchasers, and in their enclosures the oysters were piled in great heaps and allowed to die; after going through the usual process of decay, which, in so warm a climate is particularly rapid, the fleshy part having been completely decomposed, the pearls were found amongst the sand and refuse. In general, however, the oysters are purchased and divided amongst the speculators, who immediately open them, and if lucky, sell their prizes and continue their speculations upon a larger scale. Where thefts are so easily made, and a valuable article like a pearl is so easily secreted, incessant watchfulness is necessary on the part of those who employ others to open oysters; but I believe their utmost endeavours are ineffectual, as the moral character of most of those assembled at Kondátchie, affords no check to their inclinations or interest; they have been attracted, many of them from a distance, and at great risk and exertion, by avarice, and their only principle and pursuit is how to make money, and if successful, the end to them would sufficiently sanctify the means.

The persons employed to survey the pearl banks having ascertained the position of those on which the oysters are of the proper age, proceed to mark out the limits by placing buoys previous to the commencement of the fishery. If the oysters are too young, the pearls are small; and if allowed to be too old, the oysters die, the shells open, the pearls are irrecoverably lost to man, and "known but to genii of the deep."

Portions of sand taken from banks on which the oysters have died, (their shells detached from the bottom having been washed away,) contain no appearance of pearls.

The space over which the oyster-banks which are fished extend, is from twenty-five to thirty miles square, situated in the lower part of the gulf of Manár; although some are much deeper, the average depth of water on the best pearl-banks may be taken at forty feet. The pearl-oyster, although neither palatable nor wholesome, has no poisonous quality, and is said to be sometimes eaten by the poorest of those people who frequent the fishery.

None of the pearl divers are Cingalese, and only those few who come from Manár are subjects of the British Government; the remainder arrive from various towns and villages on the opposite coast of the Indian continent: the consequence of this was, that the Dutch Ceylon Government having quarrelled with the native sovereigns of the Southern Peninsula of India, they prevented the divers from resorting to the fishery, which was thus interrupted and prevented from 1768 until the taking of Ceylon by the British in 1796. Immediately after that event, a fishery was announced, and rented for sixty thousand pounds, beyond which the renter is supposed to have made other sixty thousand. In 1797, the fishery rented for one hundred and forty-four thousand. In 1798 for one hundred and ninety-two thousand. In 1799 it fell to thirty thousand; the fable of the goose with the golden eggs being exemplified in the indiscriminate destruction of the oysters on banks where they could have been but of little value. From this time up to 1806 there was no fishery at Manar, and even then it only rented for thirty-five thousand pounds.

There are some detached banks, but of inconsiderable value compared to Manár, situated further to the south, and on the west coast of the island, nearly opposite to the village of Chilaw, these had not been fished for thirty-six years previous to 1803, and then they produced a revenue of fifteen thousand pounds; they have occasionally been rented since that time, but have never realised anything approaching to the same amount. The facts above-mentioned at first sight might induce a belief that the age of the oyster was greater than is generally supposed; but there is no doubt that the present management produces a much larger amount, besides being a much less precarious item of revenue than allowing an accumulation of several years, and permitting renters to fish where they chose. Repeated examinations of the banks, and judicious restrictions of the fishery to those places where the oysters are of full size, have almost brought the pearl-fishery to be a regular annual addition to the income of the island.

In digging anywhere near Kondátchie, the extraordinary depth of oyster shells vouches for the number of ages which have successively witnessed the same persevering, difficult, dexterous, and eager pursuit of these delicate baubles. The greatest number of oysters brought in by one boat in a day, was thirty-eight thousand; the greatest number of boats employed in one day was one hundred and sixty-two; and the greatest length of time any diver that I heard of remained under water was seventy seconds. The fishery of which I am now writing, commenced on the 5th of March, and continued until the end of April 1828. Only one large and one small bank were fished: the oysters of the former at one time sold as low as seven rupees (about fourteen shillings) for a thousand; and for a short time those of the small bank rose to eighty rupees, but having been much overvalued, soon fell to one-third of that price. This fishery realized about thirty thousand pounds to Government.

Theorists have called for the abolition of what they are pleased to term "the pearl-fishery monopoly," and have had the hardihood to assert, that to throw it open would benefit the inhabitants of Ceylon; but it is to be hoped that neither vague theory, nor the sound of a word—monopoly, will triumph over common sense and justice, to deprive the public of Ceylon of this unexceptionable source of revenue. If the pearl-fisheries of the island were thrown open to all speculators, a very short period would suffice to annihilate this mine of wealth, and the only benefit would accrue to a few *foreign* adventurers who, for one season, might appropriate to themselves this portion of the revenue of Ceylon, and thus profit by the fiat of presumptuous ignorance.

Other theories which certainly require more facts, and of a different kind from those as yet brought forward in their support, have been advanced with confidence, and received without hesitation in Europe. It has been asserted that, from B.C 500, Ceylon was of the greatest possible importance in respect to general trade, and that until the latter end of the fifteenth century, it was the emporium of trade carried on between the eastern and western portions of the old world, between Africa, India, and China. I shall here state a few objections to these theories in their full extent, and also to some of the points which have been adduced in proof of their correctness. We are told that the passage which separates Manar from the opposite coast of Ceylon near Mantotte, and the Paumban passage between the island of Ramisseram and the continent of India, have "both been much deeper in ancient times." Now, with regard to these straits in the remote and obscure ages described in the Ramayan,* we find that Rama having completed the Saitubandha, or causeway through the then existing straits, marched his army across it from the continent of India to the invasion of Ceylon; but that soon afterwards great part of the coasts of that island were overwhelmed by the sea. The era of Rama is placed by Sir William Jones B.C. 1810. Cingalese history fixes the period of the death of his enemy Rawena, who they say fell by his own hand, B.C. 2387.† This is also the period assigned for the submerging of the capital, and the greatest part of the then extensive island and kingdom of Lanca, Ceylon.‡ If the Cingalese "have writ their annals true, tis there," even in histories now proved to be generally authentic, that in the third century before Christ, another irruption of the sea encroached

* Ramayan—Cingalese, Rawena-Katawa.

† Raja-wallia—Rawena-Katawa.

‡ Rawena-Katawa, Lanka Wistria, and Kadaimpota.

far on the western coast of Ceylon, destroyed many villages inhabited by pearl-divers, and formed Manár into an island, by forcing through the passage which now exists between it and Ceylon. It is near this strait, at Mantotte, that some remains of slight buildings have been called forward to vouch for the former existence of a rich and extensive city which commanded these narrow seas, and was inhabited by wealthy merchants in whom was centred the trade of the known world. Much stress has also been laid on an unfinished tank in that neighbourhood, called the giant's tank, which was intended to have been supplied with water from the river Awar-aar, formerly called by the Cingalese name, in which it is often mentioned in history, the Kolong or Malwatté-oya. The embankment which was to divert the current of the river still remains, a substantial monument of excellent masonry; but the tank itself is similar in plan, and inferior in extent to many of those which were completed by the Cingalese sovereigns of the island, to whom must be attributed the whole of the great works or extensive remains which are to be found in Ceylon; for Dalamagalan who reigned from A.D. 547 to 567, and Udaya the Second, who reigned in the tenth century are both mentioned as having formed embankments across the Malwattē-oya, and diverted its stream into various branches and tanks which they had formed. Magnitude and durability are the characteristics of these ancient Cingalese works, which were reared by the profuse expenditure of forced labour, when a numerous people were goaded to exertion by a powerful despotism. Matotte or Mantotte is sometimes confounded with Mahawettatotte, at the mouth of the Mahawelleganga in the bay of Kotiar, and nearly opposite to the principal entrance to the inner harbour of Trinkomalee.

I am not aware of any ancient remains at, or near the ports and harbours of Ceylon, except the ruins of a temple at Trinkomalee, the site of which, like that at Dewundera, has more probably been selected from its being on a conspicuous promontory, than as being in any way connected with mercantile prosperity. The Cingalese are not, probably they never were, a trading nation, and the commerce of the island, such as it was, may have been carried on by the mixed race indiscriminately called Malabars, inhabiting the southern peninsula of India, and spreading over the northern and eastern parts of the coasts of Ceylon. This race often combined in predatory incursions, and not unfrequently succeeded in conquering the greater part of the island; but the precarious tenure of sudden conquest by associated plunderers, was that alone by which they held any independent possessions in Ceylon, and against them the Cingalese carried on continual hostilities which invariably terminated in the subjugation or expulsion of the intruders. From some of these Malabar settlers or tributaries, must the mission to Rome have proceeded in the time of the Emperor Claudius; and from the records preserved of their statements, we may infer that they were not less given to what their descendants are so prone to, viz. falsehood, and exaggeration. It is said, that at the head of this mission came a Rachia or Raja — a monarch or a mendicant! A Risha may have wandered into Italy, a Raja would not have undertaken such a journey. In the continued and unsuccessful struggles of the Malabars to acquire territory and retain it in possession, we may be allowed to wonder at the alleged prosperity of the merchants, and to ask for the remains of the establishments which monopolists of trade in "the great emporium between Europe and eastern Asia," would no doubt have erected, had that trade been of any value. The remains at Mantotte and Kudramalai, a promontory believed to be the Hippuros of Pliny, will not satisfactorily answer the question. I may here observe, that Palaesimundo,* which the Rachia described to be the principal city, and to have a capacious harbour, might be fairly translated "the lowlands."

Mr. Turnour remarks, that in the historical works of the island, ships are only mentioned in the instances in which missions have been sent to the Indian continent, or the eastern peninsula,

* Most of the Kandian districts were divided into Udacia and Palacia, upper and lower; Mandhala signifies a province, thus Palaciya Mandhala is lower province.

either on political embassies, or for the purpose of conveying to the island the betrothed princess from the Indian courts, which usually supplied the consorts of the sovereigns of Ceylon. The expedition against the King of Arramana and Cambodia, in the reign of Parakráma Bahu is described in some detail; and it is there stated, that "several hundred vessels were equipped for that service in five months." This was in the sixteenth year of the reign of Prákrama-bahoo, or A.D. 1169.

If the Malabars could not establish themselves independently and permanently, still less could the Cingalese Mohammedans who, in political obscurity as well as in their pursuits, resembled very nearly the condition of the Jews in Europe, in the poorest states, and under the most rapacious and despotic monarchs of the dark ages. The record of the hostilities carried on against the Portuguese, Dutch, and English by the Kandians, after they were cooped up in the centre of the country, will show what chance less civilised and powerful traders had of maintaining their independence, or retaining their wealth, before the decay of population, and the dismemberment of the most valuable provinces of the Cingalese kingdom. We also find it recorded in the native histories, that the King Gajabahoo marched across by Ramisseram to the continent, A.D. 113, and that on his return, he visited Trinkomalee and repaired its temples. But to leave arguments and doubtful points of history for authentic documents of modern science; I shall quote from Major Sims's report of 1829, regarding the practicability of improving the Paumban passage.

"The Paumban passage, or, as it is called by the inhabitants, the Paumban river, is a narrow opening through a dam or ridge of rocks, extending from the island of Ramisseram to the opposite promontory, on the continent to the east of Ramnad." * * * "The continuation of the rocks, or dam, can be easily traced on the main land and island of Ramisseram, preserving exactly the same direction, but on both sides several feet higher than the dam in its natural position, and in uniform layers, having a small inclination to the south." * * * * "The ridges which form the dam are very much broken and displaced, and now consist of large flat masses of rocks, seldom more than two or three feet in thickness. Their shattered state, and the break or chasm which they form in the general height of the stratum of rock, would seem to indicate that the island of Ramisseram was at one time connected with the main land, and that it had been separated in the first instance by the sea, during storms, breaking over and bursting the chain of rocks which joined them, and afterwards by the water undermining and displacing the broken fragments." * * * * "This supposition corresponds with the tradition of the inhabitants, for the Brahmins of Ramisseram state, that when Achoodapah Naig was Raja of Madura, A.D. 1484, the island was connected with the continent, and that the Saumy of Ramisseram was carried to the main land thrice every year on particular festivals. During Achoodapah Naig's reign, a small breach in the rock was caused by a violent storm; but as there was no great depth of water in it, travellers still continued to cross on foot till the time of his successor, Vissoovana Naig, when the breach was much enlarged by a second storm. The Divan Ramapiah was ordered to fill up the breach, that the pilgrims of the pagoda of Ramisseram might pass without difficulty; this was accordingly done, and the repairs lasted about ten years, when a third hurricane re-opened and greatly extended the breach." * * * * "The rock of which the dam is composed, is a sandstone, varying considerably in quality and compactness, but everywhere soft and easily pierced and broken." * * * * "The dam is two thousand two hundred and fifty yards in length; it is bounded by two parallel ridges of rock, about one hundred and forty yards apart." * * * *

The circumstances above related, the facts recorded in Cingalese history, and the little knowledge possessed by those ancient writers of the western world, who have mentioned Ceylon, lead me to doubt if any very extensive commerce was carried on in the island during the early ages; and still less do I admit that "it is proved to have been the great emporium of trade between the eastern and western world." From the facts and quotations above given, I infer that the Paumban channels have gradually been becoming deeper by the action of the waves and currents upon the ledges of rock which impede this passage; and that if ever there was any channel through which large ships could pass between Ceylon and the continent, it must have been during some temporary shifting of the sand-banks between Manár and Ramisseram. This is not likely; Pliny, to be sure, mentions with some hesitation, "channels of so great a depth, that no anchor can fasten itself," while the rest of the space was not more than six feet in depth; but the remainder of the sentence will show that this was merely imperfect information, and that the channels there mentioned are the same narrow shallow passages that now exist; and that they were then navigated by the same wretched craft that is still used by the natives, under the names of dhonies, canoes, &c. "The ships are constructed so as to sail either way, in case it should be necessary to turn back while in the straits." The arguments and opinions brought forward to support the statement that large ships ever passed through the Manár and Mantotte, or the Paumban channels, appear to me quite insufficient to support such a position.

The Hindus imagine that many of the combats and scenes described in the Ramayan, occurred in this part of the island; that the rough beads, bangles, and other ornaments of very coarse coloured glass, found in great quantities mixed with the soil, in the tank and vicinity of Patsimadoe, are the remains of the ornaments of fallen warriors of that period; and that Marambu, Pomparippo, Marichicatty, Mardodé, &c. &c., preserve by their names the recollections of that great war. The Swaita-má-parwatia, the white rocks which were the key of Rama's position, the Ranabhumi, battle-field in which Rawena fell, and his splendid fort of Sri-lanka-poora, lie whelmed beneath the ocean on the west side of Ceylon.

To return from this digression to the busy scene and noisome stench of Kondátchie, and its pearls. Large pearls appeared to me to sell at prices nearly as high as what they could be purchased for in Britain; trash, or seed pearls, as the very small ones are called, sold much higher; and it was understood that this kind was principally intended for the Chinese market.

Having already seen the country between Aripo and Colombo, which I had passed through while on a coursing and shooting excursion (of which I have given an account elsewhere), and that route affording little variety or interest, I proceeded in a boat to Chilaw. About sixteen miles from Aripo, we passed the promontory of Kudra-Malai, which is conjectured, not only from the derivation of the name, but also from its position, to have been the place reached by a freedman of Annius Plocamus, in the time of the Emperor Claudius.* There are remains of a town near this promontory, but whether it was a colony of Mohammedans or Malabars, or neither, I could not make out, from the tra-

* The following is from an article in the Colombo Journal, 25th July 1832.

"Gibbon, in a note to the tenth chapter of the Decline and Fall of the Roman Empire, has inadvertently represented the freedman as farming the tribute instead of Annius Plocamus. This freedman is supposed to have preceded but a short time Hippalus, the discoverer of the south-west monsoon, which was called after his name. Of the precise situation of Hippurus we are not informed, but learn that it was a port to the northward; and it is plain that it must have been on the western coast, from the circumstance of Hippalus having been blown across during his sailing round Arabia. A conjecture has often suggested itself, which the latent etymology of the name given to the port at which Hippalus arrived, in two different languages might, with a trifling literal alteration in one of the names, seem to sanction. The name by which the port is called in Pliny, is Hippuros, ἵππουρος (the horse's tail), as Arcturus is the bear's tail; now, supposing the name to have been really Hipporos, we shall have for the name of the port, ἵππορος, instead of the former; the exact translation of which into English is horse-mountain. Now, can we find on the north-western coast, to which Hippalus was carried, any trace of such a name? We have it clearly in the name given to the highland immediately opposite to Calpentyn, in the Malabar language, Coodra-malie, literally horse-mountain, and it is remarkable that the port of Calpentyn, and the inland coast adjoining to the horse-mountain, are the only parts of the coast between Manár and Negombo into which he could have entered. At this day, vessels from the coast are often detained at Calpentyn, on their way to Colombo, without the power of advancing further against the south-west monsoon.

ditions concerning it; these traditions were wild in incident, and so absurd in dates, as to be unworthy of notice.

From Chilaw, I procured a canoe which conveyed me with great speed to Colombo, bounding over the waves without any of that jumbling motion which has caused me to feel every other kind of vessel so sickening and uncomfortable. These canoes are of a very peculiar construction; the principal part consisting of a long tree hollowed out; on this, a high mast, and still higher sail, appear quite disproportioned to the vessel, which is prevented from being upset by a log of wood called the outrigger; this is a sort of miniature of the canoe, only it is solid, and is attached and kept parallel to the canoe by means of two-curved elastic sticks. The outrigger is always to leeward, and, as both ends of the canoe are shaped alike, the change of direction is accomplished with little delay, by simply shifting the sail, and proceeding with the former stern as its head. The motion of these canoes somewhat resembles that of a horse at full gallop; and if the outrigger is well secured, they are able to keep the sea in ordinary weather, which could hardly be expected, judging from their simple form and skeleton-like appearance.

CHAPTER XII.

SHOOTING EXCURSION ALONG THE WEST COAST OF CEYLON.

To fright the animals, and to kill them up
In their assign'd and native dwelling-place.

SHAKSPEARE.

To Madampe. — Pepper Garden. — Mosquitoes. — Crocodiles. — Crocodile Charmers. — Crocodile Hunt. — Catching Crocodiles. — Ganges Stag. — Hunting. — Immense Tree. — Karativoe. — Noosing a wild Elephant. — Elephant Shooting. — Adventure. — Anecdotes. — Accidents. — Driving Elephants. — Chuny. — Wild Elephant's tail amputated.

SOON after my return from Adam's Peak, I proceeded, in company with two friends, along the coast to the northward on a sporting expedition, in the course of which I was fortunate enough to shoot, besides smaller game, pea-fowl, deer, alligators, and elephants.

Our first stage was Negombo, the next Chilaw, two considerable villages with old forts (the former commenced by the Portuguese, and both completed by the Dutch). In neither did I see anything worthy of remark. Negombo is twenty-three, and

Chilaw fifty miles from Colombo. We halted a night at Madampe, nine miles short of Chilaw, in a thriving pepper-garden, where the vines, clustered round the stems of high forest trees, produced a luxuriant cool appearance, and formed a pleasing shade over neatly kept walks, which diverged in every direction from the collector's bungaloe in which we had established ourselves. On one side of this forest-garden, extended a tank covered with water-lilies; this is the principal memorial left to show that Madampe was a residence of princes who aspired to independence, in the fifteenth century. Of the beauties of this place I should have retained a more pleasing recollection, had not the mosquitoes proved more annoying and severe than I ever felt them; and had not the number of jackals that went hunting past, or sat howling around our door, awakened whole troops of monkeys, the screaming and chattering of which completely prevented my forgetting in sleep the folly I had committed, by first lying down without closing my mosquito-curtains. Putlam is a large village, near which, on the flat shores of its shallow gulf, there is a considerable manufacture of salt; it is eighty-five miles from Colombo, and the whole of our way had been across a succession of rice-fields, jungles, and plains, through which, by taking advantage of various streams, and connecting them by a canal, there is now water-carriage, by which we had forwarded from Colombo our travelling-lumber, and the supplies necessary for our further proceedings.

The tanks and sluggish streams in the neighbourhood of Putlam and along this coast, are infested by crocodiles in great numbers; these reptiles sometimes attain the length of seventeen feet, and not having any enemy sufficiently powerful to combat against them with success, except man, they are to be found in every small piece of water, in those flat districts in which the population is scanty. In the mountainous region, crocodiles are very rarely seen; but in districts where they abound, human beings occasionally become their prey, which they generally secure while it is in a state of rest, although I have heard a well-authenticated instance of a man being seized and dragged from a small canoe in which he was crossing a river in the Mágampattoo. They destroy great numbers of deer, young cattle, and animals of all kinds which come to drink, or lie down to cool themselves in the rivers and ponds. In hunting, or coursing, it is necessary to ride well up to your dogs and advisable to fire a pistol on approaching water, as otherwise the dogs run a great risk of being taken down by crocodiles; indeed, this so frequently happens, as greatly to diminish the pleasure of hunting, and to increase the difficulty of preserving good dogs.

When a party has to pass through deep water, crocodile charmers give assurance of safety, and are always successful in bringing their employers along without accidents Such conjurors as I have seen employed in this vocation, took care that the whole party had assembled on the bank, while the incantations, accompanied by splashing of water, were in process; then, on receiving notice that the crocodiles were effectually muzzled, all rushed in together, thus creating sufficient disturbance to frighten the cowardly slothful reptiles, and to show that there may be safety as well as confidence from the manœuvres of a crocodile-charmer. That crocodiles are neither active nor courageous, may be inferred from the manner in which the natives of Putlam and some other places venture into water where they abound, and drag them to the bank by means of a strong net. This is a curious and interesting sight; but it was not without surprise and considerable anxiety that I witnessed it for the first time. We had noticed the heads and backs of several crocodiles, and immediately after the net being arranged, we perceived the crocodile-hunters, seven or eight unarmed Moormen, wade up to their necks in the water, and form a semicircular line around the spot where the animals had been last observed; for, on seeing the unusual bustle of preparation for their capture, they had gradually lowered their heads beneath the surface. The people employed in dragging the net moved their legs rapidly, and others who accompanied them kept striking on the surface of the water with poles; they proceeded in this way, gradually contracting the space within the net, until they brought three crocodiles to the shore at the place where we, armed with spears and guns, were waiting to commence the work of destruction. The most vulnerable place in which to strike a crocodile with a spear is, that part of the body which is left exposed when the creature moves its fore legs; and for this, and every other kind of attack, the spear should be so formed as to admit of its being easily withdrawn, that you may strike a more deadly blow if the first should prove ineffectual. The persons employed in dragging (although inside the net), or beating up the game, did not exhibit any symptoms of alarm, nor did much exertion appear requisite to get out of the way when the crocodiles bestirred themselves, and attempted to regain the deep cover of the tank; this they seemed determined to accomplish, on finding themselves suddenly in shallow water and closely surrounded. The best way of destroying crocodiles is, by means of hooks baited with flesh attached to a strong cord, not hard twisted, but composed of many small strings, which get between the wide-set teeth of the animal, and cannot there be cut; a block of wood to which the lines are attached serves as a float, and points out the place to which the crocodile has retired after swallowing the bait. An attendant, having laid hold of this float, pulls very gently until the animal's head appears above water; then a shot, directed between the head and neck, breaks the spine and renders the creature powerless; after which, it is dragged ashore and the tackling recovered. In this manner a gentleman killed several hundreds of these animals in one year in the Batticaloe district. Although the hard and irregular surface of a crocodile's skin is very apt to cause a ball to glance off, there is no part of any one which I saw, that would resist an ordinary-sized ball properly directed.

In the neighbourhood of Aripo, and at the plains near Marichicotta, and Pomparipo, deer* are to be met with in great numbers, and afford good sport to those who are fond of coursing, and disregard the danger of hard riding over broken ground. These deer are prettily spotted, and more elegantly formed than the fallow-deer, which, however, they much resemble; they are easily tamed, but the males become dangerous when old; even the does are apt both to butt and bite when they are full grown. Albinoes are not uncommon in this species of deer; three of them were found at the palace of Kandy, when it was taken possession of by the British forces under General Macdowall in 1803, and I have heard of several, and seen one, perfectly white; the eyes had that peculiar red colour so common in albinoes. Notwithstanding the abundance of game, there are many difficulties in the way of those who persevere in coursing; the wooded nature of the country, and coarse vege-

* The Axis, or Ganges stag.

tation of the plains, require that the dogs be fleet; they must also be strong, and high-couraged enough to speed through the prickly plants which are so common in the open grounds of Ceylon. In dry weather, the ground is intersected by numerous cracks; and wherever the deep footsteps of elephants have been formed during the rainy season, they afterwards become hardened by the sun, and are a serious and dangerous obstacle for horses to pass over. It is difficult, on account of the warmth of the climate, to rear good dogs in Ceylon, and it is still more difficult to preserve them; for their bitter enemy, the crocodile, is always to be found in numbers near those places where coursing is practicable. The sportsman must contrive to find game, and start his dogs near some small jungle from whence the deer have to cross the plain before they can reach a continued forest; break of day is the best time, and the chase once commenced, unless dogs, horses, and riders have sufficient strength and use their utmost energies, coverts, impracticable for dogs, will soon receive the game and disappoint the sportsman. If he happens to have young dogs, he may also have the additional mortification of seeing them return lame and torn from a useless attempt to follow the chase in a thorny jungle, while the cunning elders of the pack have wisely given up pursuit at the edge of the forest, and contented themselves with looking at the gallant younkers dashing into the thorny brake.

At Marichicatty we observed the natives purifying the thick, white, muddy, and unwholesome water, which was the only kind to be met with there, by means of a small nut called ambuprasadana, which is commonly found in the dry parts of Ceylon, and when rubbed down in the inside of an earthen vessel, has the effect of clearing the water by precipitating the earthy particles.

At the Mohammedan burying-ground in the village of Putlam stands a tree, called by the natives Papparapooli, the giant's taramind; six feet from the ground its solid stem is nearly forty feet in circumference, and at eight feet it divides into two branches, one being twenty-two feet, the other twenty-six feet in circumference. The height of this tree is under one hundred feet; and on inquiring of the inhabitants, they said, that according to their traditions its age did not exceed one hundred years. It is, I believe, an Adansonia, and the only one I saw in the island.

From Putlam we crossed the gulf of Calpentyn (which is here eight or nine miles broad) to the low uninhabited island of Karativoe, and there took up our quarters for two days in a dilapidated Hindu temple. This island is about nine miles long and one broad; in the middle is a large pond, surrounded by an open space covered with coarse grass, and both ends of the island are overgrown with jungle rising from a swampy soil. We had brought people with us to beat the brushwood, and having placed ourselves, and stationed the dogs on the edge of the plain, we succeeded in killing several deer, and saw some good coursing. The venison of such deer as are fat is excellent, but in general, it is not only very dry but is also insipid. The jelly made of a native fruit called lowi-lowi is often eaten in Ceylon with venison, it resembles red currant jelly, but is more acid; when the fruit of the lowi-lowi is ripe, and its red berries, (about the size of a nutmeg) are hanging in clusters as large as a bunch of grapes, amongst very thick and dark foliage, it appears one of the prettiest fruit-bearing trees in Ceylon.

Near Putlam I saw, for the first time, a wild elephant noosed by a hunter; this man had accompanied us on a shooting excursion; and having heard of three elephants in the forest, we got near enough to kill one, another was very young, and the third an old one, went off apparently unhurt. While this elephant was tearing through the jungle, the hunter kept close on the animal's flank, until with great dexterity he contrived (when the elephant was stepping over a fallen tree) to slip the noose round its hind leg, and almost at the same instant he wound the other end of the cord several times round the trunk of a tree. The sudden check threw the animal on the ground, and its capture might easily have been completed; but although the skill of the hunter was thus successfully exhibited, it was not sufficiently rewarded; the elephant was found to have received a mortal hit, and died immediately after its fall. The young one, about two years old, remained near, and was left unmolested. Before returning to Colombo, we killed several more elephants near Palam, and had some good pea-fowl shooting about ten miles inland from Putlam on the Kandy road; we also saw two leopards, and a few red-legged partridges, but did not get a shot at them.

A sportsman fairly equipped for elephant shooting, ought to have at least four barrels, and the best form of these would be two double-barrelled guns carrying balls of an ounce and a third in weight, and of strength sufficient to take a large charge of powder. I should prefer plain to rifle barrels, as they occupy less time in loading, which is sometimes of great consequence: and smooth barrels carry balls with sufficient accuracy; for shooting at a distance is never successful in this sport, and it is not advisable (if you have a choice) to fire until you are within fifteen yards of the animal; half that distance is preferable, as then your shot, if it fails to kill, will in all probability check him for a sufficient time to allow of exchanging your gun and hitting again. As the sportsman's attention must be entirely occupied in forcing through the jungle, and keeping a good look out, the person who follows close to him should have good nerves, sufficient activity, and some experience; if this be the case, the sportsman runs little risk, as his follower will hand him the loaded gun immediately on hearing the other discharged. This is done by those accustomed to it in such a way, that the sportsman is not required to withdraw his eye from the animal, whose advance might not allow him time to return to his proper position, and take a steady aim.

In this excursion along the western coast, I had given my spare guns in charge to two common Colombo coolies (baggage porters), who had volunteered for the employment, and said they were accustomed to the sport. On one occasion, at Palam, I found myself in a most disagreeable and dangerous position; but nothing could exceed the coolness, promptitude, and sound judgment with which these two men acted, under the peculiar circumstances of the case. In an extremely thick dark copse, matted with thorny creeping plants, two elephants had taken shelter after the dispersion of a herd, two of which we had killed. The mould under this copse was hard, bare, and black, and the brushwood was without leaves for eighteen inches from the ground; this was occasioned by the place being a hollow, which filled with water during the rainy season. Creeping in on my breast for a few feet, I could distinguish the legs of a very large elephant, whose head was concealed by the foliage; but another and smaller one was sufficiently visible to allow of my taking a proper aim. Looking round, and seeing the coolies close to the edge of the brushwood, and being myself, as I imagined, ready to back out and face the expected charge of the large elephant, I fired at the other and it fell dead. I then attempted to rise, but felt myself entangled and secured by numerous twigs and the strong hooked thorn, so common in many Kandian jungles, but which was then unknown to me. I had no time to repeat my efforts at escape; for I immediately felt the tangled mass of vegetation pressing forward upon me, while the big elephant rushed up almost close to where I lay, and there stood uttering that fearful shrill trumpet-like squeal with which these animals generally accompany their charge. The coolies were little more than a pace to my right, and it was towards them the elephant had rushed. They perceived my situation, and each of them thrust down a gun through the brushwood (so that the butt end was within my reach), and then ran for their lives. The elephant, already at the edge of the copse, did not pursue; for I suppose it missed and was unwilling to leave its fallen companion: there the brute remained, trumpeting, and standing with its round shapeless legs within my reach, and its head almost over me. I had a rifle, carrying a ball of two ounces' weight in my hand,—this I raised perpendicularly under the elephant's head, and, with the butt end resting on the ground, pulled the trigger; the shot took effect, the animal staggered back eight or ten paces towards the dead one, while by violent exertions, I disentangled myself from my most uncomfortable position. I now perceived Colonel L—— (who had heard the trumpeting) hastening towards me, and returned with him to see the position of an elephant which he had shot, and which had died so instantaneously, that instead of falling over, it remained where it sank down, resting on its knees and head; I afterwards heard several instances of the same thing having occurred in killing elephants.

When an elephant charges, he rushes headlong forward with the trunk upright, at the same time making a wild, loud, long-continued noise, resembling the sound of a bad trumpet, and very different from the deep hollow growl which he utters when alarmed or slightly irritated.

It is necessary to know those parts of an elephant's head, by hitting which your ball can reach the brain; for this occupies but a very small space in proportion to the size of their skulls. It is also necessary to take into consideration the height of the elephant before you, relative to the position in which you stand. A tall elephant advancing straight upon you, if the ground be level and his head erect, cannot receive a mortal hit, and it was in this way that one in the vicinity of Gampola, famed for the number of natives he had killed, is said always to have advanced; certain it is, he had often escaped the punishment intended for his numerous manslaughters, and was at last killed while charging up a steep hill at a gentleman, who, with only one gun, accidentally encountered him in the dusk of the evening. Luckily, however, advancing with the head held up, when they approach any obstacle, is not usual with elephants; and it seems natural for them to lower their heads, and curl up their trunks, when determined on overcoming anything that obstructs their progress. Afraid of injuring their trunk, they seldom strike with any great force when they make use of it; two instances are all I have known to the contrary: one of these was when a wounded elephant in running away, struck and killed with one blow of its trunk an unlucky buffalo that crossed its path. On another occasion, an elephant that had turned and broken through the line of beaters at an elephant-hunt in Mátalé, reached up in passing and killed a man who had taken refuge in a tree. The man had hold with both his hands of a branch above that on which he stood, and could easily have raised himself higher, but he was looking down, and considered himself beyond reach of danger: it was at this moment that the elephant, stretching up, struck the man with such force as to break both his thighs and hurl him to the ground; the elephant took no further notice of his victim, but passed on: the man lived but a few minutes.

A herd of elephants never charges *en masse*, although affection for their young may induce some of the females, if closely pursued, to turn upon the sportsman; and on reaching very thick jungle they generally turn round, either from feeling themselves secure of a retreat, or afraid of being overtaken in forcing their entrance. A hora alia, rogue elephant, on the contrary, invariably maintains his position, and charges intruders, and often with more cunning than can be perceived in their more amiable actions. Near the old path to Trinkomalee from Kandy, and close to the remote station of Gonáwe in Mátelé, one of these brutes had taken his position in an extensive forest, from which he occasionally sallied out and did much mischief, having, amongst other acts of manslaughter, killed one of the post-office runners. In consequence, native travellers generally passed the place (before this elephant was destroyed) in groups, which assembled at the nearest stations, and in which commonly one or more persons carried firearms. These parties the animal always avoided; but a young Malabar lad was killed by this brute with circumstances of premeditation and stealthy cunning, more consonant to the habits of the tiger. The lad had attached himself to the followers of a gentleman who was proceeding to Kandy from Trinkomalee, and was walking a short distance behind this gentleman's horse, and a little way in advance of the coolies carrying the baggage, when the elephant rushed out, seized, threw him down, and trampled on him, then passed on into the forest on the opposite side of the way. The elephant had allowed the horse and those people immediately around the gentleman to pass, and had remained quite quiet, although naturally the most restless and fidgety of living creatures, until he found an easy victim; it must also be recollected that elephants are almost invariably terrified at horses, to which it is difficult to accustom them.

There are two methods of proceeding in shooting elephants: one is to have them driven by natives towards the place where the sportsman is stationed; the other, more sportsmanlike, also more dangerous and fatiguing, is for the man to enter the jungle, in which case the only risk is to himself and his immediate followers, and he does not expose the lives of those natives who are compelled to attend,* but have neither interest nor amusement in the proceedings.

If elephants are to be driven, the sportsman must take his station on the sheltered side of the cover, as otherwise, from the keen sense of smell which these animals possess, they would avoid breaking out of the jungle at the place of his ambush. The persons employed in driving, are sent in at the opposite side, and form a curved line beyond the herd; after which, they advance yelling, shouting, and beating tom-toms. Great care is necessary to keep those persons who accompany the sportsman perfectly still, that the elephants may not be turned

* Compulsory service was abolished in 1833 by an order of the King in Council.

back upon the beaters; for the same reason, and also as it gives a greater chance of sport, the leader of a herd should be allowed to pass, as the others will then endeavour to follow at all hazards, and in the same direction. If it is a large herd which is driven, the confusion of sounds and the gradual approach of the ponderous massive tread of the elephants, produce their full effect, from the silence maintained around the anxious sportsman.

In shooting elephants by forcing up to them in the jungle, the forenoon is the best time, as then they are least inclined to move from the shade, under which they may be seen flapping their ears, crossing and rubbing their legs, swinging their bodies; in short, always moving, unless alarmed and listening, in which case they seem to trust most to their sense of smell, and move their trunk in every direction, trying to fix the point from whence they may expect disturbance. If the wind should favour them, after a short time the trunks will be found pointed in the proper direction, and the whole endeavour to steal off as quickly and quietly as they can; but never allowing any of the young ones to fall behind. Elephants in dry weather, and during the heat of the day, are seldom to be found without a leafy branch held in their trunk; this they employ in switching off the flies by which they are especially tormented. When lying down they sleep soundly, and may be easily surprised; but they do not often indulge in this mode of rest, and generally recline against a tree on which they have been rubbing themselves; with the earth which they are continually scattering over their bodies with their trunks, the trees are so marked as to enable those who are employed in watching them to form an idea of the size of the largest elephants in a herd. I seldom found the elephant-hunters mistaken in their conjectures regarding the size of the animals and numbers composing a herd, although they may not have fallen in with it; as, besides the marks on the trees already mentioned, they have a surer criterion in the footmarks, which they can trace on the hardest soil. Having entered the jungle, the sportsman must proceed towards his game from the lee-side, and with as little noise as possible; but if on his near approach the elephants have taken the alarm, and are about to move off, he must make a dash forward, before they have time to turn themselves round and commence their retreat. If unsuccessful in this, and unable to get a shot at their heads, an active man by following them closely (his progress being facilitated by the track they leave) may sometimes succeed in overtaking and causing them to turn upon him.

While relating occurrences in elephant-shooting, I must not forget the anecdote told me by a friend, one of the earliest of the real sporting elephant-shots, who, being an excellent marksman, and possessed of strength, activity, and wonderful nerve, had been particularly successful in that amusement. Being on leave in England, this gentleman happened to mention in a party some ordinary fact (I believe, that elephants were generally brought down by the first shot of a good sportsman), when, on looking round, he found the eyes of all present turned full upon him; he could easily perceive the general incredulity, and felt that he was found guilty without the possibility of making a defence. As his only resource, he determined to back out of the dilemma, and to enjoy the unbelieving ignorance of those around him, by asking, if they really thought him serious when he mentioned such a circumstance? They all declared they did not—that they were aware of its impossibility! and forthwith began quoting some passages in the war which had lately terminated against Chuny of Exeter 'Change. This had filled the newspapers and occupied their readers for sometime; and with the view and plan then published, has often proved a subject of mirth to the sportsman in Ceylon:—A, the elephant; B, a party of the Guards; also, a return of ammunition expended in the destruction of an elephant confined in a cage.

After this, it would be unreasonable for me to expect implicit credit for the fact that several individuals have killed nine elephants in one day, or to publish that fifteen wild elephants were actually docked by a gentleman in one forenoon. The tail of the elephant, like the brush of a fox, is the signal of success; and, as well as the tusks (if it be a tusker), belongs to whomsoever brings down the animal. Several laughable scenes have occurred by young sportsmen proceeding to dock the elephants before making sure of their death: and I know an instance where a gentleman, having shot an elephant apparently in good health, was surprised to find the operation had already been performed; his companion coming up soon after, and producing the trophy, was requested to point out the carcase from which he had cut the tail. He proceeded to the spot, but the marks of blood were all that remained to vouch for the fact of his having amputated the tail of a live elephant.

CHAPTER XIII.

VISIT TO KANDY.—MORAL LAWS OF GAUTAMA BUDDHA.

The rifled urn, the violated mound.—BYRON.

Abstain from all sin, acquire all virtue, repress thine own heart; this is Buddha's injunction.
Tenets of Buddhism by KITULGAMMA UNNANZE.

Exhibition of Buddha's Tooth. — Splendid Procession. — Description of the Tooth. — Its Caskets. — Its Sanctuary. — Offerings made to it. — Sacred Music. — Handsome temporary Building. — Native Dresses. — Whips. — Town of Kandy. — Burial-ground of the Kandian Kings. — Priests receiving Alms. — The Pavilion. — The Grounds and Scenery.—Moral Laws of Buddha. — Buddhist Priesthood.

IN the month of May 1828, I proceeded to Kandy, and witnessed that brilliant Buddhist festival, the exhibition of the Dalada (tooth of Buddha); an expiring blaze of the ancient worship of Ceylon, whose beams even then gleamed flickering and unstable, and will suddenly sink in darkness, or surely and gradually fade before a brighter light. From one district, at least, I know the numbers who attended at this Dalada Puja were procured by compulsion more than attracted by devotion; and that it was the dread of present punishment, not the hope of spiritual benefit, by which they were collected. I anticipate that Buddhism, shorn of its splendour, unaided by authority, and torn by internal dissension, will not long have power to retain even its present slight control over the actions of its votaries by the mere excellence of its moral laws, and that it will fall into disuse before Christianity is prepared to step into its place, which for a time will be occupied by those vile superstitions and demon worship to which the Cingalese are so prone.

Fifty-three years had elapsed since the King Kirti Sri had openly displayed the relic; and, from the revolutions which had since taken place in the country, but few people remembered the ceremony, and still fewer had seen the Dalada, which they believed to be the most sacred thing on earth, and that only to see it proved their former merits by their present good fortune.

On the 29th May 1828, the three larger cases having previously been removed, the relic contained in the three inner caskets was placed on the back of an elephant richly caparisoned: over it was the Ransiwigé, a small octagonal cupola, the top of which was composed of alternate plain and gilt silver plates, supported by silver pillars. When the elephant appeared coming out of the temple-gate, two lines of magnificent elephants, forming a double line in front of the entrance, knelt down and thus remained; while the multitude of people, joining the points of their fingers, raised their arms above their heads, and then bent forward, at the same time uttering in full deep tones the shout of Sadhu: this, joined and increased by those at a distance, swelled into a grand and solemn sound of adoration. The elephant bearing the relic, followed by

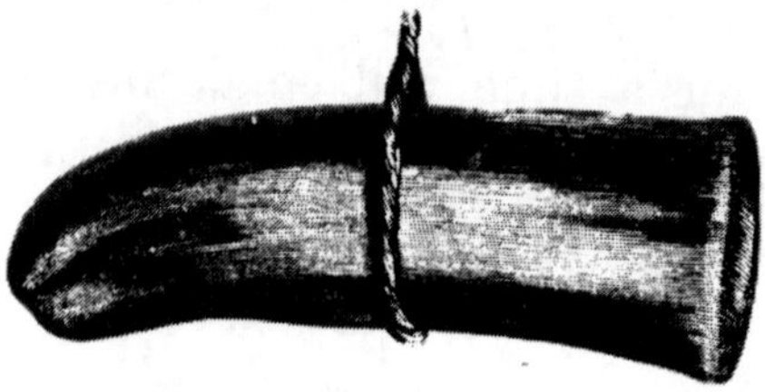

the establishments of the temples with their elephants, also those of the chiefs, after proceeding through the principal streets of the town, returned to the great bungaloe: here the first Adikar removed the relic from the back of the elephant, and conveyed it to the temporary altar on which it was to be exhibited. The rich hangings were now closed around the altar, and the three inner cases opened in presence of Sir Edward Barnes the Governor. The drapery being again thrown open disclosed the tooth placed on a gold lotus flower, which stood on a silver table: this was covered with the different cases of the relic, various gold articles and antique jewellery, the offerings of former devotees.

Whether prompted by their own feelings, or impelled by more weighty reasons to attend at this exhibition, still the relic was evidently an object of intense veneration to all the assembled Buddhists, and by those of the Kandian provinces it is considered the palladium of their country; they also believe the sovereign power of the island is attached to its possessors. It is a piece of discoloured ivory, slightly curved, nearly two inches in length, and one inch in diameter at the base; from thence to the other extremity, which is rounded and blunt, it considerably decreases in size. The Dalada, as we find in very ancient details of its adventures, was discoloured when it arrived in Ceylon: that a relic of Gautama should fade or decay was at the time urged as an argument against its authenticity; but a miracle settled the dispute, and silenced sceptics.

The sanctuary of this relic is a small chamber in the temple attached to the palace of the Kandian Kings; and there the six cases in which it is enshrined are placed on a silver table hung round with rich brocades. The largest or outside cover of these carandus (caskets) is five feet in height, formed of silver gilt, and shaped in the form of a dágoba:* the same form is preserved in the five inner cases, which are of gold; two of them, moreover, being inlaid with rubies and other precious stones. The outer case is decorated with many gold ornaments and jewels, which have been offered to the relic, and serve to embellish its shrine. In front of the silver altar on which the tooth was exposed a plain table was placed; to this the people approached one at a time, and, having seen the Dalada and deposited their gifts, they prostrated themselves, then passed on and made room for others. The offerings consisted of things the most heterogeneous: gold chains and gold ornaments; gold, silver, and copper coins of all denominations; cloths, priest's vestments, flowers, sugar, areka-nuts, betel-leaves. The Dalada was exhibited and the offerings continued for three successive days. On the second day some wretched specimens of the science of defence were exhibited before the Governor, both with fists and also with wooden swords and targets: on the fourth night there was a display of native fire-works, well made and skilfully managed. Night and day, without intermission, during the continuance of this festival, there was kept up a continual din of tom-toms, and sounding of Kandian pipes and chanque shells. The Kandian pipe is a musical

* The bell-shaped buildings raised over the relics of Buddha.

instrument in power and melody nearly resembling a penny whistle: but the chanque is a shell with a mouth-piece attached, and, under the influence of powerful lungs, is a most efficient instrument for producing a noise which was called music; its tones varying between the bellowings of a chained bull and the howling of a forsaken dog. I presume the natives consider these sounds peculiarly adapted for their sacred music, as such instruments are to be found in all temples, and may be heard at all hours, to the dire annoyance of any European who attempts to sleep in their neighbourhood.

The principal temporary building was two hundred and fifty feet in length, of proportionate breadth, and supported by six lines of pillars,—it was under this that the tooth was exhibited; and the whole was ornamented with palm branches, plantain-trees, fruit and flowers: so gracefully were these disposed, that the columns in the variety of their decorations, and some even in unity of effect presented combinations which, if transferred to stone, would rival any specimen of elaborate Corinthian architecture. In the brilliant pageantry of this festival, the rich altar and resplendent ornaments of the relic, the great size and elegant decorations of the temporary buildings, the peculiar and picturesque dresses of the chiefs, the majestic elephants, and dense mass of people, threw an air of imposing grandeur over the spectacle, to which the old temples, sacred trees, and the wild and beautiful scenery around the Kandian capital formed an appropriate landscape. These combinations were rendered still more impressive by the disturbed state of the elements; for an extraordinary gloom and tempestuous weather continued during the whole time of the exhibition, and the torrents of rain which fell at that time caused the loss of many lives, and destroyed much property, in various parts of the island.

The court-dress of a Kandian Adikar—minister of state and justice—consists of a square cap resembling a huge pincushion, sometimes made of white stiffened muslin, but in full-dress of scarlet cloth embroidered with gold, and having an elevated peak in the middle, surmounted by a precious stone. The jacket is of tissue, with short plaited sleeves, very full upon the shoulders, and fastened with amethyst buttons; over this is worn a white tippet of plaited muslin, with gold edging. On the lower part of the body, over white trowsers, which are tight at the ankle and terminated by a frill, a number of white muslin and gold figured cloths are bound in cumbrous folds round the waist by a broad gold belt; in this is stuck a knife with a richly carved handle. Gold chains are worn round the neck and hanging down upon the chest, bangles on the wrists, and immense rings, which almost conceal their small hands, complete the decoration of a Kandian Adikar.

The dress of the other chiefs differed but little from that of the Adikars, except that their caps were white and circular. The peculiar and distinguishing insignia of Adikars are their silver stick, and immense whips eight or ten feet in

length, two inches in breadth, (made of the fibres of a plant like strong hemp,) and producing a report almost equal to firing a pistol; seven of these emblems of power and punishment were borne by as many men, who announced the coming, and effectually cleared the way for the first Adikar.

Before each chief, hammered and squalled the tom-toms, pipes, and sometimes a little squeaking trumpet belonging to the district over which he presided. Each district, and in some cases each division of a district, had a separate flag, which was borne before the great man. Near him remained a confidential servant with a large silver betel-box; and he was followed by persons carrying long-handled fans, (which were used as parasols,) guns, and ornamented sticks, spears, and bows. The "tail" was composed of the people of the district, and the personal retainers of the chief.

The dress of the chiefs and their wives is very similar; only, the ladies have their cloths bound tighter to their shape, have no head-dress, and wear gold ornaments in their hair. Although some, particularly in the highest rank of females, are handsome, and most of the sex are comely when very young, yet they are comparatively inferior in appearance to the men. Both sexes, of all ranks except the lowest, have their hair long, divided smooth from the middle of the forehead, and turned up in a knot; that of the men on the back of the head, while the women allow theirs to rest on the neck as far down as the shoulders. They have expressed to me their surprise at seeing European ladies with their hair curled, as it was one of the practices which they could not in any way account for; amongst themselves, the slightest tendency to a curl in their hair being considered a blemish. The distinction of ranks amongst both men and women was designated by the length of their cloth above or below the knee; in women a farther distinction was covering the bosom, or leaving the figure entirely exposed from the waist upwards.

The town of Kandy is judiciously planned, and the present regular arrangement of the streets was marked out by the Adikars under the direction of the King; the streets all run in straight lines, but do not cross at right angles. It is situated on an angular piece of ground, with the base resting on two lakes which were formed by the late King. The buildings remaining from the time of the native dynasty are several temples of Buddha and two colleges, at one of which every Kandian priest ought to be ordained: there are also temples to the gods Náta, Vishnu, Katragamma, and the goddess Patine; but there is nothing worthy of remark either in their architecture or decorations.

In the audience-hall, now used as a court-house and church, are some well-carved pillars of halmila wood: the trees from which they were formed were cut and squared near Nalande; from thence they were dragged over a hilly country, and up a steep mountain, the whole distance being upwards of thirty miles. The other remains of the palace and buildings inhabited by the royal establishment were, without exception, mean, and equally destitute of internal comfort and external beauty; the most striking object is a low octagonal tower with a peaked roof, from a balcony in which the King exhibited himself on occasions of public festivity.

Wikrama Bahoo the Third, who reigned from A.D. 1371 to 1378, was the first monarch who settled himself even temporarily at Kandy, then called, from a large rock which projects from the hill above the old palace, Sengadda-galla-nuvara; but it did not become the permanent capital of the interior until the reign of Wimala Dharma, which commenced A.D. 1592, and it continued the chief city until the native Government fell before the British power in 1815.

The burial-ground of the Kandian Kings cannot be viewed without exciting reflections on the revolutions which alike occur to man's estate and the most ancient monarchies. Ere the last of one of the longest lines of Kings which authentic history records had so far expiated his crimes, and received his measure of earthly retribution for the cruelties he had inflicted, by suffering a long imprisonment and an exile's death, the solid tombs of his predecessors were ransacked by the hands of avarice, or riven in sunder and ruined by the swelling roots of sacred trees. This hallowed spot, where the funeral piles were raised, the last grand solemn rites performed, and the

last of earthly pomp and splendour was shown to the remains "of the race of the sun" and the rulers of the land, is now a wilderness, where decay revels and rushes rapidly on beneath dank vegetation and a gloomy shade. The tomb of Raja Singha, the tyrant who reigned during Knox's captivity in the seventeenth century, was nearly perfect, and preserved its shape in May 1828; that of Kirti Sri was then entire. In 1837 the former was a heap of rubbish, from which the stones had been removed; and the beautiful proportions, even the general form of the latter, could no longer be traced. Hopes of plunder, or unmeaning wantonness, at the time when Kandy was entered by the British, precipitated the fate of these monuments: neglected as they now are, there is nothing to retard it; and a few years will show, mingled in one common mould, the crumbling wreck of the tombs and the dust of their royal tenants.

During the continuance of the Dalada festival, the priests of Buddha, in different communities, headed by the seniors of their establishments, seemed to think it incumbent upon them to perambulate the town with their begging-dishes, and to go through the ceremony of receiving alms. These parties moved on slowly with their fans before their faces, occasionally halting to receive whatever food was offered to them, but not asking for it. It appeared to me that this was evidently more of a temporary penance than a regular practice, although to live by alms is enjoined by the rules of their order. Their sleek faces and sly looks also spoke of better fare procured elsewhere with less trouble and more certainty than wandering in heavy rain through Kandy, and waiting for supplies from the more devout portion of those professing the Buddhist religion.

An idea of the wooded nature of the environs of Kandy may be given, when I state that at this time, 1828, almost every night, elk might be heard belling in the thick jungle behind the Governor's cottage, and a leopard was drowned in a well near the middle of the town; into this it had tumbled while attempting to carry off a calf, which escaped and recovered. Since then the Governor's residence, the Pavilion as it is commonly called, has been built: although not completed to the original extent of the architect's* plan, it is a handsome and commodious building, combining in an uncommon degree the comforts necessary for a tropical climate with an elegant exterior; it is all incrusted with a preparation of fine lime, which takes a good polish, and has the appearance of white marble. This building was erected under the government and superintendence of Sir Edward Barnes; and the grounds were afterwards laid out in the time of his successor, Sir R. Wilmot Horton. From the road, which winds round the wooded hills immediately behind the Pavilion, and which is now

* Captain, now Lieutenant-colonel Brown, R.E.

known by the name of Lady Horton's road, there is a succession of landscapes, as you proceed, which I should imagine to be unequalled in richness of foliage and variety of scene. The course of the rapid Mahavilla-ganga winds below; the green hills and forest-clad mountains, rising to a height of upwards of six thousand feet, lie beyond; and this, with clumps of palmyra, tufts of cocoa-nut trees, and every variety of forest foliage, is the first of these scenes, which continue as you proceed round the walk, until Kandy and its lakes lie beneath your feet. The road has a branch to communicate with one which winds round the upper lake of Kandy, an additional distance of about two miles. The lake of Kandy is sixteen hundred and seventy-eight feet above the level of the sea. Mattan Pattanna, the hill immediately over it, is three thousand one hundred and ninety-two. The rocky ridge of Hantanna, about a mile farther off, is four thousand three hundred and eighty. Hoonasgiri Peak four thousand nine hundred and ninety, the Knuckles six thousand one hundred and eighty, Diatalawe five thousand and thirty, Aloogalla three thousand four hundred and forty, and Ettapola and Pannegaum about four thousand feet, are all remarkable features in the views seen from Lady Horton's walk.

The four great roads which enter Kandy, viz. the Colombo, Trinkomalee, Badoolla, and Kurunaigalla roads, were undertaken and most of them completed, under the government of Sir Edward Barnes.

In the neighbourhood of Kandy, as the temples are generally kept in better repair, and the propei ceremonies are more attended to, I shall describe a complete Buddhist establishment, such as the Ganga-rama (river temple) and others in the vicinity of the town. The dagoba is a solid bell-shaped building, built over some relic of Gautama; the wihare is the temple in which, before one or more statues of Buddha, the offerings are placed and prayers are chaunted; the poyagé is the house in which the priests should examine each other and instruct the people; the pansola, a dwelling for the priests. The sacred bo-tree, a slip or seed originally from that at Anurádhapoora, is planted on an elevated terrace, and surrounded with a wall on which are small altars to receive the offerings of flowers; for the bo-tree is, equally with the images of Buddha, an emblem to recall to the minds of the people the founder of their religion. The whole of these are generally surrounded by a wall, in which are numerous niches for containing lamps, to be lighted on particular festivals by those who make offerings.

Before concluding this account of my first visit to Kandy, and of the exhibition of the supposed relic of Gautama Buddha, I shall give a brief account of the Buddhist priesthood, and of the moral laws of a religion, the excellence and simplicity of which may astonish those who have only heard it mentioned to be condemned as an impure, cruel, and unintelligible portion of Paganism. That despots professing the religion of Buddha have been often cruel, cannot be denied; that its admirable laws have little power to control his nominal followers, may be admitted; yet it is unfair to charge Buddhism with the crimes of those who disobey its injunctions, defy its commandments, and dare its threats of future punishment. The history of Christianity proves how the symbol of peace may be used as the standard of war and the signal for slaughter; and it is difficult to imagine what Christianity might ere now have become, if Europe had continued unblest by the art of printing,* and had been cursed with the distinction of caste.

The religion of Gautama Buddha enjoins its followers to place reliance on Buddha, his religion, and its priesthood. It enjoins also just conversation, and strict adherence to veracity:

Just conduct, and incessantly endeavouring to counteract the effects of former sin by the practice of active virtues:

* Printing certainly checked priestcraft in its career over the subjugated minds of Christian Europe, when, from excessive use, miracles had ceased to be wonders, and the canonization of a saint was more common than the creation of a city knight. Caste, although repugnant to Buddhism, was upheld from policy by the rulers of Ceylon; and if it opposes any rapid retrogradation in the arts, it is equally effectual in preventing improvement.

Just living, earning a livelihood by honest means:

To reverence priests and your parents:

To give alms, particularly to the priesthood.*

Forgiveness of injuries is also inculcated as a matter of wisdom as well as of virtue.

This religion forbids its followers—

To envy their neighbour, or covet his property:

To follow the worship of false gods:

To commit adultery:

To indulge in unprofitable conversation, or use irritating or unbecoming language:

To destroy any animate being:

To sell the flesh of animals, or rear them for slaughter:

To trade in deadly weapons, or fabricate instruments of war, or anything to be used in the destruction of life:

To trade in poisons:

To use, prepare, or sell intoxicating liquors:

To traffic in human beings; to sell one's children, or transfer a slave:

To receive bribes:

* The priests of Buddha ought to subsist by alms only: this has induced them to clog many parts of history with the prolix accounts of alms given to priests and gifts bestowed on temples. It is not uncommon, in the account of a great monarch or fortunate individual, to find the principal part occupied by a tiresome detail of the alms he gave when animating some former body; and this is made out to be the cause of his enjoying ease and splendour in his later transmigration.

To deprive any one of his property by violence, fraud, or deception:

To tell a falsehood, or use words to conceal the truth.

Gautama thus sums up the duties of mankind:— "Abstain from all sin, acquire all virtue,* repress thine own heart." This is unobjectionable; yet how feeble, cold, and inefficient, compared with the summary of Christianity contained in the words, "Thou shalt love the Lord thy God with all thy heart, and with all thy soul, and with all thy mind; and thou shalt love thy neighbour as thyself!"

The doctrine of transmigration as believed by the Buddhists of Ceylon is, that, before attaining Neerwane, they will have to become perfect in the course of an incalculable number of incarnations in various shapes. It is thus described:† "Even as one's shadow attends only on his own person, and never on that of another, so whatever merit one may have acquired, or whatever demerit he may have incurred, adheres to that identical individual alone, and, following him into futurity, superinduces appropriate retribution."

* Gautama has compared the mortal body to a vessel externally bright and beautiful, but abounding with impurities. Again, he has compared it to a pool of water which teems with insects.

† Kitulgama Dewamitta Unanze's Compendium of Buddhism, translated by Mr. Armour.

They believe that a man may be born again as the greatest of earthly sovereigns, or as the most loathsome of the lesser insects; to revel in every enjoyment, or to suffer "all those ills that flesh is heir to."

It is unfair to conceal, and in vain to deny, that peace and pure morality are enjoined by the religion of Gautama as well as by Christianity; the latter exerts its influence over the minds of its followers not only by the perfection of its laws, but from the nature of its promises, so consonant to the hopes of man and the mercy of God. The moral duties which Christianity inculcates, the warnings in prosperity, the consolations in adversity, might all pass unheeded or unfelt, if it were not for the faint though clear light which it has shed on realms beyond the limit of the grave. That the promises or the threats held out by the religion of Gautama Buddha are insufficient to encourage to good, or deter from evil courses, may be owing to the remote period at which Neerwano is finally to be attained. Transmigration, even the animation of other human bodies, is too favourable a doctrine for those who wish to delay repentance, or the performance of strictly moral duties: he who expects to appear again in different forms will naturally reserve for them that strict propriety of conduct which may be more grateful to his future shapes than he feels it is to the body he now animates. Whatever may be the cause, the effect is certain, viz. that the moral system of Buddha has but little influence over the mass of his followers.

PRIESTS OF BUDDHA.

A novice intended for the Buddhist church is generally brought up from early youth by some priest, to whose temple, after acquiring sufficient knowledge, and undergoing the necessary examinations, he is destined to succeed: youth, however, is not a necessary qualification in the aspirant, and old men may sometimes be seen studying their rudiments with more perseverance than success. The junior pupils of a priest are often not above eight or ten years of age, as it is supposed that from early habit they will more easily become reconciled to the regularity and privations which they must, or at least ought to encounter, after entering into the priesthood; as it is easier to restrain an inclination to vices or passions, than to conquer them after they have already exerted their dominion. Although the religious policy of Buddhism requires celibacy from the priests, yet it does not suppose the form of consecration to be of that powerful and mysterious nature which endows the initiated with a character of perpetual sanctity, so that his own wish or crimes may not allow him if weak, or force him if unworthy, to retire from a situation whose ordinances he is unable to fulfil, or which his wickedness would pollute. The form of laying aside the yellow robe is simple, — little beyond throwing it into the river; and this brings no disgrace on the person who does so without crime or compulsion: in fact, from the learning they must have acquired, they are generally held in more respect than those who have always remained laymen.

The dress of a priest consists of a long yellow robe folded round the body, the end thrown over the left shoulder, and leaving the neck and right arm exposed: his head and eyebrows are shaved, but the necessity of this operation, as regards the eyebrows, is one of the points in dispute in a schism which now rages in the Buddhist church in Ceylon. In the religion of Buddha they have an institution bearing some slight resemblance to a Sunday; it is called Poya: the people ought, and the priests sometimes do observe it, and assemble four times a month at the changes of the moon, for the purpose of mutual instruction and the encouragement of religious feeling. Wasswassana somewhat resembles Lent, and continues for three months: previous to its commencement the people prepare a large building, called Banagé, (from Bana, their sacred scriptures; and gé, a house,) sufficient to protect the congregation, which assembles at night to hear the doctrines of their religion expounded by some learned priest whom they select for the occasion, and who is generally assisted by several others of less eminence in the church. The principal priest must not be absent from his station for more than six days at a time during the continuance of the Wass; and at its termination it is usual for his hearers to present him with a new robe, a fan, and walking-stick. In the Kappupuja (cotton offering) sometimes made to priests, the Buddhists clean and spin the cotton, and weave and dye the cloth before mid-day, at which time the offering of the robe is made to the priest. We find from Herodotus, that, in a feast connected with the worship of Ceres, the ministers of the solemnity had a vest woven within the space of a day.

After attending as a page and pupil on the priest of a wihare for three years, the novice may be examined, and, if found qualified, is admitted into the lowest or Samanairia order of priesthood: at the age of twenty, if he can pass an examination in one of the colleges at Kandy, he is admitted to upasampada (ordination). Every priest is attached to a wihare, which generally descends from the incumbent to the senior pupil; but some wihares are in the gift of Government, and others are at the disposal of lay proprietors. Such priests as aspire to the highest dignities in their church make themselves acquainted with the Burma and Siam alphabets, and can thus compare and study the versions of sacred Pali literature in those as well as in the Cingalese form of letters. By these qualifications, conjoined to other requisites, they may succeed in being elected to the situations of chief priests of the Asgiri and Malwatté colleges at Kandy; to one or other of which establishments every priest ought to belong. There is also a second high-priest to each of these foundations; and in the provinces some particular temples are considered to give a superior rank to their possessors while in their own district; as Anurádhapoora, Dambool in Mátalé, Ridi-wihare in the Seven Korles, and Mulgiri-galla in the southern part of the maritime provinces. Besides being correct in moral conduct, a priest cannot be ordained unless he be free from bodily deformity, and from leprosy or any visible disease. The prohibitions and ordinances enjoined as the rules of conduct to those who become priests of Buddha are extremely severe, and include all corporeal gratifications or common comforts; they are directed to look for happiness only in a correct discharge of their duties, and in the tranquillity of mind obtained by the contemplation of virtue and the hope of obtaining Neerwane. Now-a-days, besides the spiritual pride engendered by this system, and the rank which priests hold in the country, (for no native, whatever be his rank or situation, can sit in presence of a priest, nor pass one without saluting him as a superior,) they very generally evade the strict performance of disagreeable duties, and many neglect the self-denying ordinances for the more captivating employments of laymen, and the unscrupulous accumulation of property; not a few, if I may judge from their practice, consider that tranquillity of the mind may be happily promoted by comforts of the body.

CHAPTER XIV.

KANDIAN FESTIVALS.

—— Baal next and Ashtaroth,
And all th' idolatries of Heathen round.—MILTON.

Kandian Festivals. — Festival of the New Year. — Festival for Priests' Ordination. — The Peraherra. — Festival of Lamps. — Festival of New Rice. — Gods worshipped in Ceylon. — Unknown God. — Demons. — Demon Worship. — Planetary Worship. — Offerings to Ancestors. — Ceremonies at naming Children. — Marriage Ceremonies. — Funeral Ceremonies. — Floods. — Accidents. — Buddha Rays.

BESIDES the Dalada Puja, which, as I have already stated, was a rare occurrence, five annual festivals were celebrated by the King and chiefs in Kandy, with all the pomp and splendour that their circumstances could afford, or custom allow them to extort from those under their control. Although ordained for religion, and in honour of the gods, the festivals were also a source of profit to the native Kings, and a cherished rule of their policy. As the chiefs were obliged to attend, their periodical visits enabled the King to levy exactions on the estate, or to secure the person, of any influential or turbulent headman, who in his own district might have braved the power of the King and defied arrest. These five festivals are still kept up; and although they are now only tolerated, not encouraged, and without the show of regal state or compulsory attendance, still the Peraherra is an imposing spectacle.

The festival of the New Year is in April, and at that time the Cingalese indulge in the few amusements which they enjoy, and in such luxuries as they can afford. Before New Year's Day, every individual procures from an astrologer a writing, fixing the fortunate hours of the approaching year on which to commence duties or ceremonies; and to the most minute points of these instructions he religiously adheres, believing that even an involuntary omission of any prescribed act at the appointed moment would render him liable to misfortunes. The following is an abridgement, omitting the astrological lore, of one of the annual documents, prepared for my benefit by the astrologer of Mátalé, who also took care to inform me of all eclipses, and to give me special instructions in writing how to avoid those misfortunes which they might occasion. "The emblem of the approaching year will be a red lion seated erect on a horse, and proceeding from an aperture resembling the mouth of a horse; this will be at the commencement of the year, nine hours and fifty-four minutes after sunset: at this fortunate moment milk should be boiled at each of the four sides of the house." Next day I was directed to look to the north while dimbul leaves were suspended over my head, and with kolon leaves placed under my feet: then, having anointed myself with different juices and aromatic drugs, I was to dress myself in perfumed clothes of red, white, and blue colours; then to look to the south, and cause fire to be lighted and cooking to begin. On the second day, at two hours and a half after sunrise, I was to commence eating victuals prepared with pounded salt and curdled milk. At twenty-seven hours,* while looking to the east, I was recommended to begin business by paying or receiving money. The whole concluded with a prediction, that, from the situation of the planets and other cogent reasons, I might expect both good and evil to happen during the year which was about to commence.

The second festival was held in the month of May, and was principally remarkable as being more essentially Buddhist than any of the others: during this festival such Samanairia priests as passed their examinations received upasampada (ordination).

The third festival, called by pre-eminence Peraherra (The procession), commenced with the new moon, and continued until the full moon in July; sometimes longer, if the procession was interrupted

* The Cingalese divide their day into sixty hours of sixty minutes each.

by meeting with a dead body of any animal, or any object considered unclean. The procession regularly increased in splendour every night until the last; at which time it was very imposing, from the multitude of people, rich dresses, brilliant lights, and large elephants. The arms and other relics of the gods were carried either on elephants or in palanquins; and, on the last night, the casket containing the Dalada, borne by an elephant, accompanied the procession to the limits of the town, and rested at the Gedigé wihare, near the tombs of the kings, whilst the remainder of the procession passed on to the Mahawelli-ganga at Ganorooa, three miles from Kandy. There the four Kapuralls of the temples of Vishnu, Nata, Katragamma, and Patine embarked on the river in ornamented canoes, and awaited the first dawn of day: then, drawing a circle in the water with their golden swords, they filled pitchers of holy water from within the magic ring, and the procession returned to the city. The different chiefs of districts and temples, with their elephants and followers, were then permitted to return to their provinces; and there, at some particular temples, the same procession on a limited scale took place.

The fourth festival, called the Festival of Lamps, was celebrated on the day before full moon in November: the whole town was illuminated on this occasion; and the immense number of niches alongside of the canal in front of the palace, as well as in the side of the lake, being filled with lamps, had a brilliant effect from the reflections in the water.

The fifth festival was called the Festival of New Rice: it was held in January, and appears to have been intended as a propitiatory offering at the commencement of the maha (great) harvest; for the Cingalese, judging from their own feelings, consider that an offering at the commencement is more likely to secure favour than an expected thanksgiving at the end of an undertaking.

The gods to whom these processions are principally dedicated are, Saman (Vishnu), Nata, Katragamma, and the goddess Patine. Wibhisaná, who is retained as a god at Kellania and in the vicinity of Colombo, is never heard of in Kandy. Vishnu is worshipped in his form of Ramachandra, and his statues are painted blue. Of Nata's history I could learn nothing with certainty; his statues are painted white. Katragamma is the same as Kartickya (Mars), and has received the name by which he is now worshipped in Ceylon from the place where his principal temple is situated, which is at the village of Katragamma, at the south-east of the island. He is more feared than the other gods; and many of his votaries lose their health, and even their lives, in a pilgrimage through the unhealthy country which surrounds his malignant shrine. His priests are Brahmins; and, in the rebellion of 1818, they were the zealous assistants of the pretender who called himself King, and was the puppet of the rebel chief Kaepitapola.

The goddess Patine is, I believe, the same as Durga, and is invoked to protect her votaries from small-pox.

Wibhisaná was the brother of Rawana; and, having assisted Rama in his invasion of the island, was, on the defeat and death of Rawana, placed on the throne of Ceylon, and reigned at Kellania.

To the list of gods the name of Mahasen (commonly called Minneria-deyo) may be added, who, in the vicinity of Minneria, and in several parts of Mátalé, where temples have been reared to him, maintains his reputation as well as Vishnu or any of the more ancient and generally acknowledged deities. As Mahasen is a name of Katragamma as well as of the great Cingalese King, it is difficult to say whether these temples were originally dedicated to him; but I presume they were, and that King Mahasen has no legitimate claim to deification. However, in the temples of Mahasen the same warlike furniture may be found as in those of other gods; and the gigantic tanks and bridges formed under his superintendence give him a better claim to immortal gratitude than those who are only known by name as kings, heroes, and gods, although they may have conferred similar benefits on earlier ages.

When Gautama Buddha visited Ceylon, Saman

(Vishnu) appears to have been particularly worshipped, also Eiswara and Wibhisaná; and offerings were made to planets, ancestors, and demons.

The powers and attributes of the gods and demons of the Cingalese are not well defined; there are vices and crimes charged in the history of the gods, while the devils seem to respect the virtues which they do not practise, and their forbearance must be purchased by offerings and propitiatory ceremonies. The wild and wooded nature of the island, and the now thinly scattered population, naturally tend to superstition; and it may be perceived by the native histories, that, when the country was most prosperous and populous, the Buddhist religion was maintained in the greatest purity.

In the temples of the gods there is always some relic, generally connected with arms, such as bows, spears, or arrows; and if any person wished to erect a temple, he, by pretended inspiration, astrology, or other deception, proceeded to discover, with much ceremony and mystery, an arrow of the god, or some such relic, which had been hid in the spot selected for the building. The will of the god having been thus miraculously ascertained, the work was commenced; and, by permission of the King, land might be dedicated to the establishment, and have the same privileges as a Buddhist temple. The Kapuralls, or priests of a god's temple, require no other qualification than having sufficient cunning to dupe the superstitious, and bodily strength enough to enable them to go through the violent exertions and vile contortions which they exhibit, and denominate dancing and inspiration. The performance of all these ceremonies is accompanied by tom-toms, pipes, chanque-shells, halamba (hollow metal rings), and other noises, which they denominate musical. Over the principal temples are placed laymen of rank, who have charge of the revenues and are guardians of the relics; these chiefs do not take any part in the laborious exertions and insane excitement which, in this superstition, are supposed to propitiate the spirit that is invoked.

I discovered a temple in Mátalé to the Abudha Deiyo (unknown god),* and found he was patron of secret villany (Mercury).

The images of the gods are only formed of plaster and brick, neither is their workmanship or design worthy of better materials; and if this worship and its idols were to disappear, the arts would have no cause to mourn, and morality might rejoice at the extinction of an impure superstition, which has much to debase and nothing to elevate its votaries.

CINGALESE DEMONS, AND DEMON WORSHIP.

Amongst the infernal or malignant spirits enumerated by the Cingalese, some may be found as heroes who fought on the losing side in the wars of Rama and Rawana; others are national misfortunes, or bodily afflictions, to which terror has

* Acts xvii. 23.

assigned a form. Thus they have the red-eyed demon—pestilence, which carried off a great proportion of the inhabitants in the reign of Sirisangabo in the third century; also demons of the forest and the flood, tempest and malaria; demons which sport in the strong scent of unwholesome blossom-bearing trees; demons of the Sohon Pola (cemetery), who reside in tombs and rove through burying-grounds. There are, besides these, numerous personifications of natural afflictions or mental terrors. The belief in the power of these evil spirits, making them propitiatory offerings, and sacrificing a red cock* for the purpose of averting and repelling threatened misfortunes, are very general; although many, who follow these unhallowed rites in secret, loudly condemn them in public. Demon worship, although denounced by Gautama Buddha, was acknowledged by various Kings of Ceylon: Panduwas B.C. 500, Sirisangabo A.D. 239, Bojas A.D. 340, and others, made royal edicts in favour of or regulating demon worship.

PLANETARY WORSHIP.

Planets, by the Cingalese, are believed to be controlling spirits, for whom certain ceremonies and incantations are prescribed to be performed by those who at certain periods are supposed to be

* In 1305 Dame Alice Ketyll was charged with having sacrificed nine red cocks to her familiar spirit or imp.—*Croker's Researches in the South of Ireland.*

subjected to their malignant influence: these ceremonies are called Bali,* and appear to be a combination of astrology with demon worship; Bali is used to express sacrifice to the planets or to demons, also offerings to deceased ancestors. Balia is an image of clay, made and worshipped by a person suffering under sickness or misfortune: it is supposed to represent the controlling planet under which such person was born; and for this purpose, as well as on most occasions of importance, his handahana, an astrological document with which every Kandian is provided, and which contains his horoscope, is submitted to the inspection of an astrologer, who directs the necessary ceremonies.

OFFERINGS TO ANCESTORS.

Not only the Veddas, with whom it is general, but a great proportion of the population, make offerings to ancestors and disembodied spirits of the virtuous dead. The antiquity of these ceremonies may be ascertained from the Ramayan, in which we find it stated that the efficiency of a son's virtues, and a pilgrimage to Gaya, were sufficient to release a parent from hell. The offerings to ancestors appear to be intended for the double pur-

* These ceremonies are always at night, and conclude before break of day. Victuals always form part of the offering; and the whole ceremony, as well as the name, seems to be the same superstition as that of Bel and the Dragon. Bali, the controlling planets; and the Dragon, Rahu, the causer of eclipses.

pose of propitiating ancestral spirits, and relieving them from a species of purgatory.

The following account of the Rice-feast, which takes place when a child receives its name, and of the Kandians' Marriage-feast, are copied from notes furnished to me by the Honourable Mr. Turnour, and made by him when agent in Saffragam, at a time when these ceremonies were more scrupulously attended to than in later years.

CEREMONIES AT THE FESTIVAL OF NAMING A CHILD.

"The Rice-feast is so called from its being the first instance in which rice is placed in the mouth of an infant; and on this occasion the individual name is conferred on the child. The time appointed for the observance of this ceremony, as well as of the most trifling acts of ordinary life,—as the starting on a journey, the building a hut, the sowing a field or planting a garden,—must depend on the dictation of an astrologer. The selection must fall on some day in the fifth, ninth, or eleventh month after the child's birth.

"For this occasion the mother of the infant receives a measure of fine paddy, which she beats into rice with her own hands, and cooks herself. Among families of the first rank, as they are unaccustomed to such exertion, the mother holds the child on her left arm, while she drops the rice-pounder seven times on the grain in the mortar.

This is also the commencement of the ceremony with those who go through the entire process of preparing the meal. A cloth is spread, on which is laid the tender leaf of a plantain to receive the rice prepared by the mother, or the woman who represents her, should the mother be ill or dead.

"From provisions prepared by other hands a repast is served up to the relations and friends of the family who attend the ceremony, according to the circumstances of the host. When this is over, they assemble round the leaf on which the child's rice has been placed. Each according to his means deposits near the leaf a few coins, or some little trinket, which is intended as a present for the child.

"The infant is then brought forward (arrayed for the first time in the best clothing allowed to its rank) by the mother, and placed near the presents and the victuals prepared for it; from which the child is allowed to help itself according to its own taste, or rather as it may be guided by accident. The mother then places some rice in its mouth.

"The selection of the name also rests with the astrologer, in which he is guided by certain rules. From the terms by which the ruling planet of that moment is defined he has to take three initial consonants with their inherent vowels, for in chaste Cingalese, as in Pali, a scrupulous regard is paid to euphony; and these three initials are required to form a dactyle. A name so concocted must often be inapplicable to the condition in life which the infant is destined to occupy; the lower orders dare not, and the higher would be ashamed in many instances to avow the name assigned. It is not, therefore, allowed to transpire, and is only known to the astrologer and the father of the child.

"At the precise moment fixed on by the astrologer, and while the mother is feeding the child, the father approaches and whispers the name in his ear, and then blows into it: so completely is the name buried in oblivion, that not one person in a hundred is able to say what his real rice-name is.

"As the child grows up, some other name is fixed upon, referring generally to the order in which he was born, or to his complexion,—as Loku, big; Maduma, middle; Punchy, little; Ratu, red; Kalu, black: to which names, from the caste of artificers upwards, an addition is made of Naidehamy, Appoohamy, or Banda, to define his precise rank. To call these appellations rice-names, therefore, is erroneous; but it has been the universal practice to do so."

KANDIAN MARRIAGE CEREMONIES.

"Marriage among Buddhists, when contracted in due form, is preceded by the observance of many ceremonies and precautionary steps. Nothing that has a semblance of an option or pre-agency being left to the woman, the rejection of an offer of marriage is attended with more inconvenience than the ridicule cast on the rejected lover in a differently constituted society; as the objection must necessarily lie against his character, or want of equal family rank.

"To avoid this dilemma, a very convenient proceeding is adopted; it consists in getting some confidential friend to insinuate to the woman's family that a report of the marriage is abroad. If the intended bridegroom be objectionable on either of the two considerations before noticed, the family will indignantly refute the report, and the convenient friend joins in the resentment, and wonders at the idle gossip of the village; but, should the rumour be only calmly disavowed, it is understood that these objections do not apply, and a rejection on any other ground is not attended with disgrace.

"The second step is to send one of the most respectable of his relations to propose formally: at this stage a refusal is very rare, and, when it does occur, an action for defamation generally ensues.

"On receiving a favourable reply, the young woman's friends come to inspect the premises and property of the proposer: should these answer the expectations formed, a relation of the bridegroom waits on the other family with a load of four or five thousand betel-leaves. The acceptance of this present concludes the engagement, and is irrevocable by either party without incurring a legal penalty.

"The intended bridegroom then repairs to the

house of his mistress, accompanied by a few of his relations, and taking his horoscope with him. He solicits and receives her horoscope from her friends, and both are then placed in the hands of an astrologer, who decides whether the presiding planets at their respective births admit of their union. There are four ways in which configurations may take place, but an accordance in any one of them is sufficient.

"I recollect in a case tried by myself, in which a marriage was required to be proved, that the unpropitiousness of the stars could not prevent a young couple from coming together. The bridegroom's horoscope would not suit that of his intended; he produced that of his younger brother, an infant; it corresponded: the child, carried in the arms of an attendant, personified the bridegroom in the procession; and the young woman was brought home to the ill-starred youth, who dared not attend the ceremony. The marriage was pronounced legal; the evasion being only considered a pious fraud, or a suitable concession made to the will of the planets.

"In some instances the bridegroom throws a necklace round the neck of the bride at this visit, and brings her horoscope away to his own house, to be submitted to the astrologer there. The horoscopes corresponding, the astrologer is required to name a fortunate day and hour for the marriage. On that day the bridegroom repairs to the house of the bride, accompanied by as numerous a throng of relations and friends as he can bring together, (who are invited some days previously, by presenting betel to them placed on a white cloth,) and taking with him the apparel, trinkets, and other presents intended for the bride, and some prepared victuals for the guests. Before this procession moves, a messenger is sent with a parcel of betel-leaves corresponding in number with the friends who accompany the bridegroom, that the relations of the bride may know how many guests they have to entertain.

"Similar preparations are made at the house of the bride: the load of betel-leaves previously presented having answered the purpose of invitation cards, the house is decorated with white cloth, and otherwise ornamented for the occasion. When the guests approach the premises, the bride's relations, with their friends, sally out to meet the throng; taking two trays of betel-leaves with them, one for the men, and the other for the women. At their meeting betel-leaves are presented; and both parties proceed to the house, the bride's relations preceding.

"On arriving there, the bridegroom's feet are washed, if a man of rank, by a servant; and if poor, or of low caste, by a younger brother or near relation: a ring is thrown into that water, which is the fee of the washer. The guests are then seated by the host according to their respective rank, and a feast is served: should there be a great difference of rank, separate rooms are occupied during the meal. This chiefly occurs among the highest families, for the bridal party will get no one to attend their feast but their equals and inferiors; for a superior to do so, would be immediately to reduce himself to a level with that family.

"After the meal, the bridegroom's friends produce the presents brought for the bride. A board is then brought and placed in the centre of the room; it is covered with a white cloth: on this a quantity of rice is heaped, around which cocoanuts, betel-leaves, &c. are arranged so as to keep the rice in a heap; on the rice some coins are strewed, gold, silver, or copper, according to the circumstances of the family.

"On the astrologer notifying that the appointed moment is approaching, a half-ripe cocoa-nut, previously placed near the board with some mystical ceremonies, is cloven in two at one blow. The bride is then brought forward, and either by her mother or some other near relation raised up, and placed on the heap of rice, facing the direction in which the presiding planet is pronounced by the astrologer to be situated in the heavens. The mother then proceeds to strip her daughter gradually of all her trinkets and the ornamental parts of her raiment; to supply the place of these, the bridegroom brings forward his presents. He hands the bridal cloth to the mother, which is her perquisite; and in case of a divorce at any subsequent period, owing to the misconduct of the bride, the value of the bridal cloth is recoverable by the husband: all the other articles pass direct from the hands of the bridegroom to the bride. When completely decorated, still standing on the board, she hands betel to all the guests: after this ceremony, sometimes the marriage rings are exchanged, and the bridegroom then hands his bride down from the board; but more frequently, instead of the ring, a thread is drawn from the bride's cloth with which the little fingers of the contracting parties are tied together. The bride is handed down by her husband; and, when they have walked a few paces, they pull their hands asunder.

"He conducts her then to a repast prepared for them, of which one only of the near relations of each party partake; and they eat out of the same dish, in acknowledgment of their being of equal rank. After the meal, the bridegroom has to deposit some money in the dish; which, as well as the money strewed on the board, and the cloth with which it was covered, become the perquisite of the washerman. The bride is then conducted home by her husband and their friends. Until the third, and sometimes the seventh day, the married couple, and especially the bride, cannot lay aside their bridal raiment; these clothes they must have about them, awake or asleep.

"On either of those two days, early in the morning, the bride's relations come, attended by their friends, and bringing presents chiefly of eatables, the board is again placed, and the couple in their bridal dresses seated on it: a relation of each party taking a basin of water pours it on their heads at the same moment, which is followed by a goblet full of water; the bridal dresses are then taken off. After the bathing, the bride's friends pay one more formal visit, which closes the marriage rites.

"Owing to the expense, even amongst the higher classes some of these observances are omitted; and there are some which the lower castes are not allowed to adopt."

Marriages thus arranged, with a total disregard to the feelings of the girl, and where the knot is as easily unloosed as it is hastily tied, preclude the possibility of any very high standard of female chastity; even if plurality of husbands, generally brothers, and sometimes to the number of four or five, did not prevent anything like a feeling of delicacy in regard to the married state. Yet their laws are sufficiently strict, and the wife or paramour may be slain with impunity by the hand of a husband when irritated by undoubted and ocular proof of conjugal infidelity.

Returning in public the presents received at the marriage is the principal formality necessary in procuring a divorce, which is thus obtained by either party with little difficulty. Of this facility the fair sex very commonly avail themselves; and certainly are not a little capricious in their number of changes, or in the causes of dispute. The men in general are extremely indulgent husbands, and, fortunately, are not troubled with very jealous dispositions. The translation of an old saying quoted to me in the court-house of Mátalé by an unsuccessful suitor, who had claimed the aid of the law to restore an unwilling and runaway wife, will support this observation:

I've seen the udumbara tree * in flower, white plumage on the crow,
And fishes' footsteps o'er the deep have traced through ebb and flow.
If man it is who thus asserts, his word you may believe:
But all that woman says, distrust; she speaks but to deceive.

In Cingalese marriages there is no community of property between the husband and wife; and the two forms, called Beena and Deega marriage, cause a great difference in the right of female inheritance. A woman married in Beena lives in the house, or in the immediate neighbourhood of her parents, so as to be able to cook for them, and render them assistance in times of sickness or in old age; if so married, she has a right of inheritance along with her brothers. If married in Deega, that is, to live in her husband's house and village, she loses her right of paternal inheritance, and acquires new rights from the patrimony of her hus-

* A species of fig-tree, whose flowers have never been detected by the natives.

band. A Beena husband may be dismissed with little ceremony and short notice; and, in consequence, it is a common Kandian saying, "that a Beena husband should not remove any property to his wife's house, except a torch and a walking-stick, as with these he may at any time depart and find his way."

As prejudice and habit have concurred in producing the universal impression amongst Kandians that a dead body pollutes the house, they generally remove any expiring relation into some detached apartment, and place him with his head to the east. If the sickness terminates fatally, the position of the corpse is altered; the head is then turned to the west, the great toes are tied together, and the body is arrayed with the best dress and ornaments usually worn by the deceased. Only the bodies of priests, or those of the highest ranks, were permitted to be burned; others were interred in a grave with the head still to the west; and if the deceased left little property, and no relations were forthcoming, it was sometimes difficult to get persons for any hire to bear the corpse to the burial-ground.

The body of one of the principal chiefs, or any of their family, was conveyed to the funeral pile on a sort of open palanquin, borne by slaves and attended by the relations. The funeral pile consisted of alternate layers of dry and green wood, about four feet in height, secured by stakes at the sides, and with strong posts at the corners ornamented with cocoa-nut leaves. The body being placed on the pile, which is surrounded with cloths extended from the corners, the fire is kindled by the nearest relations, and the whole suddenly becomes enveloped in fierce flames and clouds of smoke. The fire is maintained until the body is consumed; and during the operation the priest, who has been called by the relations, repeats certain forms of prayer. After seven days the friends return, collect the ashes, over which a small mound is raised, and, the priest having delivered some moral admonitions, the funeral rites are over: in many cases, the mourning, except the dress of dark blue, may be said to cease with the termination of the ceremonies.

For this time the processions, and, to me, novel spectacles of native pomp in Kandy, were at an end; and the tooth, restored to its splendid tomb, has taken farewell of the public, probably for ever; for although I have since examined this relic, when it was shown to the next governor, Sir R. Wilmot Horton, and the party who accompanied him, it was in private within the temple. A public exhibition is not again likely to take place; and, if it were, not only the pomp and circumstance of outward splendour, but the enthusiasm of mind which characterised this last festival, and gave it a peculiar interest, would alike be found wanting.

The rain had now continued for four days without intermission, and the mail from Colombo did not arrive; but I had previously sent off a servant (with some baggage), who was to precede us on our return to Colombo: he, however, soon returned to give an account of the loss of the great ferry-boat on the Mahawelli-ganga, four miles from Kandy, which he had seen swamped, when about thirty people, principally priests, were drowned. Next day, being anxious to return to Colombo, a few Caffres volunteered, and took Captain H—— and myself, with our horses, across the river, which was still rolling down with great rapidity; and, as the boat was attached by a rope and pulley to a cable stretched across, we were soon hurried safely over. As we proceeded on our way, we found that many of the bridges on the road, some of them new, and one large one just completed, had been swept away; and, in consequence, we had to swim our horses over several streams, and at others, which were too rapid and rocky, to repair with planks the remains of the bridges. On the third day we were still seven miles from Colombo, and there found the country one expanse of water, in which clumps of cocoa-nut trees were standing, many of them with little of their stems, and in some places only their tops to be distinguished. The unfortunate people, whose houses or huts were overwhelmed, washed down, or floated off, (this last was a common occurrence to those huts made of cocoa-nut leaves,) were encamped in crowds under such temporary shelter of sheds, carts, or cloths, as they could devise. The rain, however, had ceased; and the extreme misery of the people was at an end. Where little clothing and less fire are required, as in Ceylon, the privations of the poor are incomparably less severe, under the accidents and calamities of seasons, than in climates of great variety and intense severity, which are called temperate.

Heavy rains happen every eight or ten years about the time of the year and moon which had been selected for this festival: their expected occurrence was in consequence delicately hinted before; and these slight notices were loudly repeated, and referred to as amounting to prophecies, when the event left the matter no longer in doubt. Living so much in the open air, the natives become good judges of the signs which precede changes of the weather; and, like all superstitious people, are apt to draw inferences from appearances in the sky regarding passing events in ordinary life.

A peculiar and beautiful meteor sometimes seen in Ceylon, and called Buddha-rays, is supposed by the natives only to appear over a temple or tomb of Buddha's relics, and from thence to emanate; it is seen by day, only in clear weather, and generally after a long-continued drought. Buddhists believe that these rays appear in the heavens as a sign to the faithful that the religion of Gautama Buddha will endure for five thousand years from the time of his death. I have often seen these bright rays sharply defined on the blue sky, and rising from one, sometimes from two opposite sides of the horizon; but on one occasion, near sunset, when in company with Captain H——, I witnessed this beautiful phenomenon arising from the four points of the compass, until the gradually expanded rays crossed in the ethereal dome.

Finding that no farther progress towards Colombo could be made without a boat, we returned to the rest-house of Mahara, and feasted on arrack and rice-cakes. Next morning, a native having procured a boat, we sailed over the rich country around Colombo, and landed near the fort,

> "While the sun look'd smiling bright
> O'er a wide and woful sight."

As I expected, so I found; that, my servant having been seen near the boat which was lost, a report had reached Colombo that I had shared the fate of the priests in the Mahawelli-ganga.

CHAPTER XV.

THROUGH MATALE TO DAMBOOL.

Sweet is the breath of Morn, her rising sweet,
With charm of earliest birds; pleasant the Sun,
When first on this delightful land he spreads
His orient beams on herb, tree, fruit, and flower.
MILTON.

Kandy to Mátalé. — Ballakadawe Pass. — Great Bee-tree. — Mátalé.—Walabanuwara. —Godapola. — King Vigeya Pála. —Venomous Snakes. — Superstitions. — Fountain of Gongawelle. — Aluewihare Rocks. — Buddhist Bible. — Cingalese Lady, One Hundred Years of Age. — First Visit to Eheylapola. — Stopped by Elephants.—Eheylapola Adikar's History; — Butchery of his Wife, Family, and Relations by the Kandian King. — Gaulama, Demon-bird. — Great Owl. — Ambokke.—Goddess Patine. — Small-pox. — Vaccination. — Parental Affection. — Curious Amusement. — Native Christian Village of Wahakotta. — Gasco Adikar, — his Fate. — Raja Singha's Treatment of the Fair Sex. — Church at Wahakotta. —Kandian Oculist.—Medical Practitioner.— Cases of Hydrophobia. — View from the Kalugalla-hella Pass. — Reach Dambool.

IN passing from Kandy to Mátalé, a distance of seventeen miles by the road formed in 1831, the Mahawelli-ganga must be crossed about three miles from the city: at the ferry, before crossing, the green hills and mountain peak of Dombara, and from the opposite side, looking back, the wooded heights and rocky range of Hantana, offer two equally beautiful and very different landscapes. From the Mahawelli-ganga the road passes through seven miles of country unincumbered with forests, until it reaches the summit of the Ballakadawe hills; from thence the eye is directed through a narrow wooded pass to the station of Mátalé, situated at a distance of five miles, and seven hundred feet lower than the top of the Ballakadawe Pass.

A tree of great size, growing near the stream in this forest pass, has for centuries marked the limits of two districts, and beyond the memory of the oldest inhabitant had obtained the name of Loku-Bambera-gaha (the great bee-tree). For eight months every year, from all its branches that stretch over the rivulet, one hundred or more swarms of bees may be seen depending; each having one large semicircular comb, of the thickness of the branch so far as it is attached, and gradually diminishing towards the edge of the circle. These insects and their labours are considered to be under the protection of a spirit, and from that circumstance remain unmolested: but in 1836, when the new road which passes near the tree was repairing, the community, having taken umbrage at some pioneers who were cutting down a hollow tree in their vicinity, sallied out, attacked the workmen, then the pioneers who were near them, and finally put to flight the whole party; many of whom suffered severely, and one carriage-bullock was stung to death. For days after this attack the bees remained in great excitement, and flying about the road in numbers, but they did not molest passengers; and at last became reconciled to the innovation on their prescriptive right of solitude.

Mátalé is an extensive valley encompassed with mountains, some of which are six thousand feet in height, but clothed with thick woods even to their summits. In the jungles are to be found cinnamon, as well as various kinds of citrons, limes, oranges, mangoes, custard-apples, and jack-fruit trees: wild plantains and cardamoms abound in some of the forests; and even coffee, though not indigenous, is now found mixed with jungle-plants, and is generally and extensively cultivated in this district. Few objects are more to be admired than a coffee-plantation at two different seasons; when in flower, and when the fruit is ripe. At the first period the stalk of every branch and twig exhibits a mass of white flowers mixed with its dark green glossy leaves; the perfume, although stronger, resembles that of a bean-field: when the fruit is ripe, the branches are loaded with berries of a rich red colour. The general appearance of a coffee-plantation is like that of a country covered with Portugal laurels and mixed with great forest-trees; as, in clearing the jungle, a portion of the shade is left to protect the plants from the power of the sun in dry seasons.

On the plain, near the station of Mátalé, commonly called Fort M'Dowall by Europeans, many foundations of houses point out the site of Walabanuwara. It was here that the King Walagambahoo established himself previous to recovering his capital of Anurádhapoora, and expelling the Malabar invaders of his kingdom, B.C. 90. Here, also, the rival Kings, or candidates for the throne, Gaja-bahoo and Siriwallaba, in the early part of the twelfth century, occasionally held their court and assembled their levies. In A.D. 1635, Mátalé and the adjacent provinces were formed into a separate kingdom for Vigeya Pála, who established the royal residence at Godapola, a small mount, to the top of which you ascend by a stone staircase of one hundred and twenty steps; the summit of this knoll is square, and surrounded by a wall with four gates. The interior buildings must have been of frail materials, as the foundations of their walls alono remain, and could be distinctly traced when lately the whole site of the palace, from the innermost chamber to the public judgement-seat at the gate, was cultivated with the surrounding parts of the royal domain. Godapola combines many advantages in its situation, and commands a varied and beautiful prospect; while its position on the verge of the Hunusgiri mountains rendered escape easy, and concealment secure. In the forest which covers these mountains, and three miles from the palace, are to be seen the ruins of a building called Kandénuwara (hill station), which had been prepared as a place of refuge in times of danger, and was occupied by the King before he finally abandoned his dominions to a younger brother, the warlike and ambitious Raja Singha. Vigeya Pála sought protection from the Portuguese, adopted their religion, and died in a monastery at Goa.

An immense variety and number of snakes, both harmless and poisonous, are found in this district, as well as in most other parts of Ceylon; but it is inconceivable how few fatal accidents happen from their bites. The hooded snake (cobra de capello) is very numerous, and frequently attains to upwards of six feet in length; but different kinds of polonga are justly considered much more dangerous, being less active in removing from your approach, and their poison being more deadly. Yet I have known a native to recover from the bite of a very large tic-polonga; he was a wedarall (native medical practitioner), and, being near his own house when the accident happened, was carried there in a state of insensibility: on rallying, he helped himself to their usual remedies, and eventually recovered; but for months after he felt great numbness, not only in the leg where he was bitten, but in the whole of that side. One part of his treatment was having a thin earthenware vessel filled with live charcoal placed on his head; as for the numerous vegetable compounds which he took internally, it is a pity that the effect of each individual plant or preparation could not be separately examined, to ascertain the efficient cause of cure.

The only death which occurred to my knowledge from the bite of a snake in the Mátalé district, during a period of nine years, was from that of a hooded snake; and I have little doubt the man's life might have been saved if he had applied to one of the native practitioners in time. He did not, however, state the cause of his illness until a day after he had been bitten; and gave as a reason, that, within that time, any one who knew of the bite and wished him evil would have their wish gratified. This is some remnant of a former superstition; probably the worship of the hooded snake, called in Cingalese, Nága. The Nágas inhabiting the western coast of Ceylon, and converted by Gautama, were probably of this class of worshippers; and in no part of the country inhabited by the Cingalese do you find the people willing to put this snake to death. In the Kandian country they often catch hooded snakes, and then convey them at night and release them on the grounds of some other village.

The pimbera, a species of python, is not uncommon; the largest I saw measured was seventeen feet in length, but I have been assured from good authority that they reach a larger size: they twine round their prey like the boa, are not much dreaded by the natives, and seldom seize any animal larger than a jackal.

In the Mohammedan village of Gongawelle, a very large spring of pure water rises in a basin of white sand, which is surrounded by a wall and overshadowed by trees. This fountain, in ancient legends, is said to have sprung up beside Seeta (Lakshmi), wife of Rama, who, twenty-four centuries before the Christian era, rested here when Rawena compelled her to journey from Lankapoora to the forests in the interior of the island.

Two miles from Mátalé, on the side of the new Trinkomalee road, are situated the Aluewihare rocks, which look as if a portion detached from the great mountain above had been precipitated into the plain, and riven by the shock into those pinnacles and rude masses which are heaped together in so extraordinary a manner. A single solitary cocoa-nut tree grows in a recess amongst their clefts, and waves its thin stem and scanty leaves over the highest of the rocks; amongst which large flights of blue rock-pigeons have hitherto found protection, from the sanctity of the place and the tenets of Buddhism. I suspect, however, that their privileges will not now be of very long continuance; and that, between the increase of fire-arms and the decay of Buddhism amongst the natives, the pigeons will soon disappear. To replace the cocoa-nut tree, I planted several in the same cleft of the rock.

Amongst the recesses of these crags the doctrines of Gautama Buddha were first reduced to writing, and under their huge masses many temples were formed at a very early period. These temples were destroyed by the British troops in 1803, and only two out of eight have been since restored. On one of the highest pinnacles is a print of Buddha's footstep, similar to that on Adam's Peak, from which it is copied; and a small hollow is formed in the rock near it, for the purpose of receiving the offerings of the pious. On a neighbouring crag are the remains of a dágoba, and amidst its scattered fragments a stone cut into twenty-five compartments; in the centre one of these the relic of Buddha had been placed, and the remaining cells in the stone had contained the offerings made when the relic was deposited. Through the middle of the Aluewihare rocks there is a broad natural street of unequal height; to reach this you must ascend a flight of rude steps, then pass through a crevice, and again ascend until you come upon a flat rock, which is pointed out as the spot where the King Walagam-bahoo assembled the priests, who here compared their texts, which were then, or soon afterwards, committed to writing, and form the Banapota or Buddhist Bible. This took place about ninety-two years B.C.; and for two hundred and fourteen years previous to that time, if not from the date of Gautama's death, his doctrines had descended by tradition only.

A member of an ancient family settled from time immemorial in the village near these temples, and to which they possess the right of appointing priests, was a lady one hundred years of age, who repeatedly walked to the court-house, and obtained my interference to control her undutiful grandsons. Even at that great age, she maintained with spirit her authority over her own estate against her troublesome descendants, and her faculties remained unimpaired by their present misbehaviour or her own former misfortunes; amongst which were numbered the beheading of her husband as a traitor by the exiled tyrant, and the hanging of her son as a rebel by the British Government.

My first visit to Eheylapola was made soon after my appointment to the military command of the Mátalé district, in November 1828, for the purpose of inspecting a detachment of troops stationed there, and with the intention of returning to my own house to dinner. At that time I had no idea of the number of elephants which infested and ravaged the country; and had started in a palanquin with eight bearers, and attended by a Lascoreen carrying a double-barrelled gun, one barrel of which was loaded with small shot. Having been delayed longer than I expected, it became dark; and on my return, when still five miles from Mátalé, a herd of elephants was ascertained to be a little way before us in the path: this, however, they abandoned on our advancing; which we did every one at the same time shouting at the utmost extent of his voice. About a mile further we encountered another herd in possession of the way: on them our clamour had no effect; and at last, as their leader showed every disposition to charge our party, we disposed of ourselves in different trees on the road side. I scrambled into one which grew on the bank of a stream, it also overhung the road; and, as the animals were evidently bound for the water, I was ready to fire at the leader, in which case I hoped to release myself and party from our present dilemma. I forgot to mention, that, in aid of our first noisy demonstration, I had fired off the barrel loaded with small shot, without producing any effect on our stubborn opponents. With a herd behind as well as before, there was no way of sending to the village, about a mile distant, to procure chules (bundles of dried cocoa-nut leaves, which make a great blaze when lighted); and we had already waited three hours, when a boy volunteered to go by a buffalo path through the forest, and reach the village. As he had to pass near the elephants, all those in the trees made a great noise to prevent the animals from hearing his footsteps; and, in less than half an hour after his departure, we were gratified by the blaze of numerous lights: as they approached, the hitherto persevering brutes in front drew off with great quietness, and about ten o'clock at night we were released from our absurd detention, and resumed our journey.

Eheylapola is situated nine miles from Mátalé, and is a large house with extensive grounds surrounded by an elephant fence: this was the usual place of residence of Eheylapola Adikar, of whom a short account may be interesting. He was the representative of one of the most ancient and influential Kandian families; and, being gifted with much shrewdness and considerable ability, became a favourite both of the Kandian King and the people of those districts which were entrusted to his authority. After having filled subordinate situations with more affability than was usual with natives of his rank, he was appointed Dessauve (collector) of Saffragam; in 1806 he became second Adikar; and, when Pilâmé Taláwe was beheaded in 1812, Eheylapola succeeded him as first Adikar. In 1814 Eheylapola having received insults from the King, which were a sure prelude to this chief's destruction, the inhabitants of Saffragam offered to support him against the tyrant; but he, ever suspicious, and already prepared, gave them no time to arrange opposition. The King immediately announced the dismissal of Eheylapola, and the appointment of Mollegodda as first Adikar. This person, now entrusted with the chief authority under the King, lost no time in collecting a numerous force, and entered the secluded district of Saffragam by the shortest way, which leads over Adam's Peak.

Eheylapola fled to Colombo; but many headmen,

who were known to be attached to his interests, or suspected of having promised him support, were sent as prisoners to Kandy, and there put to death by torture.

The King, enraged at the escape of this influential chief, and neither satiated by the number of victims nor the excess of the tortures inflicted on those he had already sacrificed, determined on a deed, the perpetration of which stamps him as the most brutal monster that ever possessed the human form, or prostituted sovereign power to the gratification of malignant passions. The wife and children of Eheylapola were seized by order of the King, and doomed to death with several of her relations. She and her children, four in number, were brought from the house where they had been confined, to the street in front of the Queen's apartments in the palace, and between the Vishnu and Nata temples: the eldest of the four children was eleven years of age, the youngest was still at the breast. Each of the children was beheaded in succession; and, the head being then placed in a rice-mortar, the mother was compelled to go through the act of pounding her mangled infants. The youngest was snatched from her breast, and the milk from its mouth actually mingled with its life-blood a moment after. It appears extraordinary that any woman could go through such a scene; still more so the fortitude and propriety of her conduct, as detailed to me by a follower and eye-witness, who at this time narrowly escaped being impaled, and was afterwards rewarded for his fidelity by Eheylapola. Some details, which are preserved in Dr. Davys' account of this transaction, my informant was not near enough to overhear; but they fully corroborate the dignity of her conduct, and show the extraordinary spirit of one of the children. The threat of disgraceful tortures in case she failed to comply with the orders of the infernal tyrant was probably the stimulant which enabled her to go through the most awful scene to which any mother was ever subjected. The butchery of the children having been completed, the mother and some female relations were led to the Bogambera tank and drowned.*

* Extract from Sir Robert Brownrigg's (the Governor) official declaration to the Kandian chiefs after the taking of the Kandian country.

After mentioning "the wanton destruction of human life" by the King then a prisoner, Sir Robert Brownrigg proceeds:—

"One single instance of no distant date will be acknowledged to include everything which is barbarous and unprincipled in public rule, and to portray the last stage of individual depravity and wickedness, the obliteration of every trace of conscience, and the complete extinction of human feeling.

"In the deplorable fate of the wife and children of Eheylapola Adikar these assertions are fully substantiated; in which was exhibited the savage scene of four infant children, the youngest torn from the mother's breast, cruelly butchered, and their heads bruised in a mortar by the hands of their parent; succeeded by the execution of the woman herself and three females more, whose limbs being bound, and a heavy stone tied round the neck of each, they were thrown into a lake and drowned."

This was in 1814; early the following year the British army took possession of the Kandian country, and the King was seized in a hut where he had secreted himself, by a party of Saffragam people, headed by Eknellegodda, a friend and adherent to Eheylapola. The British protected this tyrant from the vengeance of his subjects, and supported him for sixteen years as a prisoner at Vellore, with an allowance greater than for years he had been able to collect from the impoverished country over which he had ruled. This expenditure I cannot consider as an act of generous sympathy to a fallen monarch or brave man; but as a weak and culpable extravagance, in providing so well for an inhuman monster whom accident had raised to be a King, and whose own crimes had rendered an outcast.

Eheylapola made himself very popular with the Kandians previous to the rebellion which was raised against the British Government in 1817: he was then arrested on suspicion, and subsequently transported, without being tried, to the Mauritius; at which place he died in exile A.D. 1831, aged about fifty-six years.

From the best information, I cannot doubt the perfect knowledge and concurrence of Eheylapola in the treasons of his brother-in-law Kaepitapola, who was the principal leader in the rebellion; but his confidential followers were of opinion that his object was not so much the expulsion of the

British, as the hopes of being able in some manner to take revenge on the first Adikar, Mollegodda. He had formerly known this chief as a cruel enemy, seconding the wishes and enforcing the orders of the exiled tyrant; and now saw him, as a successful rival, continued in possession of the highest Kandian dignity under the British Government. Eheylapola, however, had declined the situation of first Adikar, offered to him by the Governor, Sir Robert Brownrigg; and his subsequent conduct renders it probable that he looked higher, and felt disappointed at the arrangements made by the British on their taking possession of the Kandian country.

It was while stopping at Eheylapola, on my way to the native Christian village of Wahakotta in January 1829, that I first heard the wild and wailing cry of the gaulama, or demon-bird; a sound which by the natives is considered as a sure presage of death or misfortune, unless they take measures to avert its infernal summons, and refuse its warning.* Although often heard, even on the tops of their houses, they assert it has never been caught or distinctly seen; and they consider it as one of the most annoying of the evil spirits which haunt their country. The veracious but sometimes cre-

* The protest of a native under fear of this bird is somewhat analogous to De Wilton's in Marmion:

"Thy fatal summons I deny,
And thine infernal lord defy."

dulous Knox, when a prisoner with the Kandians, after hearing its cry, pronounced it to be a devil.

It is probably a species of owl, of which there are many different kinds in Ceylon; but certainly its cry is far more disagreeable and melancholy (and more like that of a human being in distress) than any other proceeding from that ill-omened tribe. At Mátalé I shot an owl, which had perched on the top of the house after passing close to a person who was standing in the verandah; so soft was its noiseless progress, that, although the bird measured five feet three inches across the wings, its flight did not appear to stir the air in the slightest degree: this bird nearly corresponded with the description of the eagle-owl as given by Bewick, and the great horned owl of Audubon.

Nine miles beyond Eheylapola's house (and eighteen from Mátalé) is situated the village of Wahakotta, on the range of hills extending between the Seven Korles and Mátalé. In the forests on the side of Ambokke Kande, a mountain which forms part of this chain, are situated the remains of Rangalla Nuwara, and at its base a temple of the same name is dedicated to the goddess Patiné. This goddess, and this particular temple of Ambokke, or the relics it contained, were supposed to be of extraordinary efficacy in preventing or averting small-pox; so that, when that dreadful disease raged in Mátalé, the Kapurall (priest) of Ambokke was in constant request, and reaped an abundant harvest from the terror and superstition of his neighbours. Every village in the vicinity of an infected place, by means of presents nominally offered to the goddess, and the most valuable of which were appropriated by the Kapurall, procured his presence and the relics from the temple: these, a shield and bangle (armlet), were borne through the village, followed by all the inhabitants, and duly honoured by the noise of every tom-tom, pipe, chanque-shell, or trumpet which they could procure. The Kapurall had been at a former period afflicted with the natural small-pox, and was shrewd enough to have his own family vaccinated; after which his supposed temerity in visiting infected villages, and his good fortune in escaping contagion, were accounted for by himself, and believed by the people to arise from the protection of the goddess. His influence from this circumstance was considerable, and I had reason to believe that his selfishness prompted him to use every underhand means of checking the progress of vaccination amongst the dupes by whom he was enriching himself.

It is difficult to conceive the terror inspired amongst the natives by the certain intelligence of small-pox having broken out in the district; and on my proceeding to the village where it first appeared, in order to ascertain (before a hospital was commenced) that it was not chicken-pox, I discovered the body of a woman, who had but lately expired, lying in a field with her head close to a well. Tormented by thirst, and deserted by her friends, she had crept to the water whilst in the last agonies of this loathsome disease. By permission of her relations, I offered her property, including a portion of land, to whoever would bury the body; but nothing I could say or do would induce any one, even the most wretched pauper, to acquire independence by interfering with a corpse marked by the wrath of their gods.

The next case I saw was that of a man lying near the door of his house; and even the strongly marked and well-known features of an inferior priest of the goddess Patiné, were so disfigured, that I could not recognise them in the blind, helpless, hopeless object whom I addressed,—the same person who had a few days before been successful in preventing several of his neighbours from profiting by vaccination when I had visited the village with a medical practitioner. I turned the melancholy state of this man to the advantage of many, by contrasting the real security of those who now accompanied me, and had been vaccinated, with the hideous mass of disease—all that remained of this false teacher and factious opposer of authority. A man of weak intellect and eccentric habits, who had occasionally been employed as a labourer near my house, then came up and requested I would look into his house. I did so, and found three persons, (the oldest about eighteen years of age,) of which his family consisted, lying in a small room: they had evidently been carefully attended to by the old man, one of the very few in whom feelings of affection for his family had overcome the terror inspired amongst the Kandians by this disease, called by them Mahalaida, (the great-sickness,) and which they also believe to be a direct infliction of the gods. The father gently lifted their heads, and turned their disfigured countenances towards me: one was already dead, and another was just expiring; the case of the third seemed desperate: he civilly accepted the medicine which I offered, and joyfully received some sugar, for this is an article that Kandians use in all their own medicines, and when sick are very anxious to procure. Next morning I was informed that, on the death of his second daughter, the old man in a paroxysm of grief caught up the only survivor, and, carrying her several miles over a mountain before morning, laid her down beside a temple in another district; there he made his offerings, and then bore back his charge. The affectionate parent was rewarded by the speedy recovery of his daughter, who had probably benefited by the cool mountain air.

The small-pox at this time was checked without very great loss of life; and the active measures afterwards taken to supply vaccinators, and to induce the natives to profit by their exertions, will, it is hoped, prevent any very extensive ravages from a cause which has formerly contributed materially to the depopulation of the island, and is probably the red-eyed demon of pestilence who is recorded to have swept the country of half its numbers in the third century, and in the reign of Sirisangabo.

One of the very few active amusements which the Kandians pursue, is connected with the superstitious worship of the goddess Patiné; and is more intended for a propitiation to that deity, than considered as an indulgence, or pursued as an exercise. Two opposite parties procure two sticks of the strongest and toughest wood, and so crooked as to hook into one another without slipping; they then attach strong cords or cable-rattans of sufficient length to allow of every one laying hold of them. The contending parties then pull until one of the sticks gives way, and this event is announced by shouts from the adherents of the victorious piece of timber; which, after being gaily ornamented, is placed in a palanquin and borne through the village, amidst noisy rejoicings, often accompanied with coarse and obscene expressions. The inhabitants of Wahakotta profess the Christian religion, and are the descendants of Portuguese prisoners taken by Raja Singha, and of some of their countrymen, who preferred retiring into the Kandian country in 1640, to remaining under the Dutch Government.

My present visit to this village was for the purpose of inquiring into a dispute between the Christians and their heathen neighbours, in which I found both parties to blame. I could not trace any difference of features, character, or colour, between them and the Kandians of pure descent. These descendants of Europeans were not so dark, and were also free from the muddy complexion and rough skin so common amongst those wearing hats and styling themselves descendants of Europeans in the maritime provinces.

A Portuguese named Gasco, who had been taken prisoner when a boy, was afterwards raised to the rank of Adikar by Raja Singha; and is the author of many popular poems in the Cingalese language. Gasco was in high favour with the King, but, while still a very young man, the too decided partiality of the Queen cost him his life; the last act of which is believed to have been the composition of some verses, and these still remain as a proof that the judgment of the King was warranted by the guilt of the favourite. One of the verses contains in plainer language the following sentiments:—

> Those thou hadst smil'd on found a tomb,
> While love requited lights my doom;
> Not for soft look or faltering sigh
> I boldly dared and justly die!

Raja Singha's treatment of the fair sex may have been partly in consequence of the frailty of his Queen having still farther stimulated a selfish, cruel, and tyrannical disposition: it is thus described by Knox, who was his prisoner for twenty years.

"His right and lawful Queen, who was a Malabar brought from the coast, is still living in the city of Kandy, where he left her, but hath not been with him these twenty years.

"He hath many women about his kitchen, choosing to have his meat dressed by them. Several times he hath sent into the country a command to gather handsome young women of the Chingulayes to recruit his kitchen, with no exceptions whether married or unmarried; and those who are chosen for that service never return back again. Once, since my being in the land, all the Portuguese women who were young and white were sent for to the Court, no matter whether maids or wives, where some remain until now; and some, who were not amiable in his sight, were sent home; and some, having purchased his displeasure, were cast into a river, which is his manner of executing women: others were sent prisoners into the country, and none admitted to speech or sight of them.

"Often he gives command to expel all the women out of the city, not one to remain; but by little and little, when they think his wrath is appeased, they creep in again: but no women of any quality dare presume; and, if they would, they cannot, the watchers having charge given them not to let them pass. Some have been taken concealed under man's apparel; and what became of them all may judge, for they never went home again."

At this time, in the Christian church at Wahakotta, might be seen a small figure of the Virgin Mary wearing a silver cocked-hat (which decoration was no doubt intended to be reversed, when it would have looked like a crescent), a diminutive Christ on the cross, and both completely eclipsed by a long St. Michael wearing a tinsel kilt. Christianity, preached by the Nestorians, appears to have made considerable progress at a very early period amongst the inhabitants on the northern coasts of Ceylon; and Sir John Mandeville, in the fourteenth century, says that "in that isle (Ceylon) there dwell good folk and reasonable, and many Christian men amongst them."

In those early periods I cannot find any trace of Christianity having been introduced amongst the Cingalese natives; and conclude that the Nestorian converts were entirely confined to the mixed races inhabiting many parts of the eastern seacoasts and the northern lowlands. In later times it was from the inhabitants of the island of Manár, and the isles and coasts of the Jaffna district, that St. Francis Xavier and the Portuguese Catholics made their most numerous proselytes; for, in 1544, the person who styled himself King of Jaffna, a Malabar by descent, and a follower of Siva in religion, caused six hundred of the inhabitants of Manár, converts or followers of the Christian faith, to be massacred. The suppression of his establishments, the exclusion of his faith, and the slaughter of his followers, roused the energies of the indefatigable Xavier: yet the fleet and forces he received from the Portuguese authorities proved insufficient; and the expedition, with which he sailed from Cochin in 1545, was compelled to return, leaving the massacre of the Christians unavenged, and their persecutor unpunished.

Within a short distance of Wahakotta lived a celebrated Kandian oculist, whom I afterwards employed to cure a pony of a disease which in Ceylon is common to cattle and horses, but never attacks human beings: it is a worm that is somehow received into the aqueous humour of the eye; this it first distends, then dims its colour, and eventually destroys vision. The applications which this practitioner used were, I believe, all preparations or portions of vegetables, and seemed to give great pain to the horse; but the cure was complete, the insect was destroyed, and the eye eventually recovered its transparency.

The native medical practitioners are certainly acquainted with medicines of very powerful effect in relieving complaints of the eye; although in those, as in most other diseases, they often do mischief from their ignorance of anatomy. They are particularly successful in their management of boils and tumours (common afflictions of the Ceylon climate); and, amongst many different forms of treatment, occasionally make most daring and extensive use of the actual cautery.

The usual mode of payment to a medical practitioner amongst Kandians ensures his utmost exertions to accomplish the cure of his patient, as on that depends his own remuneration. Not trusting to the gratitude or generosity of the invalid, the fee, in money or some article, such as a cloth, brass dish, or article of jewellery, is deposited before the case is undertaken; if unsuccessful, the pledge is restored: a desperate case they will not undertake, unless paid in advance. In their medical books, along with much absurdity, it is probable that some information and many valuable medicines might be discovered by any one competent to examine their directions, and analyze the number of things which they enjoin to be compounded in the most trifling prescription: perhaps the number of ingredients is only to conceal the simplicity of the only useful component part.

The native doctors acknowledge their inability to cure hydrophobia, saying they can heal the bites, but the gods must do the rest. Three months is the time after which they consider any one safe who has been bitten by a mad dog; but in this they are mistaken. A man employed in my service who had been severely bitten by a mad dog, after a lapse of three months obtained three days' leave from me that he might go and make offerings at a particular temple, according to his vow and the advice of his doctor; he returned on the third day evidently unwell, and was soon after seized with spasms; being a man of strong constitution, he struggled for seven days before death released him from hopeless sufferings. His wife, who had been bitten at the same time as himself, was not attacked with hydrophobia, although much frightened by her own prospect and the death of her husband.

At one time, when mad dogs were very numerous in the Mátalé district, mad jackals were also to be met with; and two men, who had lain down to rest in an open shed, were severely bitten by a jackal, which, from their description, was evidently in a rabid state: as these men were travellers, I did not learn their fate; but I have known an instance of a horse dying from the bite of a mad jackal.

One day, in that same season, I discovered that three terriers, which I had inherited from the commandant who preceded me, were wandering about the house, all of them suffering from hydrophobia, and one of them so far gone as to be unable to close his mouth: in that state I repeatedly saw the animal put his head to the water; whether he contrived to lap any of it I was not near enough to ascertain. They were destroyed without having done any mischief. A few days after this, a servant standing near the door of a room in which my family were sitting, seeing a strange dog rushing in, snatched up a rice-pounder, which fortunately lay within his reach, and killed the animal at a blow; soon after, a half-armed crowd appeared, and recognised this as the mad dog of which they were in pursuit.

It was about the same time that, when riding out one evening, I met a moorman who had been severely lacerated by a mad dog; but the wounds healed up in about three weeks. Six weeks after he had met with the accident, some of his friends came to me in the court-house, to report that he was so furious during the paroxysms of hydrophobia with which he was attacked, that they had been compelled to fasten him up in a house, and had given him anything they thought would be of service to his disease through a hole in the wall; they added, that he was rolling on the ground gnawing the earth, and had been in this state for two days.

They were so anxious for me to send the man something in the way of medicine, that I advised them to try opium; and for this purpose a pill, as large as a man could take with impunity, was procured from a Malay in the neighbourhood: with this the friends of the moorman departed; and the next report was the man's death, which had taken place a few hours after their return. They all agreed that he took the opium (but they could not have seen whether he swallowed it or not); and that afterwards the man was able to drink a cup of rice-gruel, and another of coffee; that the spasms then returned, and he expired.

From the extremity of the mountains, which terminate abruptly near Wahakotta, the view over the flat country that extends to the northernmost parts of the island is extremely curious, from the many detached rocks and precipitous mountains which shoot up from amidst the forest which covers the extensive plains of Nuwarakalawia. At sunrise, (which was the time I arrived at the verge of the Kalugalla pass,) and for some time after, until the sun had obtained sufficient power to dispel the mists, partial fogs assumed the exact appearance of lakes: some of these, calm and undisturbed, reflected surrounding objects; while others, agitated by a slight breeze, dashed their mimic waves against the forest which appeared to bound these beautiful illusions.

The descent from the mountainous district at this place to the flat country beneath was through the wild, wooded, and romantic pass of Kalugalla-hella (or the hill of the Black Rock); from which I emerged at Gallawella, and, proceeding ten miles on the straight road from Colombo to Trinkomalee, reached Dambool.

CHAPTER XVI.

CAVERN TEMPLES OF DAMBOÔL.—THE KALAWA TANK. —MOUNTAIN OF MEHINTALAI.

And, as she entered the cavern wide,
The moonbeam gleamed pale;
And she saw a snake on the craggy rock,—
It clung by its slimy tail.

H. KIRKE WHITE.

Rock of Dambool. — Pilgrims. — Excavated Temples — of Maha-Deiyo. — Law-suit and Perjury. — Gigantic Statue. — Maha-Raja Temple. — Native Painting. — Passpilame and Alut Temples. — Inscription. — Extensive View. — Game. — Elephants. — Dambool Kapurall killed. — Remains of the Kalawa Tank. — Immense Embankment. — Ruins of Vigitta-poora; — its Siege, B.C. 162. *— Ticks. — Mehintalai.—Ascent by Stone Steps. — Antiquities. — Mihindu and Sumitta. — Ritigalla.—Elephant killed with an Arrow.—Tusk Elephants. — Height of Elephants.*

THE rock of Dambool, in which are the celebrated Buddhist cave temples, appears to rise about five hundred feet above the surrounding forests: on the north side it is bare and black; to the south, its huge overhanging mass, by some art and much labour, has been formed into temples. The only easy ascent to these is from the eastern side; and the steep path first passes over a bare shelving rock, then lies through a narrow patch of jungle, from which you again issue upon the bare rock near the miserable gateway which forms the entrance to the platform in front of the ancient fanes of Dambool. As I was up before sunrise, I passed various parties who had arrived the night before: some were still reposing on the rock; whilst others, who had also rested there, were already dressing themselves, and arranging their clothes before proceeding to the temples.

The first of the excavated chambers which we entered is generally called the Maha-deiyo-dewale, or temple of the great god; this appellation is derived from a statue of Vishnu, supposed to possess peculiar sanctity, and before which the most serious oaths were often sworn, and cases of importance decided without any other trial: this was when one of the parties agreed to abide by the oath of the other, to be given in a specified form before this statue of Vishnu, which is a coarsely executed figure, rather larger than life, and in the form of Ramachandra.

The following coincidence of events added considerably to the fame of this temple; which, however, was finally put an end to as a place for swearing parties or witnesses by the charter of 1832, and the consequent practice of judicial courts. For a long period disputes about property had been carried on with great personal animosity amongst the brothers of one of the principal chief's families, called Puritgelle; and one of them in a fierce dispute cut off the arm of another with a bill-hook; death ensued from this wound, and the survivor in the fray was transported. Two remaining brothers had now resolved their hostility into the legal shape of a civil suit for certain portions of land; this they pursued with the utmost rancour, and supported their respective pretensions by an uncommon proportion of perjured witnesses. Previously to the trial, both parties agreed that their witnesses should be sworn to the truth of their evidence before this statue of Vishnu; and after the examinations were concluded, the whole adjourned to the temple here, to vouch, in the presence of their god, to the truth of the falsehoods they had uttered before my court. None of them flinched from their statements, but a hooded snake was seen twisting round the statue of Vishnu while they were in the act of swearing; this circumstance was officially reported by the head-priest, and was seen by the court-messenger who was sent with the parties. At the same time I heard of the daughter of one of the parties having been bitten by a hooded snake in her father's house during his absence thirty miles off, at Dambool. The girl recovered after severe suffering and a long-continued illness.

Although the great fame of this particular temple is derived from the poor statue of Vishnu, the chamber contains a gigantic and well-executed figure of Buddha recumbent; and the statue, as well as the couch and pillow on which he reclines, is cut from the solid rock. This figure is forty-seven feet in length; at its feet stands an attendant disciple, and it is opposite to the face, in a dark corner, that the statue of Vishnu is placed. This chamber is long, narrow, and dark: Gautama Buddha's position and placid aspect, the stillness of the place, all tend to impress the visitor with the feeling that he is in the chamber of death. The priest whispered that the positions and figures were exact in resemblance and size—that such was Gautama, and such were those who witnessed the last moments of his mortality; to favour this illusion, the priest took care to keep the face shaded, by holding the lights in a particular position.

The fronts of all the temples at Dambool are formed by a wall raised under the beetling rock, and these sacred caverns are partly natural and partly excavated. The next temple into which I entered is by far the largest and the most imposing in Ceylon; it is all painted in brilliant colours, and every part is in good repair. I believe its name of Maha-raja wihare, (temple of the great King,) arises from its founder King Walagam Bahoo, having personally assisted in its formation; it is one hundred and seventy-two feet in length, seventy-five in breadth, and twenty-one feet in height near the front wall. The height from this place gradually decreases in the arc of a circle towards the floor on the interior side; but the bad effect of this formation is much diminished by a judicious distribution of the statues, and the drapery hung up to protect them from dust, or the gaze of the vulgar. In this temple are fifty figures of Buddha, many of them larger than life; also a statue of each of the gods Saman, Vishnu, Nata, the goddess Patiné, and of the Kings Walagam Bahoo, and Kirti Nissanga; Walagam Bahoo was the founder of this wihare B.C. 86. Kirti Nissanga after repairing the dilapidations occasioned by Malabar invaders in A.D. 1193, caused all the statues to be gilt, and ornamented the fanes of Dambool in such a manner, that it obtained the appellation of Rangiri, the golden rock. It is also called, in an inscription of that date cut in the rock, Swarna-giri-guháya — cave of the golden rock. Within the Maha-raja wihare there is a finely proportioned dágoba which touches the roof at the highest part; and in a small square compartment, railed in and sunk two feet below the level of the floor, a vessel is placed to receive water, which constantly drops from a fissure in the rock, and is exclusively kept for sacred purposes.

The whole of the interior, whether rock, wall, or statue, is painted with brilliant colours, in which yellow much predominates; in one place the artist has attempted to depict that portion of the early history of Ceylon which commences with the voyage of Wejaya, who is represented in a ship with only the lower masts, and without sails; in the sea are seen fishes as large as the vessel, and lotus-leaves of the natural size are spread on its surface. In representing the building of the great dágobas at Anurádhapoora, the proportions are not better preserved, and these artificial mounts of masonry are depicted but a little larger than the persons employed in completing them. The most successful attempt in historical painting is one which describes the single combat between Dootoogaimoonoo and Elala, the drawing of which is by no means deficient in spirit, and is considerably more correct in its proportions than any other of the historical compartments. The Malabar King is represented in the act of falling from his elephant, and transfixed by the javelin of his enemy. The following account of this combat is extracted from Turnour's literal translation of the Cingalese history in Pali, called the Mahawanso.

"The Raja Dutthagamini consulted with his mother. At her recommendation he formed thirty-two strong ramparts. The King displayed in each of these posts personifications of himself, with a royal standard-bearer attending on him, while the monarch himself remained in an inner fortification.

"King Elaro accoutered for battle, and supported by his military array, mounted on his state elephant, Mahapabbato, advanced on him. At the commencement of the onset, the valiant Dighajantu, with sword and shield in hand, striking terror by the fury of his attack, springing up eighteen cubits in the air, and piercing the figure which represented the King, took the first rampart. In this manner having carried all the other posts, he approached the fortification defended by Gamini the raja himself.

"The powerful warrior, Súranimilo, shouting out his own name to him who was rushing at the King, taunted him. The one (Dighajantu) incensed, and replying 'Let me slay him first,' made a leap at him: the other met the assailant with his shield, saying to himself, 'I will demolish him and his shield at once.' Dighajantu slashed at the shield with his sword: the other cast the shield at him. Dighajantu plunging at that unresisting shield, fell with it; and Súranimilo, springing up, slew the prostrate (enemy) with his sword. Phussadéwo sounded his chank, and the army of Damilos gave way: Eláro rallied it, and many Damilos were slain. The water of the tank at that place was discoloured by the blood of the slain; and from that circumstance the tank has been celebrated by the name of 'Kulattha.'

"The monarch, Dutthagamini, then making this proclamation by beat of drums, 'No other person but myself shall assail Eláro,' accoutred for combat, mounted on his well-appointed state elephant, Kandulo, in his pursuit of Eláro, reached the southern gate. These two monarchs entered into personal combat near the southern gate of the city. Eláro hurled his spear; Gamini avoided it, and making his own elephant charge with tusks the other elephant, and hurling at the same time his javelin at Eláro, he and his elephant both fell together there.

"There this conqueror in the field of victory, surrounded by his martial might, reducing Lanka under the shadow (of one canopy of dominion) entered the capital. Summoning within the town the inhabitants of the neighbourhood within the distance of a yojana,* he held a festival in honour of King Eláro. Consuming the corpse in a funeral pile on the spot where he fell, he built a tomb there, and ordained that it should receive honours (like unto those conferred on a Chakkawatti †). Even unto this day, the monarchs who have succeeded to the kingdom of Lanka, on reaching that quarter of the city, whatever the procession may be, silence their musical band."‡

The ornamental paintings in the temples of Dambool, where proportion is not of paramount consequence, are very neatly executed; and although some of the colours have not been renewed for upwards of fifty years, the whole appears bright and permanent. The Passpilame (western), and

* Yojana, a distance of sixteen miles.

† Chakkawatti, a King over tributaries.

‡ The remains of the tomb, and the custom alluded to, still exist at Anurádhapoora

two alut (new) wihares are formed on the same plan, but are inferior in size and ornament to the Maharaja wihare; in one of them is the statue of the King Kirti Sri, the last royal benefactor of Dambool, and a zealous supporter of Buddhism.

On the rocky platform, which extends in front of all the temples, a bo-tree and several cocoa-nut trees have been reared, and have attained a great size, despite their bare situation, equally exposed to tempests, and to the scorching heats and long droughts to which this part of the country is particularly liable. Besides an inscription on the rock over the entrance to the temples, and several short inscriptions in the square character called Nagara,* there is, near the Maha-Deiyo temple neatly cut in the rock, a long inscription in the Cingalese character as in use towards the end of the twelfth century. It records the power, wealth, and meritorious acts of the King Kirti Nissanga, and particularly his munificence in ornamenting the temples and gilding seventy-two statues of Buddha at Dambool. I devoted a day to the examination of the temples and their measurement, in which, after shutting out his pupils and securing the doors, I was assisted by the High-Priest. On the following morning, before sunrise, I ascended to the summit of the rock, which commands a most extensive

* Many, if not all, the letters in this character are the same as the alphabet lately discovered and arranged by Mr. Princep in his excellent journal of the Asiatic Society of Bengal.

view over the surrounding country; to the south lay the mountains of Mátalé and their intermediate valleys; the flat country immediately around was the patrimony of the temples, and under the superintendence of the priest; on the north and east lay the wooded expanse and abrupt rocks of Nuwara-Kalawia. The most conspicuous of these are, the circular rock of Sigiri, once the capital of the island; Dahiakande, near the fort of Vigittapoora, memorable for its siege two thousand years ago; and the mountain of Rittigalla, rising to a height of two thousand feet above the plain, by which on every side it is surrounded. The rock of Dambool was formerly surmounted by three dágobas; these have crumbled down, and their remains have been washed into a pond in the bare rock. Although situated only fifty feet from the summit, I believe the priests are correct in asserting that this pond was never known to be without water, even when in very dry seasons the springs for miles round were dried up.

On the west side of the rock of Dambool are the ruins of the Soma Dágoba, which was completed by Walagam Bahoo in the first century before the Christian era: the numerous inscriptions at this place appear to be a mixture of the ancient Cingalese and Nagara characters.

From the top of the rock, in a small field immediately beneath, I could distinguish a herd of elephants, with deer and wild hog interspersed;

I also perceived in the same open space pea-fowls disporting and their plumes glistening in the rays of a level sun. At this time elephants were so numerous in the neighbourhood of Dambool, that a rough ladder was placed against every large tree on the sides of the paths in order to facilitate the escape of travellers. In 1835, the Kapurall, priest of Vishnu, a shrewd and intelligent man, met his death while endeavouring to sustain his character of elephant charmer, in the face of a wounded and savage rogue-elephant. The Kapurall had accompanied a party of gentlemen, who were deer-shooting, into a copse, and they, coming accidentally upon the elephant, wounded him with balls which were not of sufficient size to prove mortal: the animal continued to charge the party; the Kapurall stood forward, and while holding up his hand in an imposing attitude, was seized by the uplifted arm, which was torn from his body, and the elephant passed on, leaving him a mangled corpse.

As Dambool lay in the centre of the district in which I was agent, it often fell in my route when visiting other parts of the country; and from hence, in 1832, I proceeded in company with Mr. Turnour to examine the remains of the Kaláwa tank, and search for the foundations of the Fort of Vigittapoora, We established ourselves at the village of Mahaellegamma, twelve miles from Dambool, near the embankment of a large tank which is in good preservation, and contains a supply of water sufficient to irrigate a large extent of rice-land. From this place to the sluice of the Kaláwa tank is seven miles; and in that direction, as well as towards the rising grounds of Dambool and Kandepallé on the one side, and Nikini seventeen miles from Dambool on the other side, the country bears the appearance of being occasionally overflowed; and probably this tract of country was all included within the limits of the immense reservoir. We found the double sluice of the Kaláwa tank in perfect preservation, built of very large blocks of hewn stone extremely well joined; and, as is the case with all tanks intended for the purposes of irrigation, the outlets for the water were on a level with the lowest part of the interior excavation.

The spill-water is a great mass of solid masonry, and the length of the principal embankment, according to the account of our guides (and also from other sou.ces of information), I believe to be about five miles; at one of the places where it had burst, I ascertained the sides of the chasm to be seventy feet in height. Other lateral embankments of still greater length, but of less height completed this stupendous work, which, in a much more contracted form, had existed for many centuries before it was improved and enlarged by the King Dásenkelleya, a short time before he was murdered A.D. 477. The remains of this tank alone, constructed under a very disturbed reign, and immediately after long continued wars with the Malabars, who had only been expelled from the capital a few years before, shows that then a great population existed under the control of a despot who could direct their labours.

A canal called Jayaganga was cut from this tank to Anurádhapoora, and is calculated to have been upwards of sixty miles in length.*

From the sluice of the Kalawa tank, after cutting a path a mile in length through thick, low, thorny jungle, we reached the remains of Vigittapoora. This place is mentioned in Cingalese history as early as B.C. 504, at which time it was the residence of the second King of the Mahawanso (great dynasty), Panduwâsa; and here he established one of his Queen's brothers, (a son of Amitódana, and cousin of Gautama Buddha), who was afterwards known by the name of Vigitta. The fort here was built by Elála the Malabar invader; and, previously to his defeat and death, it stood a siege of four months, when it was attacked by the Cingalese under the command of Prince Dootoogaimoonoo: the following is the conclusion of the siege as described in the native history, the date being 162 B.C.

The assault having been determined on, Kadol the famed war elephant of the Cingalese prince was directed against the eastern gate, up to which he rushed through a shower of weapons and weighty

* Turnour's introduction to the Mahawanso.

stones that were hurled at him on his near approach to the walls. On reaching the entrance, a party of the besieged who were stationed over the gate, commenced pouring down molten lead, which, falling on the elephant, he became ungovernable, and fled to shelter himself in a small tank near the walls. Kadol's wounds having been dressed, and his body fortified against similar attacks by cloths thickly folded, and shielded over with plates of copper, he was again brought to the assault, and succeeded in forcing the gate, at the same time that others of the assailants entered by a breach in the walls of the fortress.

Vigittapoora is situated in a marshy plain near two rocky hills; and being considered one of the most noxious places in an unhealthy district, we found it overgrown with jungle, its temple in ruins, and the dágoba, which is forty feet high, and terminated by an octagonal pillar, completely obscured by trees and vegetation: two lines of an inscription in the Nagara character are cut in one of the stones near this dágoba. The walls of the fort, not more than three feet in thickness, were easily traced, as also a ditch which surrounds them, and the tank mentioned in the account of the siege as the place in which the elephant took refuge from the missiles of the defenders. The fort appears to have been a square redoubt, each side of which, as near as we could judge, for the thick jungle prevented a minute examination, being about one hundred yards in length. The walls had been of brick raised on stone foundations, and much of the materials of this stronghold were probably employed in the construction of the dágoba, which was erected several centuries later, within its enclosure.

Whilst stooping down to examine the sluice at the Kalawa tank, I suddenly found myself completely overspread by that greatest of living torments within the tropics, viz. ticks. From the effect of their bites I suffered much inconvenience for several weeks, and was obliged to leave this very warm part of the country immediately, without waiting either to complete the business which had brought me down, or to make some farther excursions which I had projected in Nuwarakalawia. Ticks are to be found in all the dry parts of Ceylon; often banded together in lumps containing several thousand, they remain attached to some leaf, which, if touched by an unwary passenger, discharges a shower of these pestilent vermin, which soon make their presence known by bites resembling the application of red-hot needles, followed by intolerable itching. Ticks, although some times much larger, are in general about the size of a pin's head; they are round, hard, flat, and adhere with wonderful pertinacity to the skin of men or animals, into which they occasionally contrive to introduce themselves. They disregard all attempts to kill or remove them by any application except actual force; but the natives having the benefit of much practice in putting to death other animals of similar habits, pick off, and subject them to interdigital trituration with much ability and zest; their practice in this respect corresponding with that of the most classical nations of civilized Europe.

It may, however, be satisfactory to those who may visit tropical climates to know, that the longer they remain in them, the less are insects and their bites regarded ; and the sojourner of ten years standing, may hear with complacency, what he had often listened to with impatience, particularly on first landing. "Don't scratch moschetto bites," which is a warning commonly offered in sincerity by old residents, and neglected from necessity by new comers.

In September 1832, I again started to visit Mehintalai, (the ticks having compelled me to abandon that purpose the previous year, at the only time I had disposeable) and proceeded to Anurádhapoora as mentioned in the account of that place.

The road from Anurádhapoora to Mehintalai,* although now in some places only a forest track, was a carriage road B.C. 307, as the King Daveni-peatissa sent his carriage to convey the priest Mehindoo to the capital, from the mountain of Mehintalai.† The path at first leads for upwards

* This rocky mountain, or parts of it, is mentioned by various names in the native histories, viz. Piyal Kula, Missako, Chetiyo, Saegiri.

† Turnour's Mahawanso.

of a mile along the embankment of the Nuwara-wewa (city lake), and then proceeds through the jungle at the northern end of this tank: six miles from the centre of the city the path becomes much wider, and has on each side continued mounds of decayed bricks, the remains of one of the principal streets of Anurádhapoora.

Having passed two other tanks, the last of which, called Bulian-colom, is eight miles from the Sacred Tree, and reaches to the foot of the rocks, I arrived at the granite steps, which are twenty feet in length; and, although many are broken and others displaced, still by them the ascent of Mehintalai is easily accomplished even on horseback. I commenced counting these steps, but the task becoming tiresome, I referred myself for information to the resident priest, who declared the number to be one thousand eight hundred and forty. This number I have since found to coincide with ancient records, which state that these steps were completed by the King Maha Dailiya, who reigned from A.D. 8 to A.D. 20; but the amount must include the steps which lead to the highest part of the mountain, on which are the ruins of the Etwihare. Ascending from a landing-place of considerable extent, on which are the foundations of large buildings, a long flight of steps led to a more extensive flat, on which is situated the Ambastella dágoba, the dwellings of the priests, and various ruins. On every side, this spot is surrounded by masses of granite; some of these are of considerable height and difficult access, and all are sanctified by legends, attested by crumbling monuments, in which were deposited those relics which procured for Mehintalai the epithet of Solosmastané (the place of the sixteen relics).

On the consecrated pinnacles of this mountain lingers the faint twilight of an early history, which connects the records of another race and their forgotten prophets with the dawn of Cingalese literature and the permanent establishment of Gautama Buddha's religion by the priest Mihindu. The appearance of former Buddhas at this place, is mentioned in several religious legends; and although the events regarding them are few and uninteresting, yet the extent of labour, and different stages of decay which appear in the weather-worn steps (even those cut in the solid rock), evince the remains on this mountain to be the work of successive generations, and of different and far distant ages.

The principal dágoba of Mehintalai derives its sanctity from the relic it contains, viz. the Aurnaroma, a hair which grew on a mole between the eyebrows of Gautama Buddha. The Ambastela dágoba is situated on the spot which Mihindu selected for his conference with the King Deweni-piatissa, whom he here encountered on returning from the chase: the broken statue of this king, in an attitude of respectful attention now lies at a short distance from this monument, half covered with rubbish, and almost concealed by rank weeds. The bed of Mihindu is pointed out on one of the rocky pinnacles which overhang the plain; this bed is merely a level space on the rock, five feet long by two feet broad; it is elevated about an inch, as the surface around has been cut away to that extent: over it rests a mass of rock with a natural arch open at both sides. This curious eyry of a hermit must be cool: it also commands a most extensive view; but having a precipice on either side, to reach it is difficult, to recline on it would be perilous.

Mehintalai derives its present name from Mihindu, son of Dharmasoka, King of India. Mihindu was a priest of Buddha, who arrived in Ceylon B.C. 307, and was followed by his sister, the priestess Sumitta; at the same time Dharmasoka forwarded the branch of the sacred tree and many other relics of Buddha, accompanied by a numerous retinue from his capital of Patalipura. Mihindu and Sumitta, who is also called Sanghamitta, having renovated and firmly established Buddhism in Ceylon, continued in the island, and died, the former B.C. 259, in the eightieth year of his age, and the latter B.C. 258, in the seventy-ninth year of her age. The date of their arrival in Ceylon is occasionally used as an era, B.C. 307, after the death of Gautama Buddha 236 years.

The view from Mehintalai is said to extend from

sea to sea; on the west are the tanks and temples of Anurádhapoora, showing from amidst the thick forest that obscures the city; the formal-looking hill of Saingliamalai is on the far north-east, with a religious ruin on its summit ; and the high mountain of Ritigalla rises abrupt and rocky on the south-east. The native traditions are probably correct, in stating that the caves and residences of Yakkas * are still to be seen in Ritigalla, for these aborigines are mentioned as resisting at this place one of the chiefs of Dootoogaimoonoo and a numerous force, B.C. 160. I was anxious to visit this mountain and search for the remains of the Yakka habitations, but my time was limited, and I could not overcome the terrors and prejudices of those who lived in the neighbourhood; they denied any knowledge of how the mountain could be ascended, and avowed their dislike to trespassing on this stronghold of the devils. On the rocks of Mehintalai are long inscriptions in the Nagara character, which have not yet been translated ; but the letters resemble those on the columns of Hindostan, whose secrets have lately been disclosed by the judicious exertions of Mr. Prinsep and other oriental scholars on the continent of India. There are also very long inscriptions in the ancient Cingalese character, of date A.D. 222 ; some of these define the duties expected from the priests of the establishment, the manner in which the revenues are to be disposed

* Yakkas (demons), demon worshippers.

of, and the treatment to which the tenants and servants of the temple are to be subjected.

As I was returning from Mehintalai by a path that led through the bed of what was the Kalawa tank, I was much inconvenienced by the sudden setting in of the rains, which in some places laid the country under water, so that our track was only discernible from being freer of bushes than the surrounding space. The path, also, being lower than the ground near it, served as a channel for the water to flow in, and leaves, at least a foot deep in some places, were borne along by the current towards the tanks. Such a deposit may well account for the periodical unhealthiness of this district; and the sickly season for remittent and intermittent fevers, is immediately after the setting in of the rains. On several occasions, when the rain ceased and the waters ran off, fish, some of them six inches long, were found floundering in the path: it is when the country is in that flooded state that the crocodiles spread themselves about, and may be found in very small ponds and temporary puddles.

Near Mahaelligamma, I met a Veddah whom I had employed some time before to kill a tusk elephant, and as he had been successful, I was interested to see the weapon he had used, and the manner in which he had proceeded. I found the remains of the animal in a low, thick, thorny jungle, which a European could neither have crept under nor have forced through; but even with the unfavourable circumstances of position, the hunter had contrived to steal close up to the elephant, and to shoot him dead with an arrow, which, entering between the second and third ribs, had pierced the heart. The bow used by the Veddah was not of great strength; the arrow-blade was very thin, sharp, one foot three inches long, and one inch and a quarter broad at the centre, from which it tapered off to the stalk as well as the point; the shaft was made of very light wood, and was two feet and a half in length.

The Veddah informed me, that if he had been unable to strike the animal in the heart, he would have struck another arrow in the flank, in which case the elephant would soon have taken to water, and there have remained until it died. It is always easy for those Veddahs, who are denizens of the jungle, to trace the wounded animal by the foot-marks, even if it should have mixed in a large herd; nor is this so difficult as might be supposed by a person unaccustomed to examine the shape and to attend to the habits of these ponderous animals, for their features and wrinkles, defects and peculiarities, are on so large a scale as to be easily observed, and enable one, after a little practice, to recognize any elephant which he may have been in the habit of seeing.

The greatest proportion of the Ceylon elephants, particularly those with tusks, have part of their head and ears of a flesh colour. speckled with brown spots about the size of a pea, and in some the greatest part of the body is thus mottled; yet I have never heard of a white elephant having been seen in Ceylon: although they do not seem to be very uncommon in Siam.* Tusk elephants are rare in Ceylon: taking the proportion of those I caught while in charge of an elephant-hunting establishment, not more than one in fifty have tusks; and it is yet unknown whether there is any other material difference between their formation and that of the more common Cingalese elephants. All tusk elephants are males, although proportionably few males have tusks; the remainder, like the females, having short tushes, which always incline downwards, and never project more than six or eight inches beyond the mouth. Tusks on the contrary, invariably incline upwards from the middle, although occasionally almost straight; and those of a full-grown elephant vary from two to seven feet in length. Some tusks are much curved, some are turned out, while others project straight forward, or across one another in front of the trunk: the weight of tusks is as various as their appearance, and by no means depending upon their length. I have seen a pair of Ceylon tusks weighing upwards of one hundred and fifty pounds; but sixty pounds may be considered a fair weight for the tusks of a full-grown elephant.

Tavernier, who travelled in the middle of the

* Finlayson's Mission; Crawford's Embassy to Siam.

seventeenth century, says "Though the elephants of Ceylon are the smallest, they are the most courageous; yet only the first elephant which the female produces has any tusks." Several particulars concerning elephants mentioned by this traveller, have been disproved since their habits have become better known; but whether there is any truth in the above quotation I am unable to say. I never heard it in Ceylon, and am inclined to think that if the first male produced by every female elephant had tusks, tusk-elephants would be more numerous than we find them to be.

Notwithstanding the assertions I have heard and read about the great size of elephants, I am incredulous; for I have never seen but one that exceeded ten feet in height; and even in this one's height we might be mistaken, as, although a tame elephant, he was a sulky fidgety brute, and could not be correctly measured. Out of several hundred driven into kraals in my presence, only three were above nine feet in height; yet Finlayson, (who had been sometime quartered in Ceylon,) in his Mission to Siam, declares that the elephants which he had seen in Ceylon were of greater size than those of the Ultra-Gangetic peninsula.

CHAPTER XVII.

TO THE LAKE OF MINNERIA AND THE ANCIENT CAPITAL OF POLANNARRUA.

Along these lonely regions, where retir'd
From little scenes of art, great Nature dwells
In awful solitude, and nought is seen
But the wild herds that own no master's stall.

THOMSON.

Start for the ancient City of Polannarrua. — Tala-trees — their Leaves, Flowers, Fruit. — Mee-trees. — Flying Squirrel. — Flying Fox. — Jungle Path. — Accidents to Post-office Runners. — Mortality amongst Wild Animals. — Horse-keeper Killed. — Curious case of circumstantial Evidence.—Baggage-Bullocks. — Wild Buffaloes.—Lake of Minneria.—Resthouse. — Temple. — Mahasen. — Evening at the Lake. — Buffalo-Shooting.— Snipe-Shooting. — Fishing.—Minneria to Polannarrua. — Large Elephant. — Polannarrua — its Extent. — Ruined Temples. — Rock Temples and colossal Statues. — Bears. — Inscriptions. — Great Mass of Stone conveyed eighty Miles by Land. — Cingalese Royal Race.

ON my route to visit the ancient capital of Polannarrua, and search for the position of the fort of Sigiri, I was accompanied by Captain H—— and Lieutenant B——. We set out in April 1831; our first stage being to Nalandé, which, although only fifteen miles distant, yet has not the same moist and pleasant climate as Mátalé; even at a distance of five miles from the latter place, coffee gardens are more rare and less productive; cocoa-nut trees scarcer and less luxuriant. At Nalandé, land-leeches are never seen; at Mátalé they are a never-failing nuisance. Beyond Nalandé the Tala, commonly called talapat-tree by Europeans, is seldom to be met with. In some late accounts of the talapat-tree of Ceylon, there is so much exaggeration, and so little accuracy, that a few facts regarding these chieftains of the race of palms may not be unacceptable. In 1832, from one spot in the Mátalè district, the flowers of twelve tala-trees were visible, rearing their white pyramid of plumes above the continued expanse of jungle foliage; many more were in flower at the same time, and within the same range, but they were hid by the inequalities of the ground. The size of these trees, in favourable situations, varied from eighty to one hundred and ten feet in height, without the flower, which in some instances gave an addition, as nearly as I could judge, of twenty-five or thirty feet. The trunk of the tala is straight, but retains a mark wherever there has been a leaf, and the circumference near the ground is from seven to eight feet. I was unable to ascertain correctly the age of these trees, (for I believe them all to have been the seed of the same year,) but so far as I could discover, it did not exceed eighty years. With a tala-tree, the moment of its perfection is also the commencement of its dissolution; the fruit, which is about the size of a chesnut, and produced in great numbers, ripens by degrees as the flowers decay; the leaves then wither, the upper part of the trunk and the roots decay; and the only remaining part of the stem lies prostrate on the ground about twelve months after it first began to shoot up the great spike which is the covering of the flower. This spike and its branches are from two to three months in reaching their full size; the flower then begins to appear from the extreme point, and from this time until all the minute stalks and numberless flowerets are disclosed, elapse about three months more; the remainder of its existence is but a course of rapid decay. The leaves are largest when the tree is about twenty years of age, and are comparatively small when it has attained its utmost size, and exerts all its vitality to develope its flowers and perfect its fruit. The leaf is of a form which enables it, without any preparation, to be folded like a fan; it is fifteen or sixteen feet across and (with the addition of the stalk) from the point of the leaf to the extremity of the stalk, where it is united to the tree, is sometimes twenty-five feet. These leaves are used as umbrellas and for thatching houses; they are also formed into tents; and when prepared in strips, from two to three inches broad, and twenty to thirty in length, they form the leaves of Cingalese books.

The immense quantity of seed produced by every tree, is spread by the flying fox, (vampire bat,) the flying squirrel, and other creatures, over a great extent of country; these seeds all spring up, yet, unless in enclosed places very few survive, as the young leaves are greedily devoured by every animal that feeds on vegetables; it is this circumstance which has given rise to the erroneous idea, that tala-trees are not found wild in Ceylon.

The Nalande rest-house is over-shadowed by two mee-trees of great size; but the heavy and disagreeable scent of their flowers, more than compensates for the advantage of their shade. The mee-tree has a small white flower, which sometimes falls in such profusion, as to cover the ground for several inches in depth; and in those districts where mee-trees are abundant, the natives assert, and I believe with reason, that if rains wash down and accumulate quantities of flowers on the surface of the tanks, a noxious effluvia proceeds from the mass, and gives rise to malignant fevers. Aware as all the natives are of the danger, yet because the fruit of the tree yields a useful oil, the people refuse to lay the axe to the root of the evil. In Ceylon, although many are strongly scented, there are but few trees whose blossoms have a disagreeable smell; while in some jungles, particularly where the various kinds of wild jessamine, orange, and citron trees abound, the perfume in the early morning, or when the sun has gone down, is peculiarly delightful.

Around the tala, the wild mangoe, or almost any fruit-bearing tree in this part of the island (when its fruit is ripe), as evening closes the flying squirrel may be seen approaching, — now leaping from branch to branch, and when some forest glade intervenes, ascending to the highest bough of the loftiest tree. As yet there is no marked difference between it and any other squirrel; but, look again, it has sprung from the still quivering twig (a hundred feet above), and at once assumed a form as unlike what it was the previous second as can well be imagined. It now appears quite flat, about eighteen inches square, and with a long tail projecting from the middle of one side: without any farther exertion or the slighest noise, it seems to float through the air towards its object, only its flight is still getting lower, until depressing its tail when near and a little below the place it is about to alight on, the creature glides upon the branch, and in its original shape resumes its course along the boughs of the trees. Flying squirrels are very numerous in the lower parts of the Mátalé district, and do much mischief in the cocoa-nut gardens: the largest I have seen was two feet eight inches in length, including the tail, and was not inaptly described by my Scotch servant, to whom it was brought, and who had neither seen nor heard of such an animal before, as a "flying cat."

The very large and hideous-looking bat, commonly called the flying fox, abounds in most parts of Ceylon, and may be seen in thousands suspended by the wings from the branches of some decayed tree; they may always be perceived in the evening hovering round fruit-trees; and at night may be known by the flapping of their leathern wings, or, if they pass near where you stand, by their offensive smell. They generally move in flocks, and will strip a mangoe-tree of its fruit in a few hours.

From Nalandé we proceeded by the jungle-path, which, in 1831, was the only road leading from Colombo and Kandy to Trinkomalee; it passed through a wooded desert, the haunt of wild animals, and particularly elephants, in such numbers as to render travelling, without fire-arms, unsafe. Several post-office runners were killed by them in 1829-30; and the body of one of these unfortunate men was not found until after a long search, when it was discovered on the top of a thick bush near the road side, where it had been thrown by the elephant that killed him. Although the marks of the animal had been observed at a short distance from the bush, the peculiar position of the corpse prevented its being discovered, until beasts of prey assembling at the place excited attention; the mail parcel was found uninjured, and fastened round the waist of the unlucky messenger.

In October 1831, elephants, wild hog, and deer, died in great numbers in this forest, and the mortality extended to Minneria and other parts of the adjacent district, but the inhabitants were not affected. There was neither scarcity of water nor any apparent cause for this plague amongst the wild animals, but it is remarkable that in the same month of the following year (1832), Trinkomalee was visited by that awful scourge the spasmodic cholera.

From Nalandé to the lake of Minneria, is a distance of thirty-six miles, in which we halted at the post-houses of Nyakoombura, Gonáwe, and Paecolom; near the former place there is a small village with a few rice-fields, which formed the only break in a damp and dreary jungle, from whence issue streams that flow into the sea at opposite coasts of the island.

When within two miles of Nyakoombura, hurrying on to avoid nightfall, and to escape from a threatened storm of lightning and rain, we came suddenly on a pony, (which I had sent in advance some hours before,) standing over the body of my old horsekeeper as it lay stretched at full length on the back, and swimming in blood. The tempest commenced, and darkness closed on us as we were examining the locality of the catastrophe; but I compelled the unwilling attendants to convey the body to the rest-house, and there after minutely examining the ghastly corpse, we caused it to be interred. There was a mortal wound, a stab entering above and inside the left collar-bone, and passing (as we found by probing with a small cane) right down through the heart. The deceased was a very short man, and from the nature and position of the wound, my two friends and myself, in the absence of all information, formed an opinion that he had been wilfully murdered by some person, by means of a long and very sharp instrument. The mouth of the pony had been rubbed with blood, and also his foot, and then pressed down upon the white jacket worn by the deceased, for the purpose of making it appear that the horse had bitten or kicked the unfortunate man; these circumstances as well as the direction of the wound, showed design, not accident, and I was well aware that the pony was much attached to the deceased, who usually slept in the stall beside him. I immediately despatched messengers in different directions, and several persons who could not give any satisfactory account of themselves were arrested. On being brought before me they all cleared themselves of any suspicion regarding the crime for which they were detained; but one of them was recognized as a man who had stolen his master's plate and escaped, and of this crime he was afterwards convicted. For eight days no circumstance transpired that could throw any light on the subject of the supposed murder; but I then obtained proof that a confidential Lascoreen (court-messenger) who had charge of my baggage, and also the grass-cutter, had been seen very near, actually at the spot, proceeding apparently amicably in company with the deceased, and about the very time when his death must have occurred. I had already had the statements of this Lascoreen and grass-cutter, which now turned out to be false: and numerous connecting links in the chain of circumstantial evidence, induced me to commit them both for trial for the murder. Before they were sent off, the Lascoreen expressed a wish to make a second statement; and then detailed what afterwards proved to be the truth, although at the time it appeared absurd and incredible. The Lascoreen's statement was to this effect:—"That contrary to his orders, he had allowed the deceased to purchase some arack as a present for his acquaintances in the neighbourhood of Nyakoomboora, in which place he had formerly lived for some time as servant to the post-holder. The arack was carried in a long-necked French bottle, tied in a handkerchief and slung from his wrist: in passing a narrow part of the path, the bottle striking against a rock was broken in such a manner, that all that remained was the bottom (which still contained a little of the spirit) and attached to it a spike, the whole height of the bottle. This spike had sharp edges, a sharp point, and altogether resembled a Malay criz. The deceased continued to lead the pony, with the remains of the bottle still slung on his left arm, until he arrived where there was a hole or step in the road, of nearly two feet deep, formed by water in the rainy season flowing along the path and falling over the root of a tree. On this root the deceased stumbled, and pitching head foremost into the hole, fell on the spike of the bottle: he instantly pulled himself up, fell back, and expired." The Lascoreen proceeded "afraid and flurried, and recollecting that, contrary to your orders, I had allowed him to purchase arack, and that I might thus be blamed for his death, I desired the grass-cutter (who had only been hired by the deceased the day before) to deny all knowledge of the manner of the deceased's death, and to say that he was some distance before us, and that on coming up we found him dead. I then took the broken bottle and handkerchief, and threw them as far as I could into the jungle; after this, I became sick and fainted, and it must have been at this time that the grass-cutter marked the pony's mouth, and placed the animal's hoof over the wound and upon the jacket of the deceased. I had only recovered from fainting immediately before the gentlemen came up." At the time of hearing this statement I was thirty miles from the place, but immediately despatched persons to examine the surrounding jungle, and these returned bringing the long, slender, and brittle weapon uninjured, although it had been thrown to a considerable distance. Rain had fallen in torrents since the event occurred, yet the blood could still be traced in the curved side of the glass, which exactly corresponded to the cut made in the jacket of the deceased at the time he received his death-wound. In this case there were so many minor circumstances which bore strongly against the Lascoreen and grass-cutter, but which were all explained by the discovery of the handkerchief and glass dagger, that, had the latter not been found uninjured, (and its preservation may be considered providential,) the life of a valuable and long-tried servant would have been in the utmost jeopardy. So much importance did I attach to the safe conveyance of this most extraordinary weapon, that I would not intrust it to any one, and proceeded to Kandy, where I personally delivered it to the judicial commissioner. After a careful examination of the case, the charge hitherto so strongly supported by a chain of evidence was abandoned, and the parties released. This adventure had a considerable effect on my after-conduct as a judge, and also on my opinion as regards the infliction of capital punishment in particular cases.

In traversing the forest of Wagapanaha, a very few openings, and an occasional glance through the trees on our left, showed us the rugged outline and abrupt rocks which form the range called Arrawella Kande, lying near and parallel to our route. Two herds of elephants, a few pea-fowl, jungle-fowl, and troops of the large black monkey called Wandura by the Cingalese, served to afford us some amusement while passing through the forest. We also met several Moormen traders returning from the maritime provinces with salt, conveyed upon droves of loaded bullocks: these were the only beasts of burden employed, and formed the only means of conveyance for goods in the Kandian country previously to its being opened by carriage-roads, commenced under the government and direction of Sir Edward Barnes. Long before we came in sight of these droves of baggage cattle, we were made aware of their approach by the loud shouts of the drivers encouraging the animals; also by the various sounds of bells of different shapes, sizes, metals, and even of hard wood, depending from the necks of the animals. This combination of sounds no doubt affords them protection from the wild animals of the forests through which they pass; and, however rude, has a pleasing and cheerful effect when heard in the dreary jungles of a wooded district.

Six miles beyond Paecolom we passed through a low range of hills; on one of which, Nuwara Kande (the hill of the city), Mahasen Raja resided in the third century while superintending the formation of the neighbouring tank of Minneria, whose glassy lake and radiant plains soon burst on our view. As we emerged from the forest, we saw our baggage coolies (who had gone in advance) brought to a stand, and ready to take shelter in the surrounding trees from the threatened attack of a wild buffalo. This superb animal was standing in a menacing attitude, and advanced in front of a tame herd, with which he escaped into the jungle after receiving a wound from one of our party. So different was the appearance of this animal from that of any of the tame buffaloes of Ceylon, that I can hardly suppose domestication and labour could produce so marked a distinction: and many of the tame buffaloes are only so called by courtesy; and have no other claim to the epithet than their descent by the female side, an awkward shape, and being the private property of owners who catch and brand them when young. I know more than one instance where sportsmen, proud of their success in wild buffalo shooting, have had their triumph cut short, and their purse lightened, by having to pay the value of these brutes; as the owner was able to point out his mark, which had been branded on them when calves.

From the great extent and irregular form of the lake of Minneria, I could hardly imagine it a work of art; and, although its waters are now confined to little purpose, and the neighbouring plains contain but a few sickly inhabitants, better government will gradually restore cultivation, and health with increasing population smile on the "twenty thousand fields" which the magnificent and royal architect formed together with the lake which was to render them productive. Formerly there were several artificial lakes covering a much larger surface than that of Minneria, but they no longer exist, and probably never will be restored; as they would not repay the necessary expenditure required for repairs and to preserve them against accidents.

Having passed along several canals, and through many muddy rice-fields, we reached the rest-house of Minneria: placed in the worst situation which the neighbouring country afforded, it commanded no view either of the forest-covered hills or the lake which they enclosed. To reach the rest-house from any side, the approach was through mud-fields and swamps, by which it was everywhere surrounded, and by which it was in a manner cut off from the road which passed along the high and hard banks of the tank: its position excluded everything worth seeing in the surrounding country, and at the same time combined all the different causes which are supposed to produce unhealthiness. I mention this, as the rest-house and the Minneria line to Trinkomalee were abandoned on the formation of a cart-road in 1833, which passes about ten miles to the north of the lake; and it is highly probable that the very injudicious choice of a site for the rest-house may have been the principal cause why this country, so full of every kind of game, and possessing such beautiful scenery, was shunned by all except those whom duty compelled to pass through the Tamankada district.

In walking from the rest-house to the lake, we passed the Kowilla dedicated to Mahasen: it was a wretched hut, mudded up in the corner of the ruined temple which had been destroyed in the rebellion of 1817; like most others dedicated to gods, it was said to contain a bow and arrow of the deified king. Amongst the various temples which were supposed to possess peculiar sanctity, and whose guardian god would take vengeance on any perjurer who should dare to profane his shrine, Minneria was pre-eminent; and its unwholesome plains often proved the grave of the perjurer and his adversary, who was always present that he might watch his antagonist, and see that the usual ceremonies were strictly observed.

Mahasen died A.D. 302, and is called in Cingalese history the last of the Maha-wansae (powerful or great dynasty); for although the race was not extinct, and two of his sons successively ascended the throne and continued the family, yet from that period the royal race of the Surya-wansae (solar race) is denominated of the Sula-wansae or lesser dynasty. Various reasons, most of them unsatisfactory, and all of them insufficient to account for this change of appellation, are advanced by Cingalese traditions. We find, however, that after the period of Mahasen's death unfavourable seasons for cultivation, followed by famine and disease, oppressed the sinking and wasted population; who then had recourse to superstition, and invoked the deceased King as an incarnation of Kartikeya or Katragamdeyio (the Indian Mars), one of whose names is also Mahasen. They believed the supernatural power of this monarch had been sufficiently evinced by the mighty works he had executed when ruling over them; and, even before his death, the extent of the public works which he accomplished had created the impression that he was assisted by invisible agents.* It was about a century after the termination of the great dynasty that the fevered imaginations of a suffering people conjured up a dream which they adopted as a revelation, and then began to make offerings to Mahasen, claiming his protection if he were a god, and deprecating his wrath if he had become an evil spirit of power. Pestilence at that time abated; Mahasen remained an object of fear and worship; and Ceylon continued to decrease in wealth, power, and population.

On reaching the lake, its placid surface, lighted by the evening sun, reflected the varied foliage and forms of the clumps and trees on its promontories, capes, and islands; narrow creeks pierced far into the overarching forest; and, beyond the waters, rich grassy plains stretched amongst the wooded hills, over which arose in distance the grand outline of the Mátalé mountains. On the plains were scattered herds of elephants, buffaloes, and spotted deer;

* Much of what I have here recorded was suggested to me by the details and legends furnished by the Kapua of the temple of Mahasen, called also Minneria-deyio, at Naogulla in Mátalé. From him I hoped to procure more information respecting the object of his worship; but he was carried off by small-pox while I was prosecuting my inquiries. Mahasen, from the situation of his principal temple, was usually called, in Mátalé, Minneria-deyio.

the rays of a level sun were shivering on the peacock's rustling plumes; the scarlet and pink of the flamingo were multiplied in the watery mirror; flocks of every variety of wild-ducks and water-fowl rested on its surface; and apart from the others, motionless yet watchful, the solitary pelican reposed its ungainly form upon the glowing waters. King-fishers and fly-catchers, of many different sizes and degrees of brilliancy, glanced along the margin of the lake, tipped its surface, or flitted along its narrow inlets; the alarm-plover swept past, or wheeled around; snipe rose in flocks, and the bright plumage of the jungle-cocks might be seen along the verge of the thickets. As I gazed on this scene, brilliant in colour, refulgent with light, and replete with animal life, I felt how immeasurably superior were the ever-changing glories of the land, compared to the vast monotony of the calm heaving ocean, or the more threatening but still unvaried succession of its foam-crested billows. Ocean as described by Byron is vast and grand; ocean as it is, with its waste of waters, may satisfy the tranquil mind; but, alone, it cannot please the eye. Once fairly launched on the "boundless ocean," we can only see a contracted circle of dull-coloured waters, whose cheerless aspect repels the varied brilliancy, and even seems to repress the vivid colouring of a tropical sunset. To conclude this digression, the landscape before me appeared incomparably more beautiful, and the extremity of the tank of Minneria more distant, than aught I had seen on the "mighty deep."

Notwithstanding the great expanse of water in the tank of Minneria, the principal embankment was not required to be of such great extent as those of much smaller reservoirs: its outlets are on a level with the deepest parts, so that, while any water remained, the supply for the villages, canals, and rice-fields was maintained; and it is said that want of rain for two years would not have caused this lake to become exhausted. It is apparently a work by which man has successfully combated the caprice of seasons, and the revolutions of nature.

Before returning to the rest-house we killed a large wild solitary buffalo, that was discovered grazing near the margin of the lake. Wild buffaloes, although commonly found in the thinly inhabited districts of the flat country, are very rarely seen near the mountains; they are strong and fierce, and the form of their head is such, that a ball fired against it is apt to glance off. For this reason, sportsmen accustomed to buffalo-shooting prefer aiming at the shoulder; and, to insure a fair shot, the best way is for two persons to place themselves so that one may be opposite to the side of the animal when it charges at the other in front. A wild buffalo, intending to attack any one, advances in a curved line, with the head down and inclined sideways, in such a manner that one horn is advanced. Their courage and perseverance in attack are as remarkable as their tenacity of life; therefore, good guns of a large size are quite as necessary in buffalo as in elephant-shooting.

A sportsman, establishing his quarters in the neighbourhood of Minneria, would be sure at all times of finding great variety as well as extreme abundance of game: I was informed that quail and red-legged partridges are to be met with in the plains, but without dogs there was no chance of our seeing them on wing. For all kinds of shooting, except elephant and snipe, morning is the best time in Ceylon; but there is nothing so peculiar in the manner of proceeding as to require description. Well-trained cocking spaniels that could fetch and carry would be invaluable, but they do not thrive in the warm parts of the island. Snipe-shooting affords more amusement, as the bird is more abundant than any other kind of feathered game: but it is a dangerous sport; your feet in mud or water, and your head or body exposed to the rays of a vertical sun, at the same time that you are inhaling noxious exhalations from stagnant water and decaying vegetables, are combinations that cannot fail to injure the strongest constitution.

The natives of Ceylon catch quantities of fish in the tanks and rivers. In fishing for small fry they sometimes use a rod and line, with hooks baited with a single grain of boiled rice; larger fish they secure by means of wears and nets: and if in a soft bottom and shallow water, they use conical baskets made of thin slips of bamboo, which being lowered gently over the fish, the prize is secured by the hand, a hole to introduce the arm being left at the top of the basket. The fish of the Ceylon tanks and rivers are believed to be unwholesome, even poisonous at certain seasons; few of them are palatable at any time.

From Minneria we proceeded through a jungle-path towards the ruins of Polannarrua, a place which had been the capital of the island for upwards of five hundred years. Polannarrua was in ancient works called Pulastya-poora, a name connected with the most ancient legends of the country and the Hindu poem of the Ramayan; Pulastya being one of the progenitors of Rawena, King of Ceylon, in the earliest periods to which vague tradition attempts to ascend. Here, as at Anurádhapoora, superstition was probably one cause of selecting the site of a town which has no perceptible recommendation, and almost every disadvantage, for the position of the capital of the island.

The ruins of Polannarrua are now generally called by Europeans Topare, a corruption of Topaweva, the name of the tank which extends along one side of the city. The first European who noticed the remains of Topare was Lieutenant Fagan, who passed through them when in command of a detachment soon after the conclusion of the Kandian rebellion. Lieutenant Fagan published an account of the ruins which he saw, in the Ceylon Gazette of the 1st October 1820.

Four miles from Minneria we entered upon the open pasture lands surrounding a small artificial lake called Giri-tala; it is formed by a strong embankment of stone, which crosses a hollow at the top of a steep descent, terminating in level ground and damp forests. On re-entering the jungle, hewn stones, carved spouts, and steps of masonry spoke of former times, when this was one of the populous suburbs of a wealthy city. Five miles onward, through a wooded flat abounding with bears, and which is therefore never traversed by natives without fire-arms or a small axe, we discerned the water of Topaweva; and, soon after, the ruined spire of the Rankot dágoba appeared over the forest at the farthest extremity of the lake. At this time an elephant, apparently of great age, and certainly of most uncommon size, was standing in the shallow water, the miniature waves of which as they spread around him reflected and repeated the shadow of this leviathan of the forest. Near this huge animal, and projecting from the surface of the lake, were several rocks of so peculiar a form, that the whole group suggested the idea of the relics of a navy coeval with the ruins that lay before us. There were other elephants on the opposite shore; they, as the sun became powerful, sought shelter in the surrounding forest: but, during the whole of a calm and sultry day, this giant genius of the place remained in the bright light and burning sun; and, although we passed and returned on horseback along the margin of the lake, he not only did not remove, but scarcely deigned to look towards the intruders on his desert realm and soul-less city.

The power of Ceylon was already on the wane, and its monarchs styled of the "lesser dynasty," when the tank of Topaweva was formed by the King Upatissa the Second, who commenced his reign A.D. 368. This King erected many public works in various parts of the island; he also endowed numerous religious edifices: to these exertions he was stimulated both by piety and terror; the former excited by a priest of Hattanagalla, the latter by an earthquake. In A.D. 650, the King Sirisangabo the Second built a palace at Polannarrua, but it was not then considered the capital, and probably had been the place of his retirement when driven from the throne, which he afterwards recovered from the usurper Kaloona. From this time it appears to have been the occasional residence of several Kings, and towards the end of the eighth century became the capital of the island, and the insignia of royalty were removed hither from the ancient capital of Anuradhapoora.

Polannarrua, notwithstanding it was taken and pillaged by foreign invaders, and suffered often in domestic feuds, still increased in size until the period of its greatest prosperity; which was not till the twelfth century, and in the reigns of the Kings Prákrama Bahoo, and Kirti Nissanga, by whom all the principal buildings were commenced or completed. The works and the wars of these active and vain monarchs seem to have over-exerted the strength of a nation which was also weakened by internal dissension; for Ceylon, after the feverish excitement and boasted prosperity of these reigns, sank more rapidly, and Polannarrua, which had continued the seat of Government for five hundred and fifty years, was finally deserted in A.D. 1319. The temples and buildings of Polannarrua are in much better preservation than those of Anurádhapoora, although very inferior to them in point of size: the extent of the city also corresponds with the diminished resources and decreased population of the island in the twelfth century, when the rampart or fence of Polannarrua was formed, as compared with the power and splendour of Ceylon under the "great dynasty," when Wahapp built the walls of Anurádhapoora, in the first century of the Christian era. In several of the buildings at Polannarrua, particularly in two small doors, the proper arch is to be found, but the principle of it does not appear to have been understood by the Cingalese architects; as in the largest buildings, which have brick roofs, the side walls approximate as they ascend, (from each course of bricks projecting forward a little beyond the one immediately below it,) until only a small space is left, which has been completed on the principle of the wedge: the section of one of these chambers would nearly resemble a parabolic curve. I had, ten days previously to our visit, despatched people to clear paths so as to enable us to reach the principal ruins; and, soon after entering the forest, we were surprised by coming suddenly on a large building, more strongly resembling the early ecclesiastical edifices of Europe than any other which the island possesses: this proved to be the Jaitawanarama, which is supposed to be an exact resemblance of the temple built for Gautama Buddha, and in which he resided at Saewatnuwara* in Kosolratta. In front it has a small mound covered with stone pillars, the remains of the Gamsabae Mandapa; and the proper entrance is from thence, between two polygonal pillars of about fifty feet in height: these form the termination of the exterior walls of two chambers into which this temple is divided. The interior of these apartments is much the broadest; and, opposite to its entrance, a figure of Gautama, projecting from the wall, occupies the whole height of the building, or about fifty feet. On the outside, this ruin presents two rows of Gothic windows; but the upper range is closed, and, as far as I could judge, had never been intended to admit light or air, but merely to relieve the external appearance. This temple was repaired, if it was not built, by Kirti Nissanga, soon after his accession

* Buddha Gya.

to the throne in A.D. 1192. The whole length appears about one hundred and fifty feet; and its walls (which are of great thickness) are entirely composed of brick and mortar. With the exception of a stone moulding, the whole building, including the colossal statue, has been covered with polished cement, which still adheres to the entrance pillars and various other portions of this imposing ruin.

The figures of two snakes carved in stone, near the Jaitawanarama, afford the foundation for a childish legend and foolish derivation of the name of the city; and our guide asserted that the figure of a hooded snake* and a polonga were carved on the rocks in the middle of the tank.

After passing through a considerable portion of the ruins, we arrived opposite to the perpendicular face of a large rock; projecting from which, in the strongest relief, are three colossal figures of Buddha: they are in the usual positions, sitting, standing, and reclining; the last-mentioned being upwards of forty feet in length. According to minute directions which the Cingalese possess, these positions of Gautama are, and his features ought to be, retained without variation: so, also, it is with the figure of every supernatural creature which they worship; whether it be deified mortal, or dreaded demon, the shape originally adopted must be retained unaltered. The restrictions of human beings by caste are not more imperious, or better observed, than the instructions that fix the form of figures to be worshipped: the results exhibited by the mind of mortals, and the efforts of statuaries, afford parallel proofs of a mischievous interference and its withering effects. Mankind, debarred from improvement, first ceased to advance, then slowly retrograded; and sculptors (condemned to copy) fell short of their originals, yet had their failures again repeated, and their faults multiplied. Between the sitting and standing figures, the Isuramuni or Kalugalla wihare has been cut in the

* It is from polon and ná, the polonga and hooded snakes, that the native vulgar derive the name of Polannarrua.

hard rock; and in this cavern-temple part of the stone has been left, and afterwards shaped into the figure of Buddha seated on a throne: the two pillars in the front of this wihare are also part of the solid rock. These works were completed in the twelfth century, and in the reign of Prá-krama Bahoo; yet are not only undecayed, but the most minute ornaments are sharp and un-diminished by time or weather: they will probably retain the freshness of late-finished works when the religion of Gautama has faded for ever in its holy land and island stronghold.

We next visited the Dalada Malegawa (palace of the tooth), and found the outside partly obscured, and the inside nearly filled with rubbish; it is a small building of excellent masonry and neat architecture. The roof is flat, and formed of long stones; and the granite, of which it is entirely built, retains in perfection the admirable sharpness of the original cutting. It is said to have been joined together in one day under the personal superintendence of the King Kirti Nissanga, A.D. 1193. Bears in numbers find shelter amongst these ruins, and this sanctuary had only been vacated by some of them on hearing the noise of our approach. The guides, although armed with axes, as they advanced to the entrance often looked anxiously around, and requested that our guns might be kept in readiness. Before entering the building, the guide, standing on one side of the doorway, put forward his head and gave a loud call: after a sufficient pause to admit of any brother bruin, who might be within, to answer the summons or appear in person, we were permitted to enter.

The Rankot dágoba was built by the second Queen of Mahaloo Prákrama Bahoo, between the years A.D. 1154 and 1186; but the King Kirti Nissanga, who increased its height, gave it the name of Thuparáma. It is the highest building at Polannarrua; and although, in common with the other ruins, it is much overgrown with jungle, large trees, and creeping plants, yet the form of its spire may be still discerned from a distance of several miles, as the forests at this place betray, in the size of their trees, the occasional deficiency of moisture from which this portion of the island is peculiarly liable to suffer. Around the base, but forming part of the dágoba, are eight small chapels, and between each of them there is an ornamented projection. The height from the level of the platform on which these stand, to the highest portion of the existing remains of the steeple, we ascertained to be one hundred and fifty-nine feet. As the platform is considerably elevated above the surrounding country, this measurement confirms the native histories, which state that its entire height was one hundred and twenty carpenter's cubits:* this was when the golden umbrella, raised on the

* Carpenter's cubit, about two feet three inches.

summit of the spire, procured for this building the appellation of Rankot,* by which it is now generally known.

The remains of the Bannage (place for publicly expounding the Buddhist scriptures) is encircled by a fence of peculiar construction, in which the two lines of longitudinal bars are of stone, fitting in to upright stone pillars. In the Watte-daga, Poeyagé, Lanka-rama, Meres-wattya, Keeree-wihare, and several other buildings which we sought out, there was nothing worthy of remark, except that their position and remains exactly agreed with the native accounts of this city, and the date of the erection of the buildings as recorded in the Cingalese history. The Sat-mahal-prasada is a neat pyramidal building of no great height, although its name implies that it was seven stories high.

The palace is now a shapeless mass overgrown with vegetation, and situated on the bank of the Topaweva, the waters of which were conveyed through the buildings. The royal bath is still distinct; it is a circular excavation, about six feet deep, lined with hewn stones, one of which is round and raised above the rest of the pavement: this marks the spot where the Kings stood, and received the services of the numerous officers connected with the bathing and dressing departments of a Cingalese monarch.

* Rankot: ran, gold; kot, the umbrella-like termination which was usually elevated on the summit of the spire of a dágoba.

At Polannarrua we remarked several stones covered with long inscriptions, of which I afterwards obtained copies. One stone particularly attracted attention; it is shaped like the leaf of a Cingalese book, and is neatly ornamented, the writing being surrounded by a moulding of birds: this stone was brought from Mehintalai; it is twenty-five feet long, four feet broad, and two thick.

In a situation abounding with rocks and quarries, from which they could have riven masses of any size by means of wedges,—a plan by which they (even in the earliest periods of Cingalese history) procured pillars of great length, and of which abundant use has been made at Polannarrua, as we find by the marks in these quarries,—it is a matter of surprise that this weighty mass should have been thought worthy of being removed upwards of eighty miles; and it is still more wonderful how they who determined upon, found means to accomplish this feat. I had regarded the tradition which spoke of its removal by men (from a place so distant as Mehintalai) as an absurdity, until the inscription on it was translated, and showed the concluding paragraph to be, "This engraved stone is the one which the chief minister, Unawoomandanawan, caused the strong men of Nissankha to bring from the mountain Saegiri (Mehintalai) at Anurádhapoora, in the time of the Lord Sree Kálinga Chakkrawarti."

Several of the inscriptions cut in stone at

Polannarrua are of great length, in a character which is Cingalese, yet containing many letters now obsolete, but in general beautifully executed; the dates which they afford confirm the accuracy of the Cingalese histories, and the correctness with which Mr Turnour had arranged its chronology in an Epitome not then published, although compiled several years before. Of this work he was kind enough to permit me to take a copy, which was of material service in facilitating the researches which I had commenced, principally with a view of ascertaining the degree of credit which might be conceded to a history of twenty-three centuries' continuance, but which the English writers on Ceylon had condemned as fabulous.

Translations of three of these inscriptions,* in-

* With regard to these inscriptions, Mr. Turnour says, in his Introduction to his published translations of them, "The last of these inscriptions dates the accession of Sahasa Mallawa in the year of Buddha 1743, or A.D. 1200; while in the Epitome I have brought the period down to Buddha 1748: an anachronism which I should have attributed without the slightest hesitation to the imperfections explained as inherent in the chronology of native history. On referring, however, to the Mahawanso to ascertain the justness of Kirti Nissanga's claim to the extravagant praises lavished on him both as a sovereign and a warrior, I find that I have misstated the term of the reign of the regicide Mehindoo the Fifth, or Kiten Kisdás, whose short-lived reign lasted only *five days*, and not five years."

These inscriptions were not procured and put into Mr. Turnour's hands until six years after I had seen his Epitome, and four years after I had obtained a copy of it.

serted in the Appendix, are valuable for the dates which they afford, and curious as a record of the customs and recognised duties of a Cingalese King upwards of six hundred years ago: they farther exhibit in perfection the self-praise in which these monarchs indulged, and the high-sounding titles in which they delighted. It appears, however, from Cingalese history, that the warlike actions and individual prowess ascribed to the reigning Kings by these imperishable records are totally false, or so exaggerated as to bear no resemblance to the real merits of these rulers.

Another of the inscriptions records the grants made, and the titles bestowed, by a grateful King on a chief, his friend, and his mother, who had been instrumental in bringing this prince from the continent of India, and placing him on the throne of Ceylon, A.D. 1200. The chieftain was named Kooloondoottetti Abo-nawan; his friend, another man of rank, was Kumbudal-nawan:

> "Chiefs who under their grey stone
> So long had slept, that fickle Fame
> Had blotted from her rolls their name."

We find from the annals of Rajasthan,* that the purest royal blood of India, the Rajpoots of Méwar, acknowledged the equality of the Cingalese royal race in the thirteenth century, by the marriage of their King with a Princess of Ceylon. The beauty and heroism of the Princess Padmati, and the

* Vide Todd's annals of Rajasthan.

bravery of her island kinsmen, Gorah and Badul, are recorded in the annals of Méwar; when, in A.D. 1303, the red flag of the "race of the sun" sank not before the conquering Alla, until the battle-field and blood-stained walls avouched the honour of its slaughtered sons, and the smouldering remains of its self-immolated daughters rested in the silent caverns of Cheetore.

END OF THE FIRST VOLUME.